ENCYCLOPEDIA OF THE
Animal World

Vol 3   Biological control — Bull snakes

Bay Books Sydney

BIOLOGICAL CONTROL, the study and subsequent utilization of beneficial parasites, predators, pathogenic organisms and herbivorous animals for the regulation of destructive pests and weed plants. Since man began to cultivate the land, he has had to contend with a wide variety of pests which compete with him for his livestock and crops until, at the present time, it is calculated that more than 15% of agricultural and horticultural production is devastated annually by pests.

Under natural conditions, plants and animals have evolved well-balanced communities in which the various interactions between their members tend to damp excessive fluctuations of their numbers. This balance of nature is often severely upset by agricultural and forestry practices in which large areas of single species of plants or trees (monocultures) replace the previously natural, mixed and balanced environment. This conversion, with relatively unlimited food resources and lack of natural enemies, tends to favour the rapid increase of previously innocuous animals. Alternatively, the introduction of exotic species into a new country, such as the rabbit into Australia, can produce pest problems of an explosive nature, because the animal or plant is often introduced without its range of regulating factors. It is only relatively recently that some sort of check to the financial loss and human misery created by pests has been made possible with the development of pesticides, and the use of natural control techniques. Even the discovery of pesticides, heralded as the ultimate answer to the world's pest problems, has created its own difficulties. The indiscriminate use of DDT and other insecticides often destroys the beneficial predatory and parasitic insects which control pest populations, and can also lead to the evolution of genetic strains of the pest which are resistant to the insecticide. In these sorts of situations biological control methods often prove more than a working alternative.

The first large scale case of biological control was carried out against an accidentally introduced pest of citrus fruit in California. This pest, the Cottony cushion scale *Icerya purchasi,* threatened the citrus fruit industry with bankruptcy until a predacious Ladybird beetle *Rodolia cardinalis* was imported from Australia in 1888. The effects of this predator were such that the pest was virtually eliminated within two years, and the Ladybird beetle continues to control the pest as effectively today—testifying to the durability of the control.

Another striking example of the efficiency of biocontrol was the recovery of more than 50 million acres (20 million ha) of Australian pastureland overrun with several species of prickly pear cactus *Opuntia* spp which had been introduced from America. Australian scientists studied the cactus in its original geographical areas and imported several species of insects which they discovered feeding on the plant. One of them, a moth *Cactoblastis cactorum* whose larvae feed on the fleshy leaves of the cactus, was established in Australia in 1925 and within a few years had destroyed much of the weed, permitting the land to be used once more for agriculture.

Not all biological control ventures have met with such striking success, but on balance, the comparatively small outlay for the study and introduction of natural enemies can often produce enormous returns on the scientific investment.

An example of modern biological control is reflected in the concern of the Australian government following the accidental introduction of a woodwasp *Sirex noctilio* into Australia and its subsequent establishment in the pine forests of Tasmania and Victoria by 1950. This pest, which is found in many parts of the world where it does not constitute a serious menace to forestry, attacks living trees in the Australian forests killing many, and threatening the considerable timber investment of the continent. The female woodwasp drills her ovipositor into a tree to lay eggs, and also injects various substances and spores of a symbiotic fungus (which are stored in sacs in her abdomen). The fungal spores germinate and the fungal threads (hyphae) pass through the wood, providing food directly and indirectly for the developing larva which chews its way through the timber, producing a long tunnel filled with powder-like excrement. The fungus, and the other toxic substances, effectively block the tree's resistance mechanism so that it dies, although particularly vigorous trees may not succumb to the attack.

Woodwasps are associated with a wide range of natural enemies in their original environment which include insect parasites, predatory birds that feed on the adult insects, woodpeckers which dig out the wasp larvae from the infested wood, and nematode worms. These worms sterilize the female wasp by invading the eggs, and are introduced into the tree by the wasp which, instead of laying normal eggs, deposits the nematode-filled eggshells.

The survey of much of Europe, North Africa, Japan, North America and the foothills of the Himalayas has resulted in the collection of many natural enemies of this and closely related species of woodwasps. Several insect parasites of woodwasps were studied, principally ichneumon-wasps, which drill into the wood of affected trees and parasitize the maturing larvae or pupae of the woodwasp, and parasitic wasps called *Ibalia* which insert their ovipositors down the holes made by the ovipositing woodwasp and inject an egg into the young larva or embryo of the pest. When the biology of these parasites had been studied and it was certain that they were primary parasites and would not adversely affect control, they were consigned by air to Australia where they were further studied and propagated to produce large numbers before being released in the infested forests.

One of the more revolutionary aspects of modern biological control is the use of sterile insects to eradicate insect pests. The idea and its development as an efficient control tool are closely related to research on the Screw-worm fly *Cochliomyia hominovorax* which had been a serious pest of livestock in the southwestern United States since the industry began. The Screw-worm fly is an obligatory parasite which spends most of its larval life feeding in the wounds of live cattle, causing enormous losses in Georgia, Florida and Texas and, with extensive cattle shipments, causing local outbreaks throughout much of the southern United States. During the 1940's, study of the fly revealed that the females only mated once and if the males could be sterilized without affecting their mating activities, control or even eradication might be achieved. The underlying principle of this kind of control is to release sexually sterile males in numbers which are greater than exist in the natural population. By reason of their numerical dominance they have a decided advantage when competing with normal males. Experiments demonstrated that low doses of X-rays or gamma-irradiation of pupae, shortly before their emergence as adults, caused sterilization. In a pilot experiment, on the island of Curaçao in the early 1950's, complete eradication of the Screw worm fly was obtained. Encouraged by this dramatic success, the United States Department of Agriculture set up 'fly factories' to produce over 110 million flies per week, which were irradiated and released in the affected areas, sometimes by dropping them in specially prepared canisters from aircraft. From 200–800 flies per sq mile (2·7 sq km) were released, designed to cover 300 mile wide (480 km) bands because the pest had been recorded migrating up to 300 miles during its three week adult life. This intensive programme has resulted in the virtual elimination of Screw worm fly in the United States and undoubtedly the technique will be applied in other countries, such as Mexico, which have a Screw worm fly problem. The benefits to the cattle industry have been in the region of a 2,000% return on the cost of the programme.

The sterile male technique has been applied to other pests such as the Fruit fly, which destroys fruit in many tropical and subtropical areas throughout the world, and on some Pacific islands, over 90% eradication has been recorded. Irradiation of males has also been used with varying degrees of success with houseflies, mosquitoes, sheep blowfly in Britain, and codling-moth.

Since the development of irradiation techniques for the sterilization of insect pests, there has arisen the possibility of using chemicals to sterilize them or severely affect their reproductive capacity. Several chemicals have been discovered which, depending on the chemical used and its dose rate, cause complete disruption of the reproductive cycle by preventing oviposition or even egg development, causing failure of eggs to hatch, larvae to pupate, or pupae to emerge as adults. One chemical (amethopterin) was used originally in man as a therapeutic drug to treat some kinds of tumour and, not surprisingly, it was also found to affect other rapidly proliferating tissues such as the gonads of insects. This drug has been successfully tested on houseflies, sterilizing females but not affecting the males. Chemosterilants are applied by treating the food of the insects, spraying or dusting the insect, and treating surfaces it is likely to touch. The success of Screw-worm control has shown how induced sterility can decimate an insect population, and similar success may be expected following the application of chemosterilants either directly like a pesticide, or by the release of sterile males or females into the pest area.

A further approach to biocontrol is the manipulation of the pest by controlling its communications system. Most insects communicate if only to effect mating, although many have sophisticated behaviour patterns that result in aggregations for mutual defence or at a suitable breeding site. The principal method of communication is by chemical stimuli or pheromones emanating from the insect, its food source or oviposition sites. Pheromones that cause aggregations of insects for mating puposes are called 'sex attractants' and in one or two cases have been identified and even synthesized. An example is 'gyplure', the sex attractant of the Gypsy moth *Porthetria dispar*, which has been used successfully to trap males, and thus prevent mating and subsequent reproduction. The use of a pheromone to guide insects to a breeding area has been recently studied in Bark beetles *Dendroctonus* spp which attack coniferous trees. The initial attack of a suitable host tree by a few colonizing beetles results in the emission of a pheromone produced by the beetle after feeding on the tree. The pheromone is contained in the excrement, which is highly attractive to the rest of the beetle population, and the use of the chemical on unsuitable host trees or traps will undoubtedly help control the Bark beetle—one of the foresters' principal foes.

A less familiar method of biocontrol is the use of microbial organisms, bacteria, various protozoa, fungi, and nematodes, and the toxins they produce. Microbial pesticides, as they are called, were first advertised as pos-

sible controlling agents as long ago as 1873 and since then, their uses and successes have been many and varied. One of the first microbes to be used successfully was the bacterium, *Bacillus thuringiensis,* which causes disease in a variety of insect pests, and is particularly potent when the pest population is dense. This bacterium can be cultured and subsequently sprayed over the affected crops or forests by aircraft, killing the pest without affecting its natural enemies. One of the advantages of microbes, which can be utilized in much the same way as conventional pesticides, is their selectivity resulting in the pest succumbing to the diseases but not affecting beneficial animals or man. Viruses, of the nuclear polyhedrosis types, have been successfully employed in the battle against the pine and spruce sawflies which cause so much damage in forests, and also to control alfalfa caterpillars in the United States. The most dramatic result following use of a pathogen is undoubtedly the control of rabbits in Australia. The rabbit was introduced by well-intentioned settlers when the continent was first colonized. Because it feeds on the grazing lands throughout much of the country, and competes primarily with sheep that are such an important part of the country's economy, the financial losses were enormous. This situation was saved following the discovery and introduction of the myxomatosis virus which spread very rapidly.

Fungi which kill insects, such as the White muscardine fungus *Beauvaria bassiana,* have also been used with some measure of success in controlling insect populations. Once the disease has been introduced into the infestation areas, either by spraying or dusting, or the liberation of infected individuals, its rapid spread is brought about by movements of the insects within the population, including parasites and predators, and also through the dispersal effects of wind and rain.

A more bizarre biological control project is the use of organisms to disperse cattle

Noctiluca scintillans, a luminescent dinoflagellate.

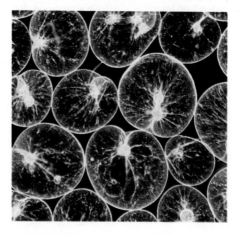

dung in Australia. This continent had no large grazing herds until the introduction of cattle following colonization and there were no native Dung beetles or other organisms adapted to deal with cow-pats, with the result that they accumulate on the pasture and remain for many years. The dung is also a breeding site of the Buffalo fly and bushfly, and leads to an increase in these noxious insects. To combat this problem, beetles were introduced from Africa, which break up the dung and bury it, or are predatory on the grubs of the flies. They undoubtedly aid soil fertility, and also reduce the risk of disease in the cattle.

What of the future for biological control? With the limitations imposed by the use of chemical pesticides and their cost of development, screening and application, the increasing use of biological control methods is inevitable. The study of ecology with its aim of a better understanding of the many and varied interactions between pests or weeds and the other members of the community will improve the likelihood of successful management and manipulation of pest populations, possibly with an enlightened combination of integrated chemical and biological control methods.   J.P.S.

BIOLOGY, the science devoted to the study of living beings and therefore primarily divisible into bacteriology, botany, and zoology. Although it is not certain that viruses are living organisms, they resemble them in so many characters and affect them so closely that virology is also included. In addition, biology is divisable into the various aspects of the subject in each group: gross structure or morphology; tissue-structure or histology; cell-structure or cytology; function or physiology and biochemistry; development or embryology; heredity or genetics; conditions of life or ecology and parasitology; behaviour or ethology and psychology; fossil forms or paleontology. Philosophers argue whether biology is completely reducible to physics and chemistry; biologists reply that biological principles have their own validity at their own level. The word 'biology' (first used in 1813) is etymologically incorrect, for the Greek *bios* means a human life and career. Grammatically, biology should be 'zoology' (Gk *zoon*—a living organism) and zoology should be 'theriology' (Gk *ther*—an animal). Phytology (Gk *phyton*—a plant) is synonymous with botany.

BIOLUMINESCENCE, the production of cold light by living organisms. It is a widespread phenomenon, about a third of the phyla of the animal kingdom containing luminescent animals. Perhaps the best known throughout the world are the luminous insects, such as fireflies, belonging to the beetle family Lampyridae, wingless

The Research Vessel *Sarsia*, from Plymouth Marine Laboratory, passing through a swarm of the luminescent dinoflagellate *Noctiluca scintillans*, forming pinkish drifts at the surface.

emales of one species being called glow-worms.

The simplest light producing organisms are bacteria. Aristotle noted that dead fish and flesh could produce light, and in the 17th century Robert Boyle showed experimentally that this could not occur without a plentiful supply of air. Of a luminous neck of veal in his cellar he remarked, 'Notwithstanding the great Number of lucid Parts not the least degree of Stench was perceivable to infer any putrefaction'. It is now known that the glow of dead fishes and meat is due to the luminous bacteria growing on them. Bacteria are the smallest lamps in the world.

Many of the older seafarers described marine phosphorescence or 'burning of the sea', the trail of light in the wake of a ship seen in tropical waters or even in temperate regions on dark nights. Darwin, during his voyage on the *Beagle* in 1832, saw a brilliant display in the South Atlantic. 'While sailing a little south of the Plata on one very dark night, the sea presented a wonderful and most beautiful spectacle. There was a fresh breeze, and every part of the water, which during the day is seen as foam, now glowed with a pale light. The vessel drove before her bows two billows of liquid phosphorous, and in her wake she was followed by a milky train'. The glow is caused by large numbers of dinoflagellate protozoa. The best known is *Noctiluca*, which has the form of a little sphere and is about 1 mm in diameter. It luminesces only when it is stimulated. Many other much smaller protozoa are also known to be luminescent.

Light production in the sea is not, however, confined to micro-organisms and protozoa. Luminous medusae were known to Pliny and descriptions of them have been recorded for hundreds of years. A large Mediterranean jellyfish, *Pelagia noctiluca* is a striking object at night. The whole outer surface of the animal including the tentacles becomes luminous on stimulation and when handled the luminous material sticks to the hand. A number of other jellyfish secrete

mucus with luminous spots. The phenomenon is not limited to planktonic coelenterates. It was recorded on the 'Challenger' expedition that a gorgonian—a Sea fan—dredged from a great depth glowed with a pale lilac light, and pennatulids or Sea pens have long been known to be luminous.

Amongst the other invertebrate groups which have luminous forms are the Ctenophora (Comb jellies), Annelida, Mollusca and Crustacea. Probably all species of Ctenophora are luminous and their presence in the plankton in large numbers may be an important factor in marine luminescence.

One of the most spectacular of luminescent worms is *Chaetopterus*, the more surprisingly because the worm spends its whole life buried in sand in a parchment tube. The whole worm glows if disturbed and even the larva is luminous. The light is formed by granules which are secreted in a luminous slime from photogenic cells scattered throughout the epidermis of the animal. Another interesting species is *Odontosyllis enopla*, the fireworm of the Bermudan coral seas. These animals swarm on the second, third and fourth days after the full moon. Both sexes are phosphorescent; the female has a strong and continuous glow and the male gives sharper intermittent flashes. The display starts 55 minutes after sunset and lasts only 15–30 minutes. During this limited period the males and females rotate together and eggs and sperm are scattered into the water.

Squids are one of the most important groups of luminous animals. They have developed varied methods of lighting, from the harbouring of luminous bacteria to the most complicated lanterns. Deep-sea forms such as *Heteroteuthis dispar*, living at 4,000–5,000 ft (1,200–1,500 m) in the Mediterranean or *Lycoteuthis diadema*, from 10,000 ft (3,000 m) in the Indian Ocean, have large luminous organs. *Heteroteuthis* is able to surround itself with a luminous cloud when it is attacked. *Lycoteuthis* has a more elaborate system of organs that shine with ultramarine blue, pearly white and ruby red light.

How is animal light produced and how is its production controlled? In general, luminous organisms can be divided into two groups according to whether the light is produced within the cell or outside from secretions, that is intracellular and extracellular luminescence. Control may involve a number of types of mechanism; thus luminous secretion may be stimulated by nerves or the material may be squeezed out by muscles. Luminous organs may be controlled by nerves or hormones.

The French physiologist Raphael Dubois may be said to have initiated the chemical study of bioluminescence. In 1887 he showed that cold-water extracts of the mollusc *Pholas dactylus* (a common rock borer) would remain luminous for several minutes. After light emission had ceased it could be restored by adding a second extract made by washing another *Pholas* in hot water and cooling the juice. Dubois concluded that the hot-water extract must contain a substrate—which he called luciferin—which was not destroyed by heating and which produced light when it reacted with an enzyme, luciferase, present in the cold-water extract.
F.J.E.

BIOMASS, the weight of living material in a population or community of animals at any given moment. It can be expressed either as live weight or as dry weight when the water has been removed from the tissues by drying at 140°F (60°C).

At present much interest in ecology is centred on the structure of animal communities and on their use of matter in the form of food. Because of the very large differences in the size of different animals, numbers alone may not be a reliable guide to the importance of any given species in the community. For example, if we were to compare the numbers of bacteria and elephants in African grassland we might conclude (if we had never seen either animal) that elephants were of no importance at all in this community. Thus in most cases converting numbers of animals to total biomass gives a clearer idea of a species' importance in this respect.

The biomass of different organisms in a community is related to their function. The largest biomass is always that of the green plants or producers which by creating organic matter by the process of photosynthesis provide the eventual source of food for the whole community. Next in total weight come the herbivores or consumers which normally, however, form only a small fraction of the weight of the green plants. Finally, the carnivores which themselves feed on the herbivores are represented by only a very small fraction of the total biomass, usually less than 1%. This type of relationship is illustrated by a 'pyramid of biomass' in which the area of each block represents the biomass of each group of organisms. The example is from an abandoned field in Georgia, USA.

The concept of biomass is also used by ecologists interested in the flow of matter and energy from one population of organisms to another in a community. Biomass, usually expressed as grams per square metre, can be used for estimating food consumption and total growth (i.e. production of organic matter) by any given organism in the community. Another advantage of using biomass is that if the energy content of the food of an animal can be obtained, then an estimate of the total energy in the food consumed, and therefore an estimate of the energy required to maintain the population, can be made.

In the past biomass estimates have been used to compare the importance of different species in a community. While this may sometimes give an idea of the importance of the species at the time of sampling, it is possible that the sample may either be taken at a peak or a trough in population numbers in such a way that the animal is either over- or under-represented in the community as a whole. For this reason such comparisons are better done on the basis of production estimates. By this method estimates are obtained of the total production of organic matter of each species in the community over a period of at least one year. This eliminates the short term effects due to seasonal fluctuations in numbers.   A.R.S.

BIOMES, geographical units or regions which are characterized by differences in the type of vegetation found when plant succession has reached a climax (see ecological succession). They are generally named after this climax vegetation, e.g. savannah biome, tropical-forest biome, tundra biome etc. Each biome in fact contains many different plant communities and associations but most of these are seral stages in the plant succession leading to the climax. An adequate definition of a biome therefore requires a good understanding of the plant community dynamics within the region. This sort of knowledge is available for only a few parts of the world, and consequently there is no universal agreement on the number of biomes in the world, and it is possible here to discuss only some of the most important. The type of vegetation that develops in a geographical region, and therefore the biome to which it belongs, is largely a consequence of its latitude and climate, and to a lesser extent its soils, the permeability of its bedrock and other factors. Since the same type of climate may occur in very different parts of the world, the regions that make up a biome are not necessarily contiguous. For instance, the Mediterranean type of climate, with hot, dry summers and warm, damp winters, occurs both around the Mediter-

ranean Sea and in California. In both regions a low, dense scrub vegetation has developed, especially characterized by the presence of small, thorny, drought-resistant, evergreen oaks. This type of vegetation is known as 'chaparral' in North America and as 'maquis' in Europe; both regions belong to the chaparral biome. Similarly the type of vegetation which is found in arctic latitudes in both Eurasia and North America is very like that found above the tree line on high mountains everywhere, even in tropical regions. This is the result of similarity of climate and these regions can be grouped together as the tundra biome, which can be subdivided into arctic tundra and alpine or mountain tundra. The species of plants found in the vegetation in different regions of a biome vary greatly, although they are frequently closely related and the form, structure and appearance of the vegetation will be very much the same.

All of this gives the impression that biomes are primarily of interest to the botanist, but the animal associations and communities of a biome, although often less conspicuous, are none-the-less characteristic. Different types of vegetation provide different types of food materials for animals, as well as different degrees of cover or shelter, and in consequence characteristic faunas develop. As with the plant communities the species forming the animal associations of a biome vary in different regions but the form, adaptations and ecology of the species involved are fairly constant. The grassland biome, for instance, has an animal species association in North America including (among many others) Ground squirrels, Pocket gophers, bison and pronghorns, and coyotes. In the African parts of the grassland biome species with similar ecology (i.e. ecologically equivalent species) include Ground squirrels, Golden moles, zebras and springboks (as well as many other large herbivores) and lions.

The principal biomes of the terrestrial environment are tundra; coniferous forest; temperate deciduous forest; grassland prairie or steppe; chaparral; desert; tropical savannah; tropical forest.

The tundra biome is circumpolar around the Arctic Circle with small outliers in mountain regions in other latitudes and in the southern hemisphere. It is the most continuous of the biomes and the easiest to define. Its vegetation is characterized by mosses, lichens ('Reindeer moss'), sedges and dwarf willows; the fauna is discussed under 'tundra fauna'.

The coniferous-forest or taiga biome lies to the south of the tundra in the northern hemisphere and is also circumpolar. The trees are mostly evergreen pines, adapted by shape and needle-like leaves to shed heavy loads of snow easily. Coniferous forest also develops on some high mountains in other parts of the world. The most prominent animals of this biome are, or more probably were, the moose and wapiti, but wolves and many species of rodents and hares are also characteristic. Amongst the birds the crossbills, which have beaks adapted for removing seeds from pine cones, are especially important and are virtually confined to this biome. The coniferous-forest biome receives many migrant birds from more southern biomes during its short summer.

The temperate-forest biome covers most of the eastern USA, western Europe and a large area of eastern Asia. In contrast to coniferous forest it is composed mostly of broad-leaved deciduous trees showing a marked seasonal cycle of leaf growth and fall. There is frequently an understorey of smaller shrubs and herbs especially near the edges of the forest or where human interference has occurred. In the animal associations of the biome many species of deer are prominent. Many mammals which were formerly characteristic of this biome have been virtually eliminated by hunting and

Pyramid of biomass, actual example taken from an abandoned field in Georgia, USA, showing the relative importance of plants, herbivores and carnivores within a community. The area in each block of the pyramid on the left represents the biomass of each group, specified on the right. The lion and stag are only symbols of carnivore and herbivore respectively.

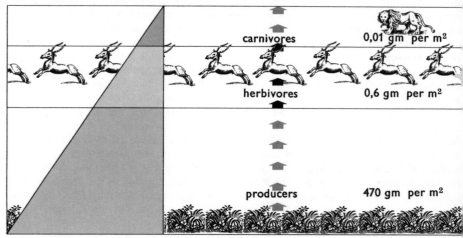

carnivores   0,01 gm per m²

herbivores   0,6 gm per m²

producers   470 gm per m²

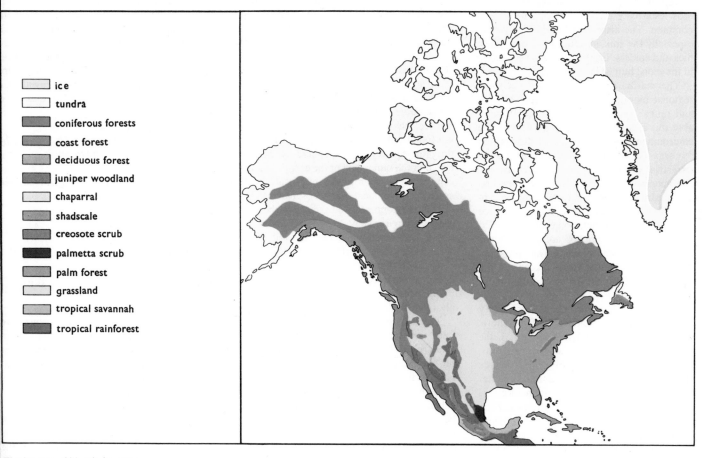

ice
tundra
coniferous forests
coast forest
deciduous forest
juniper woodland
chaparral
shadscale
creosote scrub
palmetta scrub
palm forest
grassland
tropical savannah
tropical rainforest

The biomes of North America

agriculture, including bears, Wild boar, wolf and Wild cat. Species which have adapted well to man's activities in the forest and which are still relatively common include the Red fox, badgers, squirrels, woodchucks, and weasels. High populations of insectivores and rodents occur, and owls are especially important as predators of these. The biome is very rich in bird species and woodpeckers, titmice (Paridae), thrushes, warblers (Muscicapidae) and finches are especially frequent.

The grassland and tropical-savannah biomes (steppe, prairie, pampas, savannah) are the most widespread biomes and have been of great importance to man, both as pastureland and, more recently, for cereal growing. It has been estimated that grassland previously occupied over 40% of the surface of the continents. A huge zone of grassland, the prairies, lies to the east of the Rocky Mountains between southern Canada and Mexico. Much of central Asia is covered by steppe lands. In Africa tropical grassland extends in a wide belt on either side of the Equator between the Tropics of Cancer and Capricorn. Large areas of eastern South America around the Tropic of Capricorn are occupied by pampas; most of the northern parts of the Australian continent also fall in

this biome. It is often convenient to distinguish between temperate grasslands, which are characterized almost entirely by grasses and herbs, and tropical grasslands or savannah, which tend to have more variable rainfall and a vegetation with drought-resisting properties often including areas of scrubland and small clumps of trees. The fauna is characteristically dominated by large herbivores which live in great herds, such as bison and pronghorn in North America, gazelle, asses and horses in Asia, antelopes, gazelle, zebra, springbok, wildebeest, elephant and buffalo in Africa, and kangaroos in Australia. Their chief predators are coyotes in North America, lions and cheetahs in Africa and, until it became extinct, the Tasmanian wolf in Australia. Large flightless running birds (rhea, ostrich, emu) and many small burrowing mammals are also common. Ants in temperate regions and termites in the tropics are major components of the insect fauna.

The desert biome occupies large areas between the tropics in Africa, Arabia, central Asia, India, central Australia and the western areas of both North and South America. Most deserts are areas with rainfall of only a few centimetres a year and are merely arid with a rather sparse vegetation of drought-

resistant grasses, shrubs and trees, often thorny like the cacti of the western hemisphere. More extreme deserts have rainfall only at intervals of years and practically no vegetation. Large herbivores and predators are generally rare, the fauna containing many herbivorous rodents, especially bipedal ones with hindlegs adapted for jumping (gerbils and similar forms) and also many reptiles which, with their scaly skins, have good drought resistance. Many of the vertebrates tend to be burrowing forms. Arthropods form most of the invertebrate fauna, and most of the birds are insectivorous.

The tropical-forest biome is the most complex of all biomes in terms of richness of species. Trees are mostly evergreen, tall with a continuous canopy, and there is a vigorous growth of epiphytic plants, lianas, tree ferns, liverworts etc. There is often very little ground flora due to the intense shading provided by the canopy. The fauna is rather complex and too varied to summarize briefly. It contains many species highly adapted for arboreal life (monkeys, lemurs, sloths, Flying squirrels, lizards and snakes, and frogs). Large ground-living herbivores include the tapir, capybara and peccaries in South America, the elephant and hippopotamus in Africa. Big cats, especially leopards

(Africa) and jaguars (South America) are important as predators. Parrots and cockatoos, especially tree-hole nesting forms, are common. The arthropod fauna is very rich, especially the ants, termites, bees, butterflies, flies and spiders. Earthworms are very active in the moist humus layers of the soil.

The marine environment does not show regional biomes with distinct types of flora and fauna, as does the terrestrial. Presumably this is a result of the uniformity of the environment and of the ease of distribution for organisms living in it. However, just as terrestrial biomes are distinguished by the characteristic 'life-form' of their flora and fauna, similar regions may be recognized in the sea but arranged in a depth sequence rather than a latitudinal one. In contrast to terrestrial biomes animals are usually more conspicuous than plants. The principal marine biomes that may be recognized are the oceanic, the rocky-shore and the sandy-shore biomes.

The oceanic biome of open water, away from the immediate influence of the shore. This biome can be subdivided into: 1 the planktonic sub-biome of small organisms, including unicellular, photo-synthetic plants and many Protozoa, crustaceans and invertebrate larvae, many with flotation mechanisms, concentrated in the upper waters; 2 the nektonic sub-biome of active swimming forms, occurring in a range of depths, including fishes, squids and the marine mammals; 3 the benthic sub-biome of the sea bottom, dependent for its nutrition on dead material sinking from the waters above, and including many burrowing annelids, molluscs and echinoderms. All these sub-biomes of the oceanic biome are strongly interdependent.

The rocky-shore biome of actively-eroding shores. This sub-biome is dominated by a flora of attached algae (Thallophyta) and a fauna of gastropod molluscs and balanoid crustaceans, many with mechanisms for avoiding desiccation at low tide. Zonation is a marked characteristic. A division can be made into a littoral sub-biome under the influence of tidal action and a sub-littoral sub-biome which is affected by wave action but is not exposed at low tide.

The muddy or sandy-shore biome of shores on which material is being deposited by wave action. This is an unstable habitat and the main plants are green algae which may grow in flat sheets on the surface of the sand or mud. The main animals are burrowing polychaete annelids, especially forms like *Nereis* and *Arenicola,* and burrowing or loosely-attached bivalve molluscs. Wading birds are often important as predators.

The freshwater environment is generally considered to be too fragmentary and dispersed, and insufficiently independent of surrounding terrestrial and marine biomes, for true biomes to be distinguishable. In a general way, however, most large bodies of freshwater have animal and plant communities corresponding to the planktonic, nektonic and benthic communities of the oceanic biome. I.N.H.

BIOSPHERE, comprises both the sum total of all living things inhabiting the earth and the environment in which they operate. Since living things have penetrated no more than a few feet below the surface of the earth and are found only some thousands of feet up in the atmosphere, the biosphere is concentrated in the outer shell of the earth's crust. It can be divided into the hydrosphere, or aquatic environment, the lithosphere, or terrestrial environment, and the atmosphere, or gaseous environment. The boundaries between these environments are variable and in a constant state of flux, and it is often considered that the great majority of life occurs at the interfaces of these divisions, i.e. in the surface waters of the sea and a few feet above and below the soil surface.

The term biosphere was first used by the 18th century French naturalist Jean Lamarck simply to describe the total of all life on the earth. More recently, ecologists have realized that living things are so closely integrated with their environment, and so dependent on it, that no clear distinction can be made between them, so the term is now used to cover both. Just as the word ecosystem means an integrated self-sustaining community of organisms together with its environment, the word biosphere expresses the same idea on a world, supra-ecosystem scale. The biosphere can be regarded as a series of more or less continuous ecosystems. The limits of the biosphere are set by the ability of the form of life we know to adapt to the physical conditions of the periphery. For instance, a limitation is set to atmospheric life in an upwards direction by the inability of organisms to cope with the increasing cold, decreasing density and lack of oxygen found above a few thousand feet. A limit is set to life at great depths in the soil by lack of oxygen and great density of the environment.

Within the biosphere two great biophysical processes involving interactions between living things and their environment occur. The first of these is nutrient or biogeochemical cycling. The atoms of which matter in the biosphere is made are in a constant state of movement and interchange between the abiotic (non-living) and biotic (living) components of the biosphere. Living things take chemical elements for building tissues from the environment to which the elements return when the living things die. Nearly all synthesis of living tissues from non-living components is carried out by plants. These 'vivified' materials may pass the full length of the grazing and decompos-ing food webs before returning to a non living form. Chemical elements can be re garded as circulating between two 'pools' i the biosphere, a non-living pool in whicl their rates of movement and change are generally slow, and a biological pool in which rates of movement and change are usually much more rapid. The elements are not in the same proportions in these two pools, as the table shows:

Estimated relative abundance (percentage by weight) of elements in the biosphere

	Non-living matter	Living matter
Oxyen	46	74
Carbon	0·03	11
Nitrogen	0·13	10
Hydrogen	0·01	22
Phosphorus	0·13	0·2
Silicon	28	0·05
Other elements	25	2·6

Oxygen, carbon, nitrogen and hydrogen are much more abundant in living matter than in non-living, whilst silicon and all the other elements are more rare. The forms of life that have evolved in the biosphere are seen to be very selective in the elements that they take for the non-living pool.

Energy is required for these processes of nutrient cycling, both within and between the two pools of elements and energy flow is the second large-scale biophysical process of the biosphere (see food chains and webs for more details). Energy occurs in the biosphere in a number of different forms but almost all the energy that is used by living things comes from outside the biosphere, entering it as sunshine. Most of the vast quantity of solar radiation that enters the biosphere is lost by reflection (from clouds, dust particles in the atmosphere, etc.) before it reaches the area where living things are concentrated. The amount of energy which is actually available to organisms at the land or water surface ('incident solar radiation') varies from about $2·0-2·5 \times 10^8$ calories per sq m in tropical regions. Green plants are able to combine some of this energy with elements from the non-living pool to form energy-rich 'organic' compounds and the plants themselves and all of the other organisms of the biosphere are dependent on these for energy to carry out all their physiological processes and movement. For various reasons plants are not very efficient in capturing solar energy and only 1 or 2% (at most 4–5%) of incident solar radiation is made available to the living portion of the biosphere. This energy, which is essential for all biological processes, is therefore quite scarce and there is competition amongst organisms for this resource. Scarcity of energy almost certainly controls the rate of many biological processes. I.N.H.

BIPOLARITY, a pattern of distribution in which a particular genus or species of marine animal is found at high altitudes in both the northern and the southern hemisphere, but not in between. Animals with this type of distribution prefer the colder water temperatures found in higher latitudes, and do not normally inhabit the warmer equatorial or sub-equatorial waters between. Such an animal probably evolved in one hemisphere and later succeeded in crossing the equatorial region to the other hemisphere, possibly via the colder, deeper-lying levels of water. This migration would have been made easier by the fact that cold waters exist at quite shallow depths—350 ft (100 m)—along the west coasts of Africa and South America. This is due partly to cold currents which run northwards from the Antarctic, and partly to the upwelling of cold water from the ocean depths along the edges of the continental shelves.

BIRD-EATING SPIDERS, large spiders which sometimes catch and eat birds. Very small tropical birds are sometimes caught in the strong orb webs of *Nephila* but even the giant theraphosid spiders like *Zasiodora* and *Grammostola* catch birds very rarely despite their being called Mygale or Bird spiders. See also Tarantula spiders.

BIRD FANCIER, one who keeps birds which, ideally, conform to a particular arbitrary standard of shape, size and colour laid down by the cage-bird fraternity; and in particular one who breeds birds with the aim of achieving this conformity. Bird fanciers tend to concentrate mostly on the established favourites such as the canary, budgerigars and certain other finches and parrots.

BIRDS, a class of warm-blooded, oviparous, vertebrate animals characterized by a comprehensive adaptation of the body for flight and unique in having feathers as outgrowths of the skin. This specialization, based on principles different from those exemplified in other flying animals, imposes a substantial degree of structural uniformity on members of the class. A bird is thus easily recognizable as such by anyone; even those species that have lost the power of flight retain the basic characters of the primary adaptation. Within limits, however, there is abundant diversity among the approximately 8,600 species of birds living at the time.

Adaptation for flight. Birds conform with the tetrapod structural pattern of the higher vertebrates, but have the two forelimbs modified as wings to serve as organs of flight. In consequence, they are bipedal when not airborne and the functions of a hand devolve mainly upon the head, particularly on the bill. These points hold good even for flightless birds, whether the wings have become reduced as in 'Ratite' birds or secondarily modified for swimming as in penguins.

Several other adaptations subserve the purposes of flight. Parts of the skeleton are fused to provide a rigid fulcrum for the action of the wings. The breast muscles are greatly developed to supply the motive power; and the breastbone has a keel (not in ratites) to give a greater surface for their attachment. Hollow bones are among the adaptations to give general lightness. The respiratory system is amplified by a series of communicating air-sacs in different parts of the body. The body as a whole is streamlined, when in the posture of flight. Even the fact that only one egg of a clutch is laid at a

Birds often fly in large flocks, such as dunlin *Calidris alpina* on the shores of western Europe, where they are the commonest birds.

Chick of Black-headed gull hatching.

time is helpful by minimizing sudden changes in total weight. The plumage combines efficiency in conserving heat with extreme lightness. Apart from the functions of the plumage as a body covering, and as an element in forms of display, certain feathers—notably the strong quills—extend the effective area of wings and tail.

Classification of Birds. As a framework for further consideration of diversity within the class Aves, it is necessary to have some statement of the categories into which the present-day species may be divided. (Fossil forms require separate consideration; the available picture is much less complete and

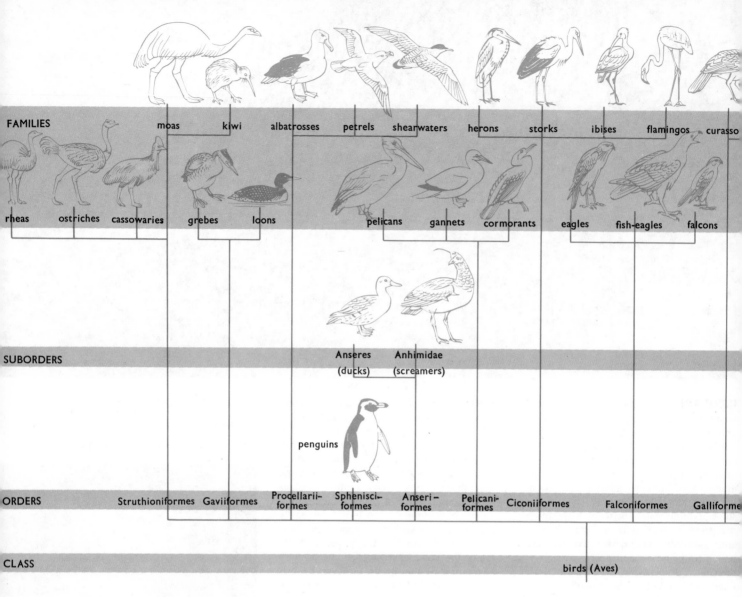

FAMILIES

moas kiwi albatrosses petrels shearwaters herons storks ibises flamingos curasso

rheas ostriches cassowaries grebes loons pelicans gannets cormorants eagles fish-eagles falcons

SUBORDERS

Anseres Anhimidae
(ducks) (screamers)

penguins

ORDERS

Struthioniformes Gaviiformes Procellarii-formes Spheisci-formes Anseri-formes Pelicani-formes Ciconiiformes Falconiformes Galliforme

CLASS

birds (Aves)

taxonomy is complicated by differences in temporal 'horizon'.) All classifications are subjective concepts and more or less controversial, but one that is widely used today divides 'recent' birds into orders as follows, beginning with the supposedly most primitive and leading up to the more highly developed:

These 29 orders are divisible into 158 families (including 2 orders and 4 families that have become extinct within recent times). In some of the families it is convenient to recognize subfamilies. About a third of the total number of families, and about half the total number of species, are included in the Passeriformes. It is common to speak of all the other orders, together, as 'non-passerine'.

Of the 154 extant families, 63 are found both in the Old World and in the New. Of these, eight are restricted to the tropics, four to the northern hemisphere and three to the southern. Of the rest, 57 are found only in the Old World and 34 only in the New World. The diagram above groups some orders of the table together to facilitate visualization.

Struthioniformes	Ostrich
Rheiformes	Rheas
Casuariiformes	Cassowaries and emu
Dinornithiformes	Moas (recently extinct)
Apterygiformes	Kiwis
Aepyornithiformes	Elephant birds (recently extinct)
Tinamiformes	Tinamous
Sphenisciformes	Penguins
Gaviiformes	Divers (loons)
Podicipediformes	Grebes
Procellariiformes	Petrels and albatrosses
Pelecaniformes	Pelicans, cormorants, gannets etc.
Ciconiiformes	Herons, storks, ibises, flamingos etc.
Anseriformes	Ducks, geese, swans and screamers

Falconiformes	Birds of prey (diurnal)
Galliformes	Megapodes, curassows, grouse, pheasants, guineafowl, turkeys and hoatzin
Gruiformes	Buttonquail, cranes, rails, bustards etc.
Charadriiformes	Jacanas, plovers, sandpipers, coursers, skuas, gulls, terns, auks etc.
Columbiformes	Sandgrouse, dodo (recently extinct) and pigeons
Psittaciformes	Parrots
Cuculiformes	Turacos and cuckoos
Strigiformes	Owls
Caprimulgiformes	Oilbird, nightjars etc.
Apodiformes	Swifts and hummingbirds

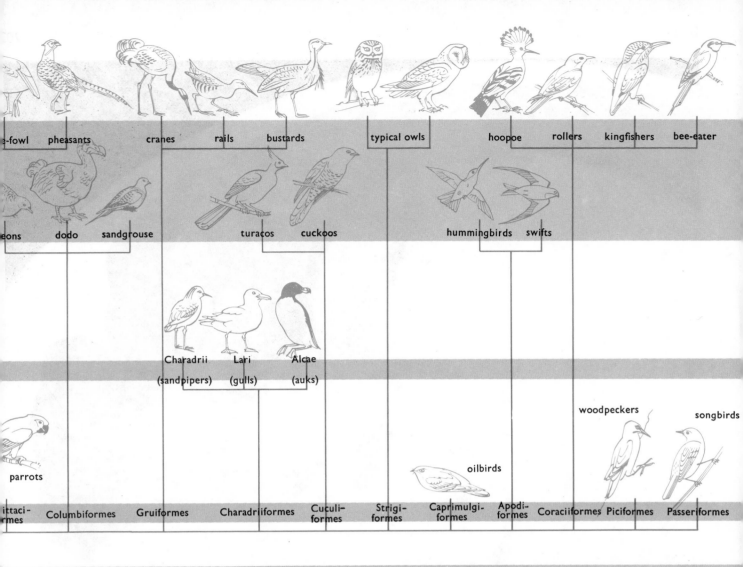

e-fowl | pheasants | cranes | rails | bustards | typical owls | hoopoe | rollers | kingfishers | bee-eater

eons | dodo | sandgrouse | turacos | cuckoos | hummingbirds | swifts

Charadrii | Lari | Alcae
(sandpipers) | (gulls) | (auks)

woodpeckers | songbirds

parrots | oilbirds

ittaci-formes | Columbiformes | Gruiformes | Charadriiformes | Cuculi-formes | Strigi-formes | Caprimulgi-formes | Apodi-formes | Coraciiformes | Piciformes | Passeriformes

Coliiformes	Mousebirds
Trogoniformes	Trogons
Coraciiformes	Kingfishers, bee-eaters, rollers, hoopoe, horn-bills etc.
Piciformes	Barbets, honeyguides, toucans, wood-peckers etc.
Passeriformes	Ovenbirds, antbirds, Tyrant flycatchers, lyrebirds etc. Numer-ous families of 'song-birds' (including Birds of paradise, crows etc.)

Dimensions. Flight imposes a limit on size, because weight increases as the cube of the linear dimension, whereas the lifting area increases only as the square. Ignoring any relatively minor advantages that can be derived from shape, it follows that the heavier bird requires, proportionately to weight, more power for equivalent perform-ance. Thus there are not, and probably never were, any enormous flying birds, The largest birds are the flightless ratite species such as the ostrich *Struthio camelus,* which may stand 8 ft (2·4 m) high and weigh as much as 300 lb (136 kg). The Giant moa *Dinornis maximus* of New Zealand, which became extinct in recent times, may have been nearly 10 ft (3 m) high if it held its neck erect and it has been estimated that *Aepyornis titan,* the largest of the likewise extinct Elephant birds of Madagascar, may have weighed nearly 1,000 lb (450 kg).

The heaviest flying bird is probably the male Trumpeter swan *Cygnus cygnus buc-cinator,* weighing up to 38 lb (17·2 kg). The Trumpeter swan, the White pelican *Pele-canus erythrorhynchos* of America and the Andean condor *Vultur gryphus* all have wing-spans of up to 10 ft (3 m), but the greatest wing-span is probably that of a bird with a lighter body, the Wandering albatross *Diomedea exulans,* in which 11½ ft (3·5 m)

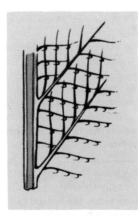

Contour feathers consist of a quill (an opaque horny tube) and a vane. The vane consists of two rows of barbs, the branches of which interlock by means of hooks, thus en-suring a rigid framework.

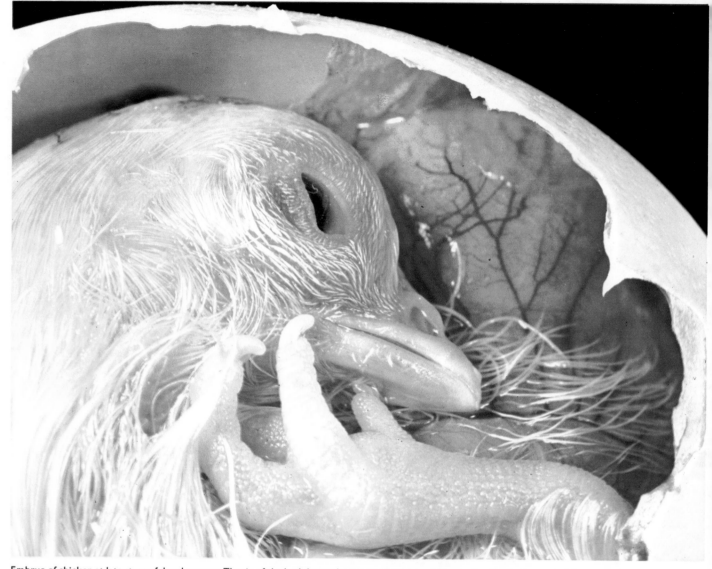

Embryo of chicken at late stage of development. The tip of the beak bears the egg tooth which will be used to break the eggshell from the inside. The network of blood vessels on the yolk sac is also clearly visible; this is used by the embryo for getting food from the yolk

has been reliably recorded. The smallest hummingbirds, such as *Klais guimeti,* may weigh less than $\frac{1}{10}$ oz (2·55 gm) and measure no more than $2\frac{1}{2}$ in (6·3 cm) in length, including a relatively long bill.

In some species the sexes differ in size, the males usually being the larger. As a rule the difference is slight, but in a few instances it is conspicuous. In the capercaillie *Tetrao urogallus* the linear dimensions of the hen. are only three-quarters of those of the cock. Sometimes the female is the larger, and in certain birds of prey this is very noticeable.

Form. The general form of the body may be elongated or compact, or anything between; but the contour is masked, to varying degrees, by the plumage. The tail, consisting entirely of feathers, may contribute a great deal to the bird's appearance and there is a great variety in tails, both in shape and in length. Similarly with length of leg: the long legs of, for example, storks (Ciconiidae) and herons (Ardeidae) are associated with the

habit of wading in shallow water or marshy ground; other instances are the cranes (Gruidae) and the avocets and stilts (Recurvirostridae). The long and powerful legs of ratite birds are for swift running. A long neck tends to go with long legs and may be a conspicuous feature, especially if associated with a large bill.

Apparent form may be affected by the posture in which the body is held, from a horizontal to a more upright stance, depending largely on how far back the legs are set. And the neck may be extended forwards, or forwards and upwards, or be held almost vertically. Herons hold their long necks partly retracted in a curve, but extend them upwards when alerted. Similarly, appearance in the air may depend on manner of flight, on the shape of the wings and on how the long neck and long legs are held. The neck is commonly extended forwards as, for instance, in storks and cranes, but it may be retracted, as in herons. The legs are usually

retracted in flight, but in storks, herons and others they are trailed behind.

Plumage. A separate article is devoted to the unit of plumage, the feather, but plumage as a whole must also be considered. It serves as a protective and insulating cover for most of the body surface; it helps to streamline the shape of the body and so to reduce friction in air or water; and parts of it are essential components of the apparatus of flight. The care and renewal of the plumage are considered separately under preening and moulting in birds,

The colouration of the plumage is the most noticeable feature to the observer, and the pattern plays a very large part in the recognition of species. In many instances the plumage is cryptic, providing a protective

A pair of White storks *Ciconia ciconia* at their huge nest of sticks on a roof-top in Europe. Although held in respect, even affection, and despite human efforts to help them, the number of storks is decreasing.

camouflage; in others it is mimetic or contributes to an aggressive appearance. Bright colours and specially shaped plumes play an important part in display and thus have a value in sexual selection. The sexes may be more or less alike in appearance, or one, usually the male, has bright hues while the other is plain. Immature birds of most species are duller than the adults, or than the brighter of these, and very young chicks have a downy plumage. Sometimes a bright breeding plumage, in one or both sexes, is replaced by a more sober dress in winter.

Pheasants (Phasianidae), ducks (Anatidae), finches (Fringillidae) and Birds of paradise (Paradisaeidae) are among the many groups that provide striking examples of sexual dimorphism in plumage colouration. The Rock thrush *Monticola saxatilis* of Europe, the Scarlet tanager *Piranga olivacea* of North America, and the Splendid fairy wren *Malurus splendens* of Australia well exemplify bright plumage in the male during the breeding season only, the winter plumage resembling that of the female. In some other birds, such as the ptarmigan *Lagopus mutus* and the Grey (or Black-bellied) plover *Pluvialis squatarola,* the sexes are similar but both undergo striking seasonal changes. Again, there are species in which the sexes are both brightly coloured throughout the year, e.g. the Cuban trogon *Priotelus tennurus* the Carmine bee-eater *Merops nubicus* and many others, notably in the tropics. In the Eclectus parrot *Lorius roratus* of Australasia, unusually, both sexes are permanently brightly coloured but quite differently, the female being predominantly red and the male predominantly green.

Locomotion (other than aerial). Powers of aquatic or terrestrial locomotion are highly developed in many species; and for flightless birds special ability in another mode is almost a prime essential, although there are a few exceptions such as the nocturnal kiwis (Apterygidae). Penguins (Spheniscidae) and many other birds are much at home in the water, swimming not only on the surface but below it and sometimes diving to depths of as much as 200 ft (70 m). In some, such as the auks (Alcidae) and the Diving petrels (Pelecanoididae), the wings, although not modified as flippers, are used for propulsion under water. More commonly the legs alone are used, the wings being held more or less close to the sides. Notable swimmers not already mentioned include the divers or loons (Gaviidae), the grebes (Podicipitidae), many of the ducks (Anatidae), a few of the rails (Rallidae), the cormorants (Phalacrocoracidae), the finfoots (Heliornithidae), and the dippers (Cinclidae). Many others, such as the remaining ducks, geese and swans, habitually swim on the surface and may 'up-end' in shallow water to feed from the bottom. Pelicans (Pelecanidae), gulls (Larinae, Laridae) and phalaropes (Phalaropodidae) are also regular

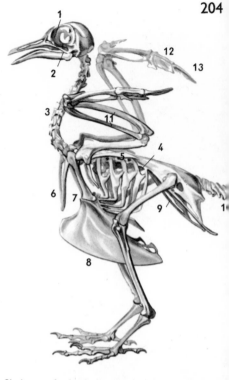

Skeleton of a bird: 1. scleral ring, 2. quadratojugal, 3. vertebrae, 4. rib, 5. scapula, 6. furcula (fused clavicles), 7. coracoid, 8. sternal keel, 9. pelvis, 10. caudal vertebrae, 11. radius and ulna, 12. 1st finger (bastard wing), 13. 2nd finger.

Below left: Nest of oystercatcher *Haematopus ostralegus,* scratchedinto the surface of the ground and lined with shells, pebbles and scraps of dried plants.

Below right: Fieldfare *Turdus pilaris* at nest.

Honey-buzzard *Pernis apivorus*, of Europe.

The Nicobar pigeon *Caloenas nicobarica* has neck feathers, or hackles, like those of a barnyard cockerel.

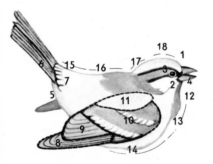

Topography of a bird: 1. forehead, 2. lore, 3. eye, 4. beak, 5. crissum (circumcloacal), 6. tail feathers, 7. tail coverts, 8. primary wing feathers, 9. secondary wing feathers, 10. wing coverts, 11. scapulars, 12. throat, 13. breast, 14. abdomen, 15. rump, 16. back, 17. nape, 18. crown.

surface swimmers. Doubtless almost any bird can swim in an emergency.

There are also birds that plunge into water from a height, whether from the air or from a perch, to catch their prey; but although they may be momentarily submerged they usually resume their flight immediately. Examples of the plunging mode are gannets (Sulidae), tropicbirds (Phaethontidae), terns (Sterninae, Laridae) and kingfishers (Alcedinidae)—also the Brown pelican *Pelecanus occidentalis* of the New World.

The most obvious adaptation to an aquatic life, found in the majority of the groups mentioned above, is webbing of the feet. The web usually extends between the three forward-directed toes; but in the Pelecaniformes it unites all four toes. As an alternative to webbing, the separate toes may be fringed or lobed, as in the grebes, phalar-opes and coots (Fulicinae, Rallidae). Birds that dive from the surface or plunge from aloft tend also to have physiological adaptations which make it possible to reduce specific gravity.

On the ground, most non-passerine birds walk or run and some of them are highly proficient in this form of movement. The ratite birds are, of course, pre-eminent, and the ostrich is credited with a top speed of about 40 mph (64 kph). Other particularly strong runners are the tinamous (Tinamidae), bustards (Otididae), some of the Galliformes and many of the Charadriiformes. Some aquatic birds and others with short legs can manage little more than a waddle, and the divers (loons) have the legs set so far back that they merely push themselves along over very short distances. They never attempt to go far on land.

Relatively few of the Passeriformes habitually walk or run; these include most of the crows (Corvidae), the starlings (Sturnidae), the larks (Alaudidae) and the wagtails (Motacillidae). The other members of the order commonly 'hop', making a series of short jumps with the feet together. The pittas (Pittidae) make long bounds. Many birds that usually hop also walk on occasion.

Progression on more or less vertical surfaces, such as tree-trunks or rock-faces, calls for climbing, and in some groups the feet are specially adapted for this type of movement; there may also be a stiff tail to lend support. The woodpeckers (Picidae) are the most familiar of several examples.

Eight types of birds' feet showing how the shape is linked with habits: 1. perching (chaffinch), 2. climbing (woodpecker), 3. swimming (duck), 4. walking (chicken), 5. wading (heron), 6. seizing (owl), 7. swimming (coot), 8. walking on snow (ptarmigan).

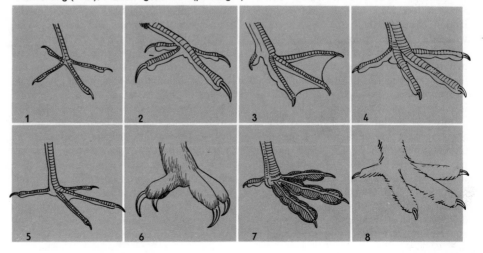

Adaptations for terrestrial locomotion, and for standing or perching, are to be found in the number, arrangement and size of the toes. No bird has more than four toes, and one of these is often greatly reduced or absent. The ostrich is unique in having only two toes. The most common arrangement is for three toes to be directed forwards, while the hallux, if present, is behind. But all four toes may be directed forwards as in the swifts (Apodidae), which cling to vertical surfaces, or the hallux may be capable of turning either backwards or forwards, as in the mousebirds (Coliidae), or it may be the outer forward toe that has this capacity, as in most owls (Strigiformes). Or, again, the toes may be arranged permanently in pairs (zygodactyl); in the woodpeckers (Picidae) and parrots (Psittacidae), among others, it is the first and fourth toes that point backwards, but in trogons (Trogonidae) it is the first and second. There is also the syndactyl foot of the kingfishers and others, in which the third and fourth toes are partly united into a broad sole.

The foot in the Passeriformes is adapted for perching on small branches or the like; the three front toes and the one hind toe are all well developed and freely mobile, so that the perch can be firmly gripped. The zygodactyl foot of parrots and others is also very effective for perching. Some birds that walk on soft ground have very long toes to distribute the weight, as in the lily-trotter *Actophilornis africanus*. Some birds that wade, or walk on soft ground, have webbed feet although they do not ordinarily swim, for example the storks. The feathered toes of the ptarmigan *Lagopus mutus* in winter plumage provide the bird with 'snow-shoes', and there are other examples among its kin.

Habitat. The mode of life of a bird is largely an adaptation to the nature of its chosen habitat. However, some species show notable versatility in utilizing a variety of habitats, although others seem to be successful only in a particular combination of circumstances or are dependent on the presence of some apparently essential feature such as a certain food plant. The greater the specialization, of course, the less is the competition with other species making generally similar demands on the environment. These demands relate to nesting opportunities and feeding opportunities of suitable kinds; and in the breeding season both must be available in sufficiently close proximity.

Birds as a class have exploited almost every possible type of habitat that the world presents; only the icy polar wastes and the most arid deserts defeat them, for even the widest expanses of ocean provide many of them with food outside their breeding seasons. Roughly, the habitats can be divided into terrestrial, aquatic (freshwater), and marine. The first can be subdivided in

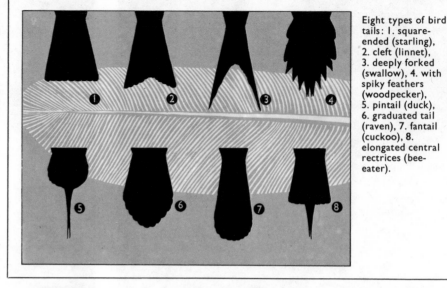

Eight types of bird tails: 1. square-ended (starling), 2. cleft (linnet), 3. deeply forked (swallow), 4. with spiky feathers (woodpecker), 5. pintail (duck), 6. graduated tail (raven), 7. fantail (cuckoo), 8. elongated central rectrices (bee-eater).

accordance with the vegetation cover. Thus there are arboreal birds, inhabiting forests or woodlands or scrub consisting of bushes, and other birds that inhabit dense herbage. In contrast there are birds that live in open country with short or sparse vegetation, or among stones and rocks or on cliffs. Most of these terrestrial birds find their food in the vegetation or on the ground; some prey on smaller birds caught on the wing or on flying insects, but this food supply is, of course, a product of the terrain below.

The preferences of freshwater birds may be for marshes, for shallow pools, for larger stretches of water, or for swift-running streams. These species may seek their food by wading, by up-ending, or by swimming and diving in the manner already described. Marine species, all breeding on coasts or islands, may be roughly grouped as inshore, offshore and pelagic in their feeding habits. The first generally keep within sight of land, at any season, and often come ashore to roost at night; examples are to be found among the gulls, cormorants and marine ducks. The birds in the second group live continuously at sea except when breeding, but tend to keep within the limits of the continental shelf. They are mostly fish-eaters and include the gannets and the auks. The true pelagic birds, such as the albatrosses and petrels (Procellariiformes), range widely over the ocean and they feed mainly on squids and planktonic organisms.

Not all bird habitats are truly natural. Many species have adapted themselves to environments that have been greatly modified and sometimes wholly fabricated by mankind; and this evolution must, in some areas, have occurred within the last few centuries. Many birds now find their most congenial habitat in suburban gardens, and others on cultivated farmland. Some show a preference for buildings in their choice of nesting sites. It is quite exceptional today, for

instance, for the swallow *Hirundo rustica* to nest anywhere else. The deliberate improvement of a habitat by the provision of artificial nest-boxes is another aspect.

Food. Some bird species can be described as omnivorous, so wide is the range of their food choice. This is true of many of the crows and gulls, for example. Many vary their diet with age or season or under pressure of circumstances. Relatively few are so highly specialized that they are dependent on the availability of only one particular source of food, but this is true of the Snail kite *Rostrhamus sociabilis*, for example, which lives entirely on molluscs of the genus *Pomacea*.

With such provisos, however, one may broadly characterize the food preferences of species, and often of whole families, as being for vegetable or animal food, and for particular kinds of whichever is favoured. Thus, a vegetarian species may live mainly on hard seeds or nuts, or on soft fruits or herbage; or it may drink nectar from flowers (but this often contains small insects) as do the hummingbirds (Trochilidae) of the New World or the sunbirds (Nectariniidae) and the honey-eaters (Meliphagidae) of the Old World. A carnivorous species may eat a variety of small animals found on or in the ground or water; or it may be wholly insectivorous; or it may hunt larger prey, including mammals, birds and reptiles; or it may catch fish; or, again it may subsist on carrion, as do the vultures of the Old World (Aegypiinae, Accipitridae) and of the New World (Cathartidae). A few, such as skuas (Stercorariidae) and the frigatebirds (Fregatidae), are piratical, robbing other birds of newly caught prey, and the oxpeckers *Buphagus* spp may be described as truly parasitic. There are also innocuous relationships, where the bird benefits from the actions of another species of bird or a mammal which disturbs the bird's prey, as with the Cattle egret *Ardeola ibis*. The dependence of honeyguides (Indicatoridae) on ratels or men is of special interest.

Adaptations to feeding habits are to be found in the shape of the bill and in the anatomy of the digestive system. It is true, however, that in a minority of birds the feet play an essentially manual part in dealing with food, witness the talons of the owls (Strigiformes) and diurnal birds of prey (Falconiformes). The parrots (Psittacidae), titmice (Paridae) and a few others use the feet for holding, or in some cases even for conveying food to the mouth. Some birds, notably the Galliformes, use the feet for scratching the ground to find food just below the surface.

A few examples of adaptive bill forms are: the conical bills of seed-eating finches (Fringillidae), the strongly hooked bills of birds of prey, the chisel-like bills of woodpeckers, the slender decurved bills of the nectar-drinkers already mentioned, and the very small bills —associated with a wide gape—of aerial insect-catchers such as the swifts (Apodidae).

The plovers and their kin (Charadriiformes) tend to have rather long, or very long, bills adapted for probing the ground, but these show a variety of forms—straight as in the snipe *Gallinago gallinago,* decurved as in the curlew *Numenius arquata,* recurved as in the avocet *Recurvirostra avosetta,* curved sideways (to the right) in the unique case of the Wry-bill plover *Anarhynchus frontalis* of New Zealand. Another New Zealand bird, the now extinct Huia *Heteralocha acutirostris* (Callaeidae), was peculiar in having a very different form of bill in the male and the female.

There is likewise a variety in the adaptations of the bill to catching fish—the dagger-shaped bill of herons, the hooked bill of the cormorants, and the saw-edged mandibles of the mergansers *Mergus* spp. The bills of some of the aquatic birds that feed on small organisms are broad, and may be furnished with internal ridges—the shoveler *Anas clypeata* is notable among the ducks, the spoonbills (Plataleinae, Threskiornithidae) live up to their name, and the flamingos (Phoenicopteridae) have one of the most extraordinary of all. The skimmers (Rynchopidae) have the lower mandible much longer than the upper, forming a projecting scoop.

Some birds are nocturnal or crepuscular in their feeding habits and, when they are predatory, as are the owls, (Strigiformes), this calls for special adaptations in vision and hearing.

Reproduction. Most bird species are monogamous, in that they form pairs either for the rearing of a brood, for the season, or for life. Some are polygamous, but polyandry is rare. The extent to which the sexes share parental duties varies widely. In some species there is almost complete equality in the division of labour, but in others the male is less assiduous or takes part only in certain phases, such as feeding the young. In others again the male is inattentive to domestic tasks. In a few, such as the phalaropes (Phalaropodidae), the roles of the sexes, apart from laying, are almost reversed. Where this is the case, the female is the dominant partner and may be the bigger and more brightly coloured bird. Parasitism, in which the incubation of the eggs and the rearing of the young is foisted onto birds of another species, occurs in six families, the

cuckoos (Cuculidae) of the Old World being the best known example.

Many birds, including most passerines, are solitary nesters, whether they be gregarious at other times or not. The pair, in these cases, vigorously defends its chosen 'territory' against other individuals of the species. The male sings in its territory both to attract a mate and to warn off intruders (see bird song).

Some gregarious species, however, nest in colonies. These may be of very great size, with the nests crowded together. This is true of many seabirds, of which the gannet *Sula bassana* and the Sooty ('wideawake') tern *Sterna fuscata* are examples. It is true also of various herons, storks, pelicans and the like and these often form mixed colonies of several species—a wonderful sight, for example in the trees around an African village. Some colonies of flamingos on the shores of brackish lakes, are of spectacular extent.

Nesting sites are as diverse as habitats. They may be in trees, bushes or herbage; among rocks or on cliff ledges; in holes; in reed-beds or floating on the water; or on open ground. The nests themselves may be no more than hollows in the ground or a little lining material in a natural crevice or burrowed hole. Or they may be more or less elaborate structures of herbage, sticks, stones, mud, or other materials, and sometimes of substantial size. A nest may be abandoned after it has served its purpose or it may be used in successive years, with necessary repairs or cumulative additions. Some birds, regularly or occasionally, adopt old nests of other species.

Laying tends to be so timed that the young will hatch when their food supply is

Birds sometimes are very colourful: left, aracari *Pteroglossus hypoglaucus*, right, Bleeding-heart pigeon *Gallicolumba luzonica*.

most abundant. Breeding seasons thus vary in accordance with the food preference of the species. In the tropics there is often some breeding throughout the year. See also eggs and incubation.

The condition of the young when hatched differs between one group and another. Nice (1962) has defined four categories, with several subdivisions. The 'precocials' are hatched with their eyes open and with a covering of down, and they leave the nest almost immediately: they may be independent of their parents as in megapodes (Megapodiidae) such as the Mallee fowl *Leipoa ocellata*; they may follow their parents but find their own food as in ducks and plovers; they may follow their parents and be shown food by them as in some pheasants; or they may follow their parents and be fed by them, as in rails. The 'semi-precocials' are born in a similar condition but are less mobile, remaining in the nest for a time and being fed by the parents, as in the gulls. The 'semi-altricials' are hatched with a covering of down but are unable to leave the nest; they may have their eyes open as in diurnal birds of prey or closed as in owls. The 'altricials' are hatched with their eyes closed and with little or no down, and they are unable to leave the nest until ready to fly. This is characteristic of the Passeriformes.

The 'pullus' (chick or nestling) stage is followed by that of the fully-grown juvenile bird. Its period of immaturity may last only until the next breeding season, or the next but one, or it may last for several years. The losses of eggs, pulli and juveniles is very high for most species, and the average further life for adult song-birds (Passeriformes) is only one or two years, for some gulls two or three years, for the swift *Apus apus* four or five years, for the Yellow-eyed penguin *Megadyptes antipodes* nine or ten years, and for the Royal albatross *Diomedea epomophora* perhaps 30–40 years. Reliable statistics for wild birds under natural conditions are, however, available for only a few species. The potential age which an individual bird *may* attain is something different; even in a wild state. As shown by ringing records, a Herring gull *Larus argentatus* has been known to exceed 30 years and, to take an example from the other end of the scale, a Blue tit *Parus caeruleus* eight years. Greater ages have been recorded among captive birds. Very roughly, the potential life-span is correlated with size. PHYLUM: Aves. A.L.T.

BIRDS, FOSSIL, birds preserved in the form of fossils. These may be very old and completely fossilized, as in the case of *Archaeopteryx,* or they may be relatively recent and incompletely fossilized as with, for example, the remains of the Great auk, moas and dodo, which are known as sub-fossils.

Archaeopteryx from the Jurassic period some 150 million years ago is the oldest known fossil bird and the most important, for its remains show both reptilian and avian features. The statement that 'birds are only glorified reptiles', attributed to various people, including T. H. Huxley, is a just one. *Archaeopteryx,* though undoubtedly a bird, was reptilian in so many of its skeletal features that if it were not for the clear fossil imprint of feathers it would probably be classed as a reptile—as in fact it once was. Birds and mammals, therefore, had a common ancestry in the reptiles, though the mammals arose much earlier than the birds.

There can be little doubt that *Archaeopteryx,* or a creature like it, was ancestral to more recent birds. But the fossil record is, understandably, incomplete and estimations of the number of good species over the past 150 million years vary from under $\frac{1}{2}$ million (James Fisher) to over $1\frac{1}{2}$ million (Pierce Brodkorb). For only rarely have birds died under conditions favourable for fossilization. Only when the carcasses fall into still or slowly moving water is there a chance of them becoming covered with suitable sedimentary material for preservation. However in addition to fossil material from the 8,600-odd species of living birds, an additional 850 or more species are known from fossils only.

An important factor in the discovery of fossil material has been the occurrence of 'graveyards' wherein large numbers of animals were overcome by some unusual environmental circumstance. The most famous of such graveyards is that in the tar pit of Rancho La Brea in Los Angeles where thousands of animals became trapped during the Pleistocene period in asphalt pools. In one of these pits 30,000 bones of 81 species of birds have been found.

An outline of the bird remains so far recorded from various areas is as follows. The deposits of 65 million years of the Cretaceous period have as yet yielded few fossils, though in these deposits were found the famous—if somewhat misnamed— 'toothed birds'. The next oldest specimen to *Archaeopteryx* is the thigh bone of a possible goose from the Lower Cretaceous of France.

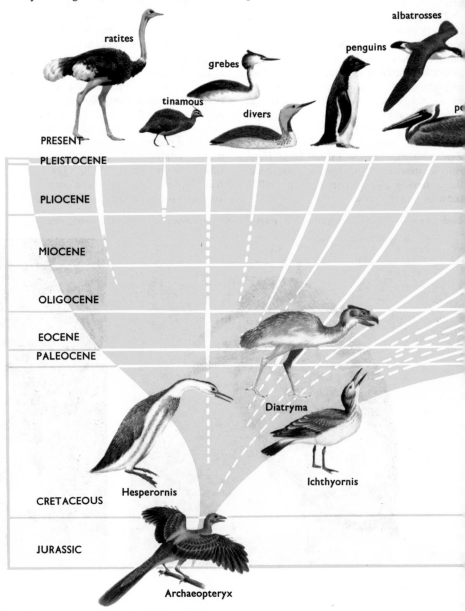

This is followed by a number of bones of possibly two species of pigeon-sized sea bird from England, perhaps ancestral to the divers.

The Upper Cretaceous has been slightly more prolific, largely by reason of the finds in the Niobrara chalk beds of Kansas. We know that when these beds were the bottom of an inland sea there were at least six species of tern-like birds flying and probably fishing there. These have been given the generic name *Ichthyornis* and one of them, *I. victor*, is known from almost complete skeletons. These species have long been thought to be toothed, but re-examination shows that their supposed jaws were those of a contemporary reptile. Another of the traditionally toothed-birds from the same area is *Hesperornis*, 6 ft (1·8 m) long and flightless. This bird was an accomplished swimmer, being like the divers in appearance though it was probably more closely related to the grebes. The fossil evidence with respect to teeth is slightly more positive in the case of *Hesperornis*, one skull being in good enough

condition for us to be fairly sure that teeth were in fact present.

Two other birds, closely related to *Ichthyornis* and *Hesperornis* respectively, have been found in the Niobrara. Otherwise, our knowledge of the Upper Cretaceous avifauna is restricted to little more than a handful of specimens. These include one or two preflamingos from Sweden; an ancestral cormorant from Transylvania; a pre-ibis from Alabama; and diver and flamingo relatives from Wyoming.

70 million years ago the Cretaceous period was replaced by what we now call the Paleocene, thus ending the great Mesozoic era and beginning the Cenozoic in which we live today. This was a period of great change. Oceans appeared, new land masses were raised and much of Europe and North America was tropical. During this time the great reptiles were replaced by birds and mammals and the end of the Cretaceous must have been a time of considerable avian development, for from the Paleocene we have fossils belonging to the modern families

of cormorants, rails, sandpipers and divers.

After 10 million years of Paleocene came the 20 million years of the Eocene; the period, possibly, of maximum radiation of avian types. We have evidence from this period of many more families, including vultures, hawks, herons, cranes, bustards, gulls, auks, flamingos, partridges, kingfishers, starlings and swifts. The beds of the Paris Basin alone have yielded 40 species of 25 genera. Of particular note are the first known remains of a true penguin from the early Eocene of New Zealand and the enormous, flightless, and probably predatory, diatrymids of Europe and North America. These birds stood up to 7 ft (2·1 m) tall, were very powerful, and had a massive hooked beak on a skull the size of that of a horse.

Avian evolutionary radiation did not end with the Eocene but the main lines of development were already drawn and we will now concentrate on the more biologically significant among these.

By the end of the Miocene, some 11 million years ago, the majority of avian

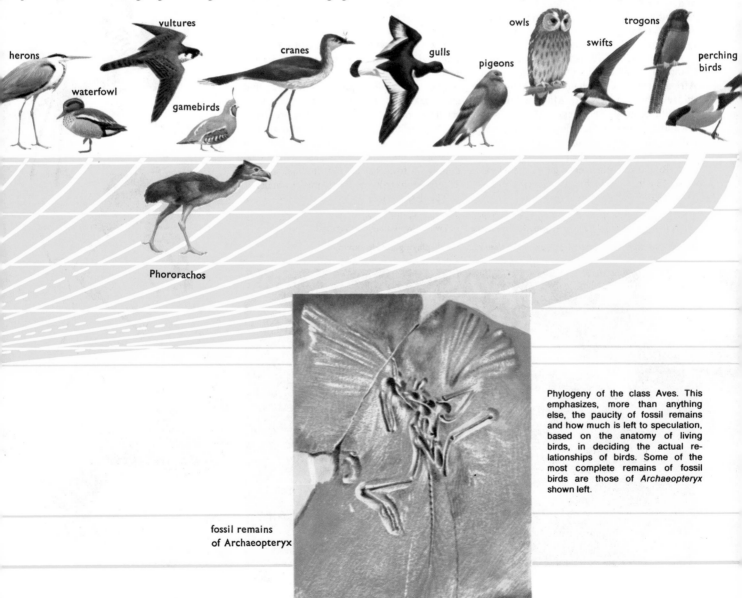

herons   vultures   cranes   gulls   owls   swifts   trogons   pigeons   perching birds
waterfowl   gamebirds   Phororachos

fossil remains of Archaeopteryx

Phylogeny of the class Aves. This emphasizes, more than anything else, the paucity of fossil remains and how much is left to speculation, based on the anatomy of living birds, in deciding the actual relationships of birds. Some of the most complete remains of fossil birds are those of *Archaeopteryx* shown left.

families and many of the genera were probably in existence, as shown by the fossil record in many parts of the world. When the Pliocene ended 1 million years ago the bulk of the modern genera must have been well established and the Pleistocene which followed was, for the birds, largely a time of stabilization or extinction.

The fossil record confirms that the most important and latest radiation has been that of the Passeriformes, the great order of perching birds which contains more than half the species of birds and a third of the families. This order developed very rapidly during the Pliocene and since then has been the dominant avian line in almost all parts of the world.

The Pliocene was also a period of expansion for some of the large flightless birds, such as the emus, ostriches and moas. The moas are interesting in that while usually regarded as being extinct (there is the intriguing possibility that some small specimens may survive, hidden in the New Zealand jungles) their remains exist in unfossilized and sub-fossil as well as fossil form. These remains reveal a series of 20 or more species varying from turkey-sized birds to some growing to a height of 12 ft (3·6 m).

Another group of large flightless birds found in fossil and sub-fossil form is the African family of Elephant birds, Aepyornithidae, which survived in Madagascar into the 19th century. The biggest of these was not quite as tall as the tallest moa but was bulkier, and with a weight of up to 1,000 lb (450 kg) was probably the heaviest bird of all time. Remains of their eggs give dimensions up to $13\frac{1}{2}$ in (34 cm) by 9 in (23 cm) and a capacity of 2 gall (9 litres).

Finally we may consider a more successful flightless group, the penguins, with 17 living species and many more known from fossils. A fine fossil series shows us that after the early Eocene the penguins increased in size, two Miocene species standing, respectively, rather more, and rather less than 5 ft (1·5 m) high. The largest living species is the Emperor penguin, standing up to 3 ft 6 in (1 m), and the smallest is the Little blue, standing only about 14 in (35 cm). Clearly, the penguins did not concentrate on sheer size, and this may have been contributory to their continued success. The fossil record assists greatly in our understanding, not only of the avian past, but also of birds still living today.

P.M.D

BIRDS OF PARADISE, a family of about 40 species of strongly-built perching birds famous for the brilliantly coloured and elaborately shaped plumes used in display. They are closely related to the bowerbirds and may well belong to the same family. Birds of paradise range from 5–40 in (13–100 cm) long. Their legs and feet are rather stout and their tails vary from short and square to very long and wire-like. The bill may be fairly heavy with or without a hooked tip or long, thin and sickle-shaped. In some species the sexes are much alike but others show such marked sexual dimorphism in plumage that each sex was originally described as a separate species. Birds of paradise are found in the forests of New Guinea and nearby islands, with a few species in northern Australia and the Moluccas. They feed mainly on fruit, but also on insects, spiders, Tree frogs, lizards and other small animals.

The less ornate Birds of paradise have

1. *Paradisea apoda* (Greater bird of paradise); 2. *Paradisea rudolphi* (Blue bird of paradise); 3. *Cicinnurus regius* (King bird of paradise); 4. *Seleucidis melanoleuca* (Twelve-wired bird of paradise).

Prince Rudolph's blue bird of paradise *Paradisea rudolphi*, displaying upside-down.

black plumage with little or no decoration, as in the Paradise crow or Silky crow *Lycocorax pyrrhopterus* of the Moluccas in which both male and female are blackish with no ornamental feathers. The sexes of Mac-Gregor's bird of paradise *Macgregoria pulchra* are also similar, black with orange patches on the wings and orange overlapping wattles around the eyes. In Princess Loria's bird of paradise *Loria loria* the sexes are different; the female dull olive-brown and the male black with iridescent patches on wings and face. In the more ornate species the female remains dull brown or grey, while the male has elaborate crests or long plumes on the body or tail. One of the more ornate species is the 12-wired bird of paradise *Seleucidis melanoleuca* in which the male is black and yellow with yellow feathers on the flanks that end in 6 in (15 cm) tips that bend forwards. The King bird of paradise, the smallest species, has long curling, central tail feathers which are wire-like with 'flags' at the tips. The body is red above, white below. Another remarkable species is the King of Saxony bird of paradise *Pteridophora alberti*. Mainly black and yellow, the male has two long wire-like plumes set with small blue 'flags' trailing from the head. These are 18 in (45 cm) long, twice as long as the bird. Perhaps the most ornate, and bizarre, is the Superb bird of paradise *Lophorina superba* which is black with a bright bronze, green or mauve gloss and has an enormous 'cape' of long feathers on the nape which are raised in display.

The breeding habits of many species are not known but it seems that the more plainly coloured Birds of paradise are monogamous and the males assist in rearing the young. Brilliant plumage has developed in polygamous species where the sexes meet only for mating. The drab female raises the family alone, while the males are free to develop their spectacular plumage because there is a reduced need for camouflage in birds that do not sit on the nest. On the other hand, the development of plumes and colours is enhanced by the increased competition in communal displays. The males of the plainly coloured species, such as the Trumpet birds or manucodes *Manucodia,* chase the females through the trees and display to them, but the ornate males usually gather to display in particular places, sometimes with several males in one tree. The combination of displays and calls of several males is probably more successful in attracting females than the same number of isolated males. The males spread their plumes, flap the wings, sway and posture, and even display hanging upside down, as in the Greater bird of paradise *Paradisea apoda*. The King bird of paradise hangs upside down with spread wings and walks along the undersides of branches.

The nests are cup-shaped and are built in

Red plumed or Count Raggi's bird of paradise *Paradisea apoda raggiana*.

thick creepers or in forked branches, but the King bird of paradise nests in tree cavities. The clutch is of two pale pink to brown eggs.

It would be expected that the development of distinctive plumage would have reduced the chances of interbreeding but 19 hybrids have been recorded between different species, 14 of which were between species in different genera. This suggests that Birds of paradise in different genera are much more closely related than has been thought and the apparently profound differences in plumage are the result of 'run-away' evolution due to the polygamous habits of Birds of paradise. However, in the mountains of New Guinea, where Birds of paradise are most abundant, few species have overlapping ranges and the species in a particular genus are often isolated from one another in different mountain masses. Furthermore the genera tend to replace each other at different altitudes on any one mountain mass. FAMILY: Paradisaeidae, ORDER: Passeriformes, CLASS: Aves.

D.T.H.

BIRDS OF PARADISE became known when the survivors of Magellan's voyage around the world brought some skins back to the King of Spain. The Spanish court were so impressed with the splendid plumages that they decided that such birds could only have come from paradise. Even in the 19th century naturalists studying plumes imported for the feather trade refused to believe that some plumes were real, the manufacture of artificial plumes then being a common trick. Yet more strange, it was considered that, as the imported bodies had no legs, Birds of paradise must spend all their life in the air. No one thought of examining the carcases for signs of mutilation but elaborate hypotheses were invented. It was suggested that the birds of paradise floated effortlessly, feeding on the dew of heaven. They mated by the male wrapping his wire-like tail feathers around the female and she laid her egg in a hollow in his back.

Barn owl *Tyto alba* with a vole.

BIRDS OF PREY, theoretically, incorporates any bird that preys on other animals but as this would include herons, storks, pelicans, gulls and other fish-eating species, and insectivorous species, such as shrikes, the term is normally applied only to two orders of birds: the diurnal birds of prey (order Falconiformes) including New and Old World vultures, ospreys, kites, hawks, buzzards, eagles, Secretary birds and falcons; and the nocturnal birds of prey (order Strigiformes) including all owls.

Similarities between the two groups caused systematists at one time to place them together. Both have hooked bills for tearing flesh, and powerful taloned feet for grasping, holding and killing prey. They share, in addition, sexual size dimorphism, the males usually being smaller than the females, which is associated with the predatory habit. In Old and New World vultures, which do not normally kill anything, the sharp talons have atrophied and males are as large as, or larger than, females. All such behavioural and anatomical resemblances between owls and falconiforms are, however, the result of convergent evolution towards the common predatory way of life. In all modern classifications owls are not placed close to falconiforms, though recent anatomical work suggests that they may be distantly related to falcons (*Falco* and related genera). The similarities again may be due to convergent evolution, however.

The Falconiformes are not obviously closely related to any other birds. They are normally placed between the aquatic ducks and geese on one side and the gamebirds (*Galliformes*) on the other, resembling

neither to any great extent. A generalized Bird of prey, perhaps akin to present day New World vultures (Cathartidae) is known from Eocene times, 60 million years ago. The Falconiformes are thus probably an old group, long specialized for their particular function.

Present day falconiforms are divided into four main family groupings. (1) The New World vultures, of which there are six species, including condors, turkeys and King vultures. They are regarded as primitive and not closely related to Old World vultures, resembling these mainly in scavenging habits and their weak feet. They differ from other falconiforms in, for example, the possession of pervious nostrils and rudimentary hind toes. They make no nests, laying eggs on ledges, in hollows or on the ground. The inside colour of the egg-shell is yellowish-white.

(2) Ospreys, hawks, buzzards, kites, eagles and Old World vultures. The specialized osprey is placed in its own family Pandionidae but all others are perhaps best placed in one large intergrading family

White-backed vulture *Pseudogyps bengalensis* replaces the griffon in southern Asia.

Steller's sea eagle *Haliaetus pelagicus*, of north-eastern Asia, has by far the heaviest beak of all the Sea eagles.

Accipitridae, with about 206 species. This is divided by some authorities into subfamilies, e.g. Snake eagles, Circaetinae. Accipitridae vary from enormous eagles and vultures to tiny sparrowhawks (*Accipiter* spp). The largest genus is *Accipiter,* with about 45 species. All Accipitridae and Pandionidae make nests, usually of sticks, in trees or on cliffs, occasionally on the ground. The inside shell-colour of their eggs is greenish blue or greenish.

(3) Secretary birds, Sagittariidae, with one living species *Sagittarius serpentarius,* are confined to African grasslands. This peculiar long-legged terrestrial raptor is unique in its habit of hunting on the ground. It resembles Accipitridae in making a large nest, in mode of display, in the greenish egg-shell colour and its hooked beak. The feet, however, cannot grasp and carry prey, but are used to kill it. Most experts consider the Secretary bird a specialized falconiform, but it may be more closely related to South American cariamas (Cariamidae) akin to cranes and bustards.

(4) The Falconidae, with 60 species includes caracaras, milvagos, Laughing and Forest falcons (*Micrastur*), falconets and true falcons (*Falco*). This family differs from other diurnal Birds of prey in a number of characters. The sequence of wing moult is different, the droppings are allowed to fall below the perch, not being squirted clear and in all but caracaras and milvagos no nest is made, the eggs being laid in a scrape, a

hollow, or another large bird's nest. The inside colour of the egg-shell is reddish.

Thus the Falconiformes are a very diverse order, probably polyphyletic, that is, derived from more than one ancestor. Within each of the larger families, Accipitridae and Falconidae, there is great diversity of form, habit, size, type of prey taken and specialization of feet and bill. The difference between a nearly terrestrial omnivorous caracara and a Peregrine falcon is nearly as great as that between, for instance, an insectivorous Cuckoo

An immature goshawk *Accipiter gentilis* at the nest.

falcon (*Aviceda*) or Snail kite (*Rostrhamus*) and a highly rapacious eagle or goshawk.

The owls, on the other hand, are much less diverse in form; none could be mistaken for anything but an owl. Again they are a very distinct order not obviously related to any other. All owls have very large eyes almost or quite immovable in tubular sockets, soft plumage permitting silent flight, a more or less developed facial disc and, in many species, asymmetrical ear structures which enable the bird to pinpoint sound in

almost total darkness. They share with the falconiforms the hooked tearing beak and the clutching taloned feet, but these organs are considerably less varied and specialized than in Falconiformes. Further examples of convergent evolution for specific functions include the rough spiculed feet of fish-eating owls which resemble those of ospreys and Fish eagles.

The Falconiformes hunt in daylight, by sight, sometimes aided by hearing. They kill living prey and often feed upon dead animals, especially the Old and New World vultures (which seldom or never kill) and caracaras (*Polyborus*). Even in vultures the sense of smell is lacking and is not used to locate prey (except to a slight degree in some cathartids). Eyesight is proverbially acute, with resolving power up to eight times that of the human eye. Most species are wholly diurnal, but one, the Bat hawk *Machaerhamphus* hunts all its prey (bats) in an hour or so at dusk. Some insectivorous or bird-eating falcons and accipiters are also crepuscular, probably because their prey is active at that time. Bat hawks, Forest falcons *Micrastur* and some other forest species have abnormally large eyes to assist vision in poor light. Forest falcons and harriers *Circus* also have larger ears than normal, enhanced by specialized feather structures forming a partial facial ruff. Forest falcons are seminocturnal, living in deep gloom, while harriers feed on small animals in dense grass, both situations where unusually acute hearing could be advantageous. In every other species sight is by far the most important of the senses.

Falconiforms show many specialized variations of bill and feet to aid in catching or killing particular prey. Bird-killing sparrowhawks and some eagles have long legs, with long needle-sharp talons, permitting a long stretch and a wide grasp. Eagles that kill large mammals (e.g. Crowned eagles *Stephanoaetus*) have thick powerful legs and very strong talons. Ospreys and Fish eagles have spicules on the soles of their feet, for grasping slippery prey, and Snake eagles *Circaetus* have short thick toes which perhaps enable them to grasp and, almost instantly, disable venomous snakes; they are not immune from snake venom. Other more specialized adaptations include the extraordinary hooked bills of Snail kites (*Rostrhamus, Chondrohierax*) which may be used to impale molluscs emerging from the shell, or the marrow-scoop tongue of the lammergeier *Gypaetus* which feeds mainly on bones. There are also many variations of wing shape to allow soaring flight, speed in a dive (falcons) or, for instance continuous high-speed gliding (bateleur). All forest species tend to have broad rounded wings and long graduated or rounded tails, giving manoeuvrability in flying among trees.

Owls hunt mainly by night, though a few species hunt by day. They depend far more on hearing than do the falconiforms. In some species, such as the Barn owl *Tyto* this is so highly specialized, with asymmetrical bony ear structures, that the owl can catch a moving mouse entirely by ear in pitch darkness. The eyes lack the resolving power of diurnal raptors, but are sensitive to movement in poor light. Facial discs, more strongly developed in strictly nocturnal species, presumably aid in concentrating light and perhaps sound. The soft plumage not only enables owls to approach their prey unobserved, but also to hunt without the noise of their own flight distracting their own attention from other small sounds indicating prey. In owls that hunt in daylight facial discs, specialized ear structures, etc. are all reduced, and in fish-eating owls (*Ketupa, Scotopelia*) further specialization includes spiculed feet and bare legs. The legs of most tropical and arctic species alike are feathered to the toes.

Although owls vary from huge Eagle owls to tiny Scops owls and owlets, no owl is as large or powerful as the largest eagles and vultures, nor can they kill such large prey. No owl feeds regularly on dead animals; probably this is because dead animals do not move and so cannot be located by ear. No owl makes its own nest, and all lay white eggs in cavities, hollow trees, or other birds' nests. Females are normally larger than males and owls, like falconiforms, lay eggs at intervals of one to several days, so that a brood may contain both downy and full-feathered young.

Although, theoretically, over the available range, large or small falconiforms and owls are capable of killing a great variety of animals, birds and insects at any time of the day or night, in practice the distribution of many species, particularly forest owls, is so local that many prey animals escape avian predation altogether. An abundant food supply may not attract a diurnal or nocturnal raptor to take advantage of it. Moreover, the rather strongly territorial habits of many raptors ensure that they maintain home ranges much larger than strictly necessary for their minimum food needs, so that they are not density-dependent upon the numbers of their prey. It follows that, with few exceptions (among migratory or nomadic species that respond to local concentrations of food supply by gregarious habits or laying larger clutches) no Bird of

prey exerts sufficient hunting pressure on the food animals severely to restrict their numbers. The effect is, broadly, to take a proportion of the surplus that would die in any case, and to smooth out the cyclic fluctuations in prey population to some extent. L.H.B.

BIRDSONG, term used to cover a wide variety of vocal utterances of birds which convey information connected with breeding, usually to other members of the same species. A few birds are mute, for example storks and certain pelicans and vultures, but most birds produce vocalizations of one kind or another. In one group particularly, the 'song birds' (suborder Oscines of the order Passeriformes), the vocalizations have become arranged to form a recognizable series of notes, usually of more than one kind, which have a certain relationship one to another. This relationship is relatively fixed and a specific pattern of vocalization results, known as the bird's 'song'.

It is not always easy to distinguish between bird 'song' and bird 'calls'. Call notes are usually single notes, or the same note repeated, as in the flight calls of finches and the feeding calls of tits, but certain vocalizations, which functionally come under the category of song, are little more than repeated call notes. Examples include the song of certain plovers and doves. Birds such as these could not, in fact, have a song like that of the true song birds, for only the latter have a sufficiently complex syrinx (the avian voice-box) for the production of diverse and variable sounds. The song of non-oscines, therefore, is of necessity restricted to simple arrangements and modifications of call notes.

In true song birds there may be, in a single species, a complete range of vocalizations from simple call notes to full song, with relatively simple patterns of call notes in between. Or, at the beginning of the breeding season before the full song has developed, the song may be little more than a few simple notes. True song, however, is usually readily recognizable as such by reason of its musical complexity.

The principal distinction between song and other types of bird vocalization is the context in which they are produced. In the majority of cases song has a reproductive connotation. It is a very important part of territorial behaviour, being used in the establishment, demarcation and defence of the breeding territory of most song birds. The

Birdsong has inspired many composers. Here, Beethoven clearly used one of the blackbird's most famous musical phrases in a violin concerto.

Beethoven   blackbird

The Reed bunting *Emberiza schoeniclus* is singing while clinging to a reed. It makes a lot of effort to produce what is not more than a short song.

other resonating structures with the bill, the noisy beating of wings which accompanies the crow of cock pheasants, and the wing-clapping performed by pigeons in their display flight.

Since the Second World War the study of bird song and other vocalizations has received considerable impetus from the use of the sound spectograph, an apparatus which produces sound spectrograms (graphic representations of sounds with accurate detail of frequency or pitch and amplitude or loudness, as well as duration). The studies of W. H. Thorpe and his associates on the vocalizations of finches, particularly the chaffinch *Fringilla coelebs* and other birds show how much can be achieved by the use of a special tool.

The chaffinch develops the ability to learn its proper song during the first year or so of life, with a peak ability of a few weeks towards the end of that period. After 13 months it can learn no more, but during the peak learning period it may learn up to six separate songs from adjacent territory owners. The usual song of the chaffinch is partly innate and partly acquired. A chaffinch reared in isolation will sing a simplified 'basic' song of the species, lacking the embellishments typical of the song of wild chaffinches. If two chaffinches are reared together, but otherwise in isolation, they develop abnormal but almost identical songs, each having been influenced by the other. Such learning characteristics have been used for centuries by bird fanciers who, by exposing finches and other birds to bird 'tutors', or tunes played on musical instruments, particularly the bird flageolet, have been able to produce unusual or particularly accomplished songsters.

The song of the chaffinch is a relatively simple one, of some two seconds duration, structured in three basic phrases, developing through a crescendo to a terminal flourish, likened to a sound picture of the run-up and delivery of a bowler in cricket. In some other species the song is much more complex. In the European robin, for example, the repertoire of the species contains over 1,300 different motifs, several hundred being used by one individual. This great diversity is largely the result of combinations and permutations of the elements which go to make up the motifs; temporal changes in the organization of the motifs are also used, and it also seems that the robin is able to improvise to a certain extent around the theme of each motif.

The robin provides us with an example of bird song which to most human ears is pleasantly musical. Whatever the definition of music, the songs of many species of birds are regarded as musical by many people. The European blackbird, the nightingale, the Pileated tinamou of Central America, the

male frequently sings from special song posts so that its hearers are able to locate it more readily. If, at the beginning of the breeding season, a male bird, newly-arrived in an area, hears another male singing vigorously and repeatedly from the same tree, it will be aware that in all likelihood the singer is a territory owner. And the newcomer will therefore seek a territory elsewhere. Song can thus be regarded as a means of avoiding combat for territory. Only when territorial space is too limited for all the breeding pairs, and to a lesser extent at the territorial boundaries of adjacent pairs, is there open combat.

Song also seems to be important in the maintenance of the pair-bond and the synchronization of appropriate breeding activities during the breeding season. Like other reproductive activities it is governed by the balanced secretion of sex hormones in the testes and ovaries, and is properly regarded as a significant part of sexual display.

Bird vocalizations, other than song, however, are employed in circumstances which are largely, or entirely, non-sexual. Examples include the flight calls and feeding calls already mentioned, and the considerable number of vocalizations used in communication between parents and young. Thus they concern the basic processes mediating the survival of the individual, rather than maintenance of the species, which is the primary concern of song.

Mention must be made here of certain of the instrumental sounds produced by birds which, if it were not for their form of origin, would come under the category of 'song'. Functionally, those instrumental sounds connected with breeding display can certainly be regarded as a form of 'song'. These include the 'drumming' of snipe when the wind thrums through the outer tail feathers of the swooping bird, the drumming of woodpeckers when they rapidly strike branches or

Pied butcherbird of Australia and the Rocky Mountain solitaire, are but a few of the many which have been singled out for some aspect or other of their song which is highly attractive to human ears.

The timing of the units which make up the song is clearly one of the important factors in its effect on both birds and humans. Usually this timing is unique to one species only: the acceleration in the song of chaffinch or Willow grouse, the type of variability seen when we compare the two notes per second of the chiff-chaff and the 300 notes in eight seconds of the Winter wren, or the speed changes combined with motif changes in the nightingale or Blackcap warbler.

But in some species more than one individual is involved in the song. In several species of oven-birds (Furnariidae) and motmots, (Momotidae), both members of the pair sing together, in duet. This is taken even further in some other groups in which the members of a pair alternate their contributions to the joint song with extreme accuracy of timing, for example in some Tyrant-flycatchers (Tyrannidae), wrens (Troglodytidae), shrikes (Laniidae) and barbets (Capitonidae). In many of these species the timing of the two contributions is so accurate that it appears to be the song of one bird only.

Mimicry is another way in which a bird may make use of other birds' vocalizations in its song-pattern. The ability of parrots, crows, and mynahs to mimic is well known, but several species of birds incorporate the vocalizations of other birds, and other sounds too, into their normal song in the wild. The starling *Sturnus vulgaris,* the Marsh warbler *Acrocephalus palustris,* the mockingbird *Mimus polyglottos,* and the Spotted bowerbird *Chlamydera maculata* are outstanding examples. A mockingbird has been recorded singing parts of the song of at least 30 other species and a starling nesting in the roof of the present writer's house mimics at least 22 other species of British birds, as well as sheep, dogs and humans. But the most accomplished mimics are probably the Australian birds of paradise, lyrebirds and bowerbirds which mimic not only a wide variety of other birds and mammals, but also a galaxy of inanimate sounds from motor horns to water sloshing in a bucket. The function of such a highly developed ability is unfortunately unknown at the moment of writing.

Next to the possession of feathers and the advantages thereof, possibly the most outstanding characteristic of birds as a whole is their use of vocalizations in song. They have developed song to a higher degree than any other group of animals, excepting man, and in the majority of species it plays a fundamental part in their existence.   P.M.D.

Bison bull, immediately recognizable by its heavy forequarters and low slung head.

BISON *Bison bison,* or buffalo, the largest land animal in America, the bulls weighing up to a ton or more (907 kg) and standing 5 to 6 ft (1·5–1·8 m) at the shoulder. The huge head, which appears extra large because of the long hair; the great hump on the shoulders; the dark brown woolly hair covering the forequarters; and the small naked hips are characteristic of the bull. Females are smaller and less striking. Both sexes have horns, but those of the bull are more massive. The calves are a light tawny colour in contrast to their dark brown parents.

The sight of vast herds of bison and Pronghorn antelope stretching across the plains and prairies of the North American continent before 1800 must have rivalled that of the ungulate herds in East Africa today. Eastward from the prairies the bison's range extended to Pennsylvania and Virginia, westward it extended to eastern Oregon, and from northern Alberta it extended southward just into northeastern Mexico.

During the breeding season from July to September, the bulls leave their male herds and mingle with the cows and calves, the strongest bulls tending individual cows until copulation is completed. Cows are sexually mature at two and a half years, and normally produce a single calf after a gestation period of about nine months.

The total population of bison was probably some 60 to 70 million animals when white man first arrived in America. Despite their great abundance, the bison probably roamed mostly in groups of 20–30 individuals and only occasionally in herds of 100 or more, and the herds seem to have migrated only to the limited extent of perhaps 200 to 300 miles (300 to 500 km), rather than making the long northward and southward treks described in early accounts.

The American Indian depended upon the buffalo for food, clothing, and shelter, and buffalo chips (dried droppings) provided a source of fuel on the open plains. It was partly to subdue the Indian that mass slaughter of these animals was encouraged during the westward expansion of civilization in the 19th century. Conservation efforts around 1900 spared the bison from extinction, and there are now about 25,000 remaining, 60% of which are in the 11-million acre (nearly 4·5 million ha) Wood Buffalo National Park near Great Slave Lake in Alberta, Canada, where they roam the immense boreal forest, muskeg and grassy plains. The largest herds in the United States are in the National Bison Range in Montana (350 animals), the Witchita Mountains Refuge in Oklahoma (1,250), Yellowstone National Park (700), the Badlands National Monument in North Dakota (500) and Custer State Park in South Dakota (1,300). Many private ranchers keep sizable herds of buffalo. Careful harvesting of the existing herds is essential, and systematic regulation of numbers is a well-established policy. Under the present system of protection and management the bison is assured of survival as a species in natural environments and on ranchlands. FAMILY: Bovidae, ORDER: Artiodactyla, CLASS: Mammalia.   H.K.B.

BISON SLAUGHTER.

Occasionally archaeologists uncover remains that give an exciting and vivid picture of how prehistoric man lived. The fossilized remains of nearly 200 bison uncovered in Colorado was one such find. Careful excavation showed that the bones were lying in a silted up gulley and, by comparing evidence from the dig with knowledge of the Plains Indians in historic times, it was possible to piece together the fate that befell these bison some 8–9,000 years ago. The skeletons lay piled up and all were facing in one direction, showing that they had been stampeded into the gulley, while flint spear heads suggested that flanking parties of Indians had prevented the bison from running around the gulley. Dismembered skeletons showed how the carcases had been butchered in a similar way to that employed by modern Indians. The tongues and internal organs were cut out and eaten on the spot. The meat was cut off in sections; head, 'hump,' ribs, pelvis, legs and so on. Some was eaten then and the rest dried for future use. The number of bison butchered (those at the bottom of the pile were hardly touched) and the Indians' known capacity for meat (15–20 lb/33–44 kg could be eaten by one man in one day at such a feast) made it possible to calculate that the Indian band numbered about 150 and that the kill kept them supplied for about one month. Prehistoric Indians must have had a well developed social organization.

BITTERLING *Rhodeus sericeus,* a 3 in (8 cm) carp-like fish from lowland waters of Europe, the breeding cycle of which involves a freshwater mussel. The bitterling is normally silvery but in the breeding season the male develops violet and blue iridescence along the flanks and red on the belly, the fins becoming bright red edged with black. In colour, the female is less spectacular but develops a long pink ovipositor from the anal fin. It is this ovipositor, a 2 in (5 cm) tube for depositing the eggs, that gives a clue to the extraordinary breeding biology of the bitterling. Most fishes of the family Cyprinidae merely scatter their eggs, but the female bitterling carefully deposits its eggs inside a freshwater mussel, hence the need for the long ovipositor. The male then sheds its milt and this is drawn in by the inhalant siphon of the mussel and the eggs are fertilized inside. Normally, one has only to touch these mussels and the two halves of the shell are snapped shut. The female bitterling, however, conditions the mussel by repeatedly nudging it with its mouth. This remarkable nursery for the eggs is clearly of great value to fishes that would otherwise lose a large percentage of the eggs through predators. It is difficult to see how this association between the mussel and fish arose, but in return the mussel releases its larvae while the bitterling is laying its eggs. These fasten onto the skin of the bitterling, which carries them around until they change into young mussels and fall to the bottom.

Attempts have been made to introduce the bitterling into England but they have not been successful.   FAMILY: Cyprinidae, ORDER: Cypriniformes, CLASS: Pisces.

The bitterling *Rhodeus sericeus,* a carp-like freshwater fish from Europe, inspecting a freshwater mussel.

BITTERNS, fairly large birds with a distinctive booming call, usually restricted to reedbeds and marshes. The cosmopolitan subfamily of bitterns comprises two genera *Botaurus* and *Ixobrychus,* the genus *Botaurus* containing the Eurasian bittern *B. stellaris,* the Australian *B. poiciloptilus,* the American *B. lentiginosus* and the South American *B. pinnatus* which replace each other and together form a superspecies. Of the genus *Ixobrychus,* the Least bittern *I. exilis* of North America, the Little bittern *I. minutus* of Europe, Asia, Africa and Australia and the Chinese little bittern *I. sinensis* form another superspecies.

The bittern *B. stellaris* is resident in British and European marshes while the smaller American bittern is a rare vagrant to Europe having been recorded in the Channel Islands, the Faeroes, Iceland, at least once in Germany and over 50 times in Britain.

The sexes of all the *Botaurus* species have similar plumage, that of the bittern *B. stellaris* being soft golden-brown and owl-like, heavily mottled with black above, longitudinally streaked below. A mane of long feathers on the neck and throat can be erected at will. Their necks and legs are shorter than those of herons. The 3 in (7·5 cm) bill is yellowish-green, the eyes yellow and the legs and feet pale green. They have powder-down patches on the breast and rump, one pair fewer than the herons, and the toothed middle claw is used to apply powder-down to the contour-feathers in preening. The finely divided particles of the disintegrating filaments of powder-down coagulates slime which coats the plumage when bitterns feed on eels. The bittern measures 30 in (76 cm) and weighs about 3 lb (1·3 kg).

Distribution is restricted by nesting requirements to reedbeds and rank vegetation by sluggish water. The extensive marshes of North Jutland, the 'plassen' of Zuid-Holland and Utrecht, Austria's Neusiedler See and

Male and female bitterling, renowned for the way they co-operate with a mussel in breeding.

the Danube marshes provide typically ideal haunts for many bitterns. In Europe bitterns breed from 60°N to the Mediterranean basin and very large numbers are present in the USSR.

The history of the bittern in Britain offers a good example of the factors acting against a bird species. Drainage, and perhaps gunners, brought about a cessation of breeding in Britain for nearly 50 years prior to 1911 when a pair were discovered in Norfolk. Since then bitterns have bred regularly in Norfolk and Suffolk and recently in Cambridgeshire but the highest concentration is now in Lancashire, where six or seven pairs nest at Leighton Moss. The number of pairs that a reedbed can accommodate is not known for certain for, while there is evidence that a female does not require an extensive area from which to collect enough food to rear her brood and that several pairs may breed fairly close together, fighting and injured birds have been observed which suggests territorial battles may occur under conditions of overcrowding.

In Britain and the Netherlands severe winter weather takes a heavy toll of resident bitterns, suggesting that not many from these areas migrate. Birds from colder areas probably do migrate, however, as an increased population in countries bordering the Mediterranean is apparent during winter months. As wanderers in winter they occasionally appear on 'flashes' above colliery subsidence or on the Cheshire mere where they formerly bred.

At any hour of the day or night from February to late June the male utters a resonant boom which may be repeated from three to six times and is notable for its carrying power, which is certainly over 1 mile (1·6 km).

The nest is built up above water level on matted roots in a reedbed and is constructed of reeds and sedge, lined with finer material. Three to six olive-brown eggs, without gloss, laid at intervals of two or three days, are incubated by the female alone. The young, too, are fed entirely by the female. Small mammals, birds (including young reedlings), water insects and crustaceans are all eaten but the principal diet appears to be fish, mainly eels, and frogs.

Extremely furtive, bitterns hunt within the reedbeds, grasping the stems as they progress although, occasionally, one will venture out onto open water. When flying over the reedbeds they skirt the tops of the stems with a slow wingbeat, quickly dropping back into cover.

The protective colouration is much enhanced by the bird's habit, when disturbed, of standing rigid with bill pointed skywards, presenting to the intruder the striped undersurface which blends so well with the surrounding reeds as to render the bird virtually invisible.

The American bittern *B. lentiginosus* is not so restricted to reedbeds as is the Eurasian species and is often observed feeding in open wet meadows. Its plumage lacks the black on the upperparts which are finely vermiculated and the primaries are uniform grey-brown without barring. It is smaller, only 23 in (58 cm) long. The American bittern ranges over the northern half of the United States and southern Canada in summer and migrates south for the winter.

The Little bittern *Ixobrychus minutus* is the only European member of a genus containing a dozen species. Sluggish rivers, backwaters, even small ponds satisfy this bird's nesting requirements and they nest practically throughout Europe, building

sometimes just above water level and sometimes in willows up to 10 ft (3 m) above the water. It is thought to have nested in East Anglia during this century although no nest has ever been found and it is now an irregular visitor, usually between April and October.

The Least bittern *I. exilis*, of the United States, is similar in appearance and habits but slightly smaller. Members of this genus are generally migratory and are sexually dimorphic. Even when standing in a concealing pose with bill and neck outstretched this inconspicuous bird does not exceed 14 in (35 cm). In contrast to the streaky dark brown of the female, the crown and back of the male are greenish-black. Extremely skulking and mainly crepuscular they usually feed on worms, insects, frogs, molluscs, fish and, it now appears, the eggs and young of small birds. Unlike the larger bitterns they frequently perch on branches of bushes overhanging ponds. FAMILY: Ardeidae, ORDER: Ciconiiformes, CLASS: Aves.   F.A.L.

BITTERN BINOCULAR VISION. The habit of standing with bill pointed upwards does more than conceal a bittern among the reeds; it also allows it to see directly to the front. The eyes are on the sides of the head and, when at rest, there is a blind spot in front of the head. With the bill pointing upwards, however, and the eyes turned inwards the bittern can look under its chin. In this position there is probably an overlap between the fields of view of the eyes, giving binocular vision. Both pupils are clearly visible to an observer in front of the bittern, giving a 'cross-eyed' effect. Similar behaviour has been recorded in other birds.

BIVALVE MOLLUSCS, molluscs such as oysters, mussels, cockles and clams, in which the shell has calcified from two centres and so is composed of two valves, each usually the mirror image of the other. The valves interlock by means of teeth placed dorsally near the oldest part of each valve, an area known as the umbo, and said to be hinged together; they are also linked, in the same region, by an elastic ligament which may lie either inside or outside the two halves of the shell. It is compressed in the former position, stretched in the latter when the valves close, and on removal of the closing force the ligament reacts to open the shell: dead bivalve shells, therefore, always gape. The closing of the valves is brought about by adductor muscles, the fibres of which run from the inner surface of one valve to that of the other.

Little bittern looks like a miniature Night heron. It haunts the reed-beds and scrub all over Europe.

Bittern, also an inhabitant of reed-beds throughout Europe, is famous for the booming call of the male during the breeding season.

The extraordinary 'toothy grin' of a File shell *Lima scabra*.

FAMILIES	Awning clam	Ark shell	shipworm	Papery lantern shell	mussel	scallop	oyster	Pearl muss
	Nut shell	Leda shell	piddock	Lantern shell	Duckbill shell	Pen shell	Saddle oyster	Swan mussel

SUBORDERS — Filibranchia

ORDERS — Protobranchia — Septibranchia — Lamellibranchia

CLASS — Bivalve molluscs

There are usually two such muscles, one near the front end, the other towards the hind end. Since the attachment of the muscle fibres interferes with the further secretion of shelly material their site of attachment is marked by an impression visible in the dry shell.

As in all molluscs the shell is secreted by the mantle (the covering of the visceral hump) and by its extensions (the mantle folds or skirt). In bivalves the mantle folds have enlarged, one on the right, one on the left, and enclose the entire body of the animal on each side. As a consequence, the shell covers the whole animal too, and when the valves are adducted the mollusc is completely enclosed. The valves, like the mantle folds, also lie right and left. The edge of each mantle flap secretes a periostracum or layer of conchiolin, a horn-like material. Onto the inner side of this layer the outer surface of each mantle fold, near its margin, adds calcareous material, usually as crystalline aragonite.

The body of the bivalve consists of a foot, by which the animal moves about, and a visceral mass. The head and its appendages have been lost.

The Protobranchia, the most primitive bivalves, including *Nucula* and *Yoldia,* commonly live in soft mud or sand below tidemarks. In them, the valves have an extensive hinge with many simple, interlocking teeth. The foot is muscular and can be protruded in front. Its tip is split and can be pulled apart into right and left halves which provide an anchorage. When their two pairs of muscles contract, the animal is pulled forwards through the substratum. Respiration is through any surface thin enough to allow gas exchange including most of those within the mantle cavity.There is, however, a pair of gills each consisting of an axis carrying a double row of rounded ciliated leaflets. The *cilia on these are responsible for sucking a current of water into the front end of the mantle cavity and pushing it out behind.

A pair of labial palps lie on either side of the mouth. Each is a triangular flap with the apex drawn out into a long palp proboscis. The two proboscides can be pushed out between the valves into the surrounding sand or mud where they pick up minute edible particles. They are then drawn back into the mantle cavity and the particles passed over the palps to the mouth. There is a pair of U-shaped excretory organs, known as coelomoducts. The nervous system consists of cerebral and pleural ganglia lying together on each side of the mouth, visceral ganglia at the hind end of the body and a pair of pedal ganglia, fused to form one, in the front end of the foot. There are no eyes but there are statocysts, and numerous other sense organs.

A second small group, the Septibranchia, including *Poromya* and *Cuspidaria* are carnivorous and feed on small crustaceans. They live in deeper waters. They are similar to the protobranchs except in the way they feed. Within the mantle cavity on each side, lies a horizontal perforated septum which moves up and down like a piston sucking in any small animals which come near the shell opening. These are then wrapped around by the labial palps and swallowed.

In the rest of the bivalves, the lamellibranchs, the gills have been converted into

Various living bivalves dredged from shell gravel.

food collecting organs, or sieves. These are lined by cilia which maintain a current of water through the mantle cavity whenever the shell is open. As the current passes between the gill filaments other cilia strain any particles it may carry and still other cilia carry the food forwards to the labial palps. These sort the bulkier food particles from the smallest, which are the only ones eaten. The larger, rejected, particles are then embedded in mucus and ejected from the ventral part of the mantle cavity as strands known as pseudofaeces. Lamellibranchs have a crystalline style in their stomach, a rod of protein with absorbed *enzymes, and in marine species there seems to be a rhythm of feeding secretion and absorption involving crystalline style, digestive gland and the opening and closing of the valves in relation to tidal rhythms.

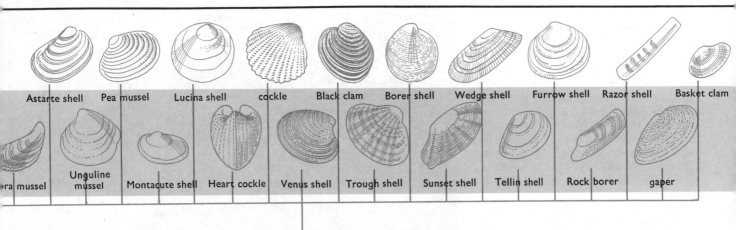

Astarte shell   Pea mussel   Lucina shell   cockle   Black clam   Borer shell   Wedge shell   Furrow shell   Razor shell   Basket clam

ra mussel   Unguline mussel   Montacute shell   Heart cockle   Venus shell   Trough shell   Sunset shell   Tellin shell   Rock borer   gaper

Eulamellibranchia

Scientific names of families for which the common name of a species has been used in the diagram: Nut shell - *Nuculidae,* Awning clam - *Solenomyidae,* Leda shell - *Nuculanidae,* Ark shell - *Arcidae,* piddock - *Pholadidae,* shipworm - *Teredinidae,* Lantern shell - *Thraciidae,* Papery lantern shell - *Periplomatidae,* Duckbill shell - *Cuspariidae,* mussel - *Mytilidae,* Pen shell - *Pinnidae,* scallop - *Pectinidae,* Saddle oyster - *Anomiidae,* oyster - *Ostreidae,* Swan mussel - *Unionidae,* Pearl mussel - *Unionidae,* Zebra mussel - *Dreissenidae,* Astarte shell - *Astartidae,* Unguline mussel - *Ungulinidae,* Pea mussel - *Sphaeriidae,* Montacute shell - *Montacutidae,* Lucina shell - *Lucinidae,* Heart cockle - *Isocardiidae,* cockle - *Cardiidae,* Venus shell - *Veneridae,* Black clam - *Cyprinidae,* Trough shell - *Mactridae,* Borer shell - *Pectricolidae,* Sunset shell - *Asaphidae,* Wedge shell - *Donacidae,* Tellin shell - *Tellenidae,* Furrow shell - *Semelidae,* Rock borer - *Hiatellidae,* Razor shell - *Solenidae,* gaper - *Myidae,* Basket clam - *Erodonidae*

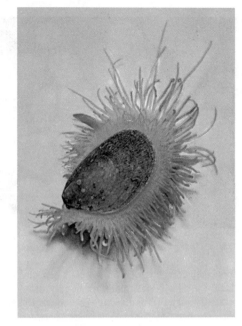

Side view of gaping File shell *Lima hians.*

The lamellibranchs occur in two grades: (1) Filibranchia, with no fusion of neighbouring gill filaments which are held together only by interlocking cilia; (2) Eulamellibranchia, in which extensive interfilamentar and other fusions occur. They differ from protobranchs in having an axed-shaped foot (hence an alternative name for them, Pelecypoda) and in having the cerebral and pleural ganglia on each side united. In some primitive lamellibranchs, such as *Glycymeris,* the teeth of the shell are as in protobranchs, but on most lamellibranchs the teeth in each valve are different in shape and size.

The common freshwater mussels, *Anodonta* and *Unio,* are typical of the kind of life followed by many lamellibranchs. They plough their way through soft sediments at the bottom of rivers or lakes by means of their foot, which can be elongated to penetrate the mud, expanded at the tip to anchor the mussel and then shortened so as to pull the animal forwards. Entry of water to the mantle cavity is limited to the rear end immediately below where the exhalant stream leaves. These points are kept above the surface of the mud so that food and oxygen are continuously available.

Many species have siphons, tubular processes drawn outwards at the points where the inhalant and exhalant water streams lie and formed by the fusion of right and left mantle edges. Siphons can be extended to considerable distances from the shell edge or, if the animal is disturbed, withdrawn completely into its shelter. Siphons allow their owner to burrow deeply into sand or mud without losing contact with the water above which is necessary for continued existence. The gaper *Mya,* which abounds in muddy sand, especially around estuaries, in water

12–18 in (30–45 cm) deep, maintains a current of water through the mantle cavity when covered by the tide by means of two long, conjoined siphons. *Scrobicularia* and *Tellina,* which live about 4 in (10 cm) deep in mud and sand respectively, have two long, separate siphons. The exhalant one projects out of the sand straight into the water, the inhalant one curves down to suck up organic matter on the surface of the mud or sand. In many of these burrowing lamellibranchs the free edges of the mantle folds fuse with one another as in *Mya,* leaving only a small opening for protrusion of the foot.

The possession of siphons also allows lamellibranchs to adopt a boring mode of life,

Thin tellin *Tellina tenuis,* showing siphons.

cutting tubular holes for themselves in shales, limestones or wood. The piddock *Pholas* and *Hiatella,* the date-mussel *Lithodomus,* all burrow into rock, the shipworm *Teredo* into wood. Except in the date-mussel, which secretes an acid mucus which dissolves the rock, lamellibranchs rasp the rock or wood into which they bore by rotary movements of the shell, on the outer surface of which lies a series of parallel ridges forming a kind of file. The foot clings to the wall of the burrow and provides a base on which the rocking motion occurs. *Teredo* uses the wood chips for food, supplemented by particles drawn in through the siphon; it lines its borehole with a calcareous lining. The opening to the burrow

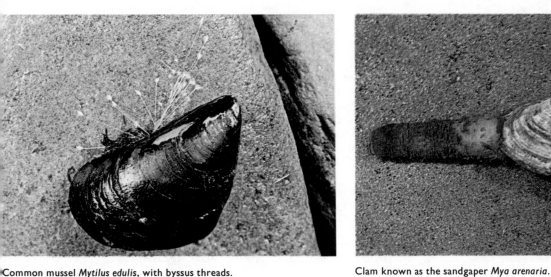

Common mussel *Mytilus edulis*, with byssus threads.

Clam known as the sandgaper *Mya arenaria*.

remains the size of a pinhole so that wood badly infested with shipworm can nevertheless seem externally sound.

Not all burrowing or boring lamellibranchs have long siphons. The cockle *Cardium* has only short ones and burrows shallowly; the razorshell *Ensis,* on the other hand, though also with short siphons and tied to the surface for feeding, can, if disturbed, dig deeply and rapidly into the sand with its powerful, cylindrical foot.

The most familiar of lamellibranchs are the Edible mussels *Mytilus,* which live in crowded masses on exposed rocky shores. They are attached to the rock, and to each other, by tough byssus threads secreted by a gland at the base of the foot and hardened rapidly by exposure to sea water after attachment to the rock. Other surface-living forms are the oysters *Ostrea* and the saddle-oysters *Anomia* which have one valve cemented to the substratum and so are immobilized. These have a more rounded shell with a single centrally placed adductor muscle which is the original rear muscle. The scallop *Pecten* spends much of its life lying free on the substratum but when disturbed is able to swim vigorously, either backwards or forwards, by flapping its valves.

Lamellibranchs usually shed their eggs and sperm into the sea, where fertilization occurs. The larvae early develop a bivalved shell and, on the head region, have ciliated lobes forming a velum with which they feed and swim. The velum is lost at metamorphosis when they fall to the bottom as spat. Successful spatfalls do not occur each year and most lamellibranch populations reflect spatfalls several years apart.

The freshwater mussels incubate the fertilized eggs within one of the gills where they develop to a stage known as a glochidium larva. When these leave the parent they must attach to the skin of a fish and live parasitically on it prior to metamorphosing into miniature adults.

Oysters, mussels, cockles and a variety of clams are favourite human food. Most of the populations exploited are wild, but oysters have been cultivated for centuries in some parts of Europe, as may in future other clams. CLASS: Bivalvia, PHYLUM: Mollusca.   A.G.

BLAAUWBOK *Hippotragus leucophaeus,* also called Blue buck, an antelope closely related to the Sable and Roan antelopes; always rare, restricted to the Swellendam district of the Cape of Good Hope, it was extinct by 1799.

Blaauwbok were 41–46 in (104–116 cm) high, with relatively short, strongly curved horns 20–24½ in (50–61 cm) long, with 20–35 rings; the horn section was oval, with the median side flattened. Ears were about half as long as the head, or slightly more, straight and untufted unlike the Roan antelope. The neck bore a short, forwardly-inclined mane and there was no throat fringe. The male and female were similarly coloured, blue-grey with a brownish tinge, the belly being slightly lighter, with no sharp border between the two colours. The face pattern was indistinct, with the nose darker than the rest of the face.

Although various authors have tried at one time or another to place the blaauwbok as an extreme southern subspecies of either the Roan or Sable antelopes, it seems clear from the work of Erna Mohr that it differed from these two at least as much as they differ from each other; notably, it was the only member of the genus *Hippotragus* with a nearly obsolete face-pattern. The blaauwbok was the first of many South African mammals to suffer at the hands of man; the quagga, Burchell's zebra, Cape lion and the huge Cape Black rhinoceros followed it into oblivion, and the blesbok, bontebok, Cape elephant and Red hartebeest narrowly escaped the same fate; the blaauwbok was, however, the only one which failed to see the

19th century. FAMILY: Bovidae, ORDER: Artiodactyla, CLASS: Mammalia.   C.P.G.

BLACK BASS, freshwater fishes of North America belonging to the genus *Micropterus.* The Large-mouthed black bass *M. salmoides* and the Small-mouthed black bass *M. dolomieu* both reach about 2 ft (61 cm) in length and are good sporting fishes. The two species were introduced into Europe in 1883 but neither has been particularly successful. They are most commonly found in southern Europe. In England they have not become naturalized except for a small colony of Large-mouthed black bass which is apparently thriving in Dorset. The same species was also introduced into East Africa and has done well in ponds and lakes in colder areas above 4,000 ft (1,200 m). Bass were chiefly introduced into Europe for sport but they have not found favour with European anglers because they seem to be very wary and retire to the deepest parts of lakes when they grow to any size.

Bass have strong teeth in the jaws and are predatory fishes which lurk amongst stones or weeds and pounce on their prey (fishes, frogs, etc.) occasionally playing with their food as a cat does with a mouse. Both species are nest builders, constructing a large shallow nest which in the Small-mouthed bass is lined with leaves. FAMILY: Centrarchidae, ORDER: Perciformes, CLASS: Pisces.

BLACKBIRDS, certain dark-plumaged songbirds of the thrush family, Turdidae, in Europe and the oriole or troupial family, Icteridae, in North America. One of the commonest birds in Britain is the blackbird *Turdus merula.* American blackbirds include the Yellow-headed blackbird *Xanthocephalus xanthocephalus,* the Red-winged blackbird *Agelaius phoeniceus* of swamps and marshes and Brewer's blackbird *Euphagus cyanocephalus* of prairies and meadows. The Rusty

Male blackbird, glossy black with orange bill.

blackbird *Euphagus carolinus* ranges to within the Arctic Circle and the Melodious blackbird *D. dives* is an outstanding songster.

The name 'blackbird' is used less commonly, and sometimes confusingly, for other birds in both Europe and America. ORDER: Passeriformes, CLASS: Aves.

BLACK BREAM, or Black sea bream *Spondyliosoma cantharus,* a marine fish of the eastern Atlantic and Mediterranean; family Sparidae; not related to the freshwater bream, which is a carp-like fish. The Sea breams, which include the gilthead *Sparus auratus* and the gold-line *Sarpa salpa,* are deep, compressed fishes with sharp cutting teeth at the front of the jaws, often with molar-like teeth at the rear. The Black bream has a deep body which is iron-grey above and silver on the flanks with numbers of dark horizontal bands. It reaches 2 ft (61 cm) in length and when abundant is considered good eating. The young fishes approach close to the shore and may enter ports and estuaries. FAMILY: Sparidae, ORDER: Perciformes, CLASS: Pisces.

BLACKBUCK *Antilope cervicapra,* the most common Indian antelope, closely related to the gazelles. Females and young are yellow-fawn with a white belly and white eye-ring; after three years of age, the male begins to turn black. In the south of India males are usually dark brown; in all cases the true sable livery is assumed only during the rut, after the rains. Only the male has horns: these are ringed, closely spiralled, 25 in (65 cm) long in the south, shorter in the north. Blackbuck stand 32 in (80 cm) high, and weigh 90 lb (40 kg).

The blackbuck is found on all plains of peninsular India, south from Surat, and east into Bengal, west into Punjab and Rajputana. Herds number 20–30, and are led by a female; during the breeding season, the bucks split the herds up into harems; a buck struts about in front of his harem making short challenging grunts, with head thrown up so that the horns lie along the back, and the face-glands widely open. The main rut occurs in February and March, but some

breeding occurs in all seasons. Gestation is 180 days.

Once there were 4 million blackbuck in India; they were hunted by Maharajahs with tame cheetah. Now there are some thousands, but they are thin on the ground. They occur in all plains country, entering both open forests and grasslands, as well as in cultivated areas. They graze in the morning, lie up during the heat of the day, and feed again in late afternoon. Eyesight is very keen. When alarmed, the herd moves off in light leaps and bounds, like gazelles, then breaks into a gallop. FAMILY: Bovidae, ORDER: Artiodactyla, CLASS: Mammalia.

BLACK CORALS, colonial polyps belonging to the phylum Cnidaria, also called *Thorny corals.

BLACKFISH, a name used for two very different fishes, one freshwater and the other marine.

1 Alaska blackfish *Dallia pectoralis,* a small freshwater fish related to the pike and found in Siberia, Alaska and northern Canada. It has a large mouth and the dorsal and anal fins are set far back on the body enabling it, like the pike, to accelerate rapidly towards its prey. Although it only reaches 8 in (20 cm) and in appearance is not very distinctive, it has been of immense interest to zoologists and naturalists because of its alleged ability to withstand being frozen. These blackfishes were formerly said to be able to survive after being frozen solid in ice for the entire winter. Laboratory experiments at the Steinhart Aquarium in California, have shown that when individuals were frozen solid for 12 hours and were then slowly thawed, they were capable of movement after some hours and later swam normally. Nevertheless, they died the following day. It is most likely that the speed of freezing and of formation of ice crystals in the cells of the body are of critical importance in the ability of these fishes to revive. FAMILY: Umbridae, ORDER: Salmoniformes, CLASS: Pisces.

Alaska blackfish with a reputation for freezing.

2 Blackfish *Centrolophus niger,* and its close relative the Cornish blackfish, *C. britannicus* are marine stromateid fishes related to the barrelfish. These species are found in the eastern North Atlantic and Mediterranean.

In *C. niger,* which reaches 3 ft (90 cm) in length, the body is elongated and purplish-black but paler on the head and belly. Little is known of the feeding habits of these fishes but young specimens have been found which had fed on pollack.

In certain parts of the British Isles the name blackfish is also used for ripe female salmon. FAMILY: Stromateidae, ORDER: Perciformes, CLASS: Pisces.

BLACKFISH, also an alternative name for the *Pilot whale *Globicephala melaena* of the North Atlantic.

BLACKFLIES, a family of small black flies belonging to the order of true flies. The same name is used for some aphids which, like the Bean aphis, are black, but in this account we are only concerned with the genus *Simulium.* The species of *Simulium* are hump-backed flies, $\frac{1}{25}-\frac{1}{4}$ in (2–6 mm) long, with relatively broad wings in which the veins are more marked towards the front edges. The females feed on blood and their bites are extremely painful. In warm countries they are of economic importance because their vast numbers make them a great nuisance and their bites may lead to loss of condition and sometimes death in domestic animals. They can also act as transmitters of disease and it is as vectors of a filarial worm, *Onchocerca,* that they are best known in Africa and Central America. This worm can enter the eye and cause 'river blindness', which affects a large proportion of the population in some parts of Africa.

The term 'river blindness' stems from the abundance of the flies near waterways, the larvae living in well-oxygenated, unpolluted running water. They live underwater attached to stones by a sucker on the tail end and feed by filtering minute plants and animals from the water which flows past them. To accomplish this mouth brushes are present which look rather like a moustache and in which the small organisms get entangled. Each larva also has a sucker towards the front so it can move by looping along using the two suckers alternately. One species, *Simulium neavei,* has larvae which no longer live on stones but adhere to the backs of freshwater crabs; another species rides on dragonfly larvae.

There are six larval stages and at the end of these the larva spins a cocoon of silk which holds the pupa and prevents it from being swept away by the current. The pupa has two tufts of gills arising from the thorax which give it a rather characteristic appearance. Finally, the adult emerges in a bubble of air and rises to the surface, flying off immediately to avoid being washed away.

Blackflies are most effectively controlled by eliminating the larvae from streams.

Indian blackbuck, antelope that springs like impala.

DDT can be released into the water, but this affects many other organisms as well as the *Simulium*. A method with less widespread effects involves using DDT adsorbed on to fine clay particles. This is dropped into the water and washes down with the current. Some of it is filtered out by the *Simulium* larvae together with the organisms they feed on so that the larvae are killed, but other animals in the stream using different methods of feeding are not affected by the poison. FAMILY: Simuliidae, ORDER: Diptera, CLASS: Insecta, PHYLUM: Arthropoda.   R.F.C.

BLACK GROUSE, two striking species of birds of the grouse family: *Tetrao tetrix* of northern Europe, including Britain, and *T. mlokosiewiczi* of Eurasia. The male Black grouse, or blackcock, is 21 in (53 cm) long and has a glossy blue-black plumage with an unusual lyre-shaped tail set off by white under-tail coverts. There are also white markings on the wings and a bright red wattle above each eye. During the breeding season males from adjacent territories gather at traditional display grounds, or 'leks', for daily displays in which the tail is spread and raised, the wings partly opened and a variety of calls and posturings performed. The female Black grouse or greyhen, 16 in (40 cm) long, has the rufous-brown cryptic plumage typical of female ground birds. She becomes more interested in the lek behaviour as spring progresses, eventually mating with one of the displaying birds and then leaving to rear the brood alone. See grouse. FAMILY: Tetraonidae, ORDER: Galliformes, CLASS: Aves.

BLACK-HEADED GULL *Larus ridibundus,* a smallish gull (family Laridae) found through much of Europe. It is 15 in (38 cm) long and may be distinguished in flight by the white leading edge to the wings. It has a dark red bill and legs and, in summer, a chocolate brown head. In winter the head is white with a dark marking behind the eye. Young birds before their first winter are mottled grey-brown above, but have the pale leading edge to the wings. The Black-headed gull is common in many areas, in town and cities as well as open country, and inland as well as on the coast. It nests in colonies on the ground in marshes or on islands, moorland, shingle beaches, sand-dunes and other similar situations. Other features of its life-history are very similar to those of other gulls. FAMILY: Laridae, ORDER: Charadriiformes, CLASS: Aves.

Black-headed gull at nest on low-lying marsh.

Black widow spider of North America, one of the few spiders dangerous to man. Its bite, while extremely painful, is fatal in a small percentage of cases only.

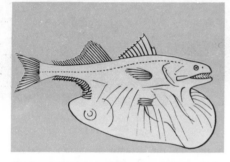

Black swallower, capable of swallowing a fish its own size or even bigger.

BLACK SWALLOWER *Chiasmodus niger,* also known as the Great swallower, is a deep-sea fish related to the weeverfishes. It is a small species reaching 6 in (15 cm) in length with two dorsal fins and a moderately long anal fin. Its most striking peculiarity is its ability to swallow fishes larger than itself. A fish of 6 in (15 cm) is able to swallow a prey of 10 in (25 cm). It manages this by means of two modifications. The first is an enormously distensible stomach. When the stomach is empty, the Black swallower has the shape of a slim mackerel, but when it has eaten, the stomach bulges out and the prey can usually be seen coiled up inside. The other aid to this method of feeding is the jaws, which are also distensible and elastic. Fishes usually swallow by using the muscles in the throat, but the Black swallower eases itself along the prey by using its jaws in much the same manner as a snake. Inching itself forward, it finally manages to cram the

whole fish inside. Living in the deep seas where all animals are relatively scarce and well spaced out, the swallower must be able to take prey when the opportunity is presented, whether the prey be small or large. FAMILY: Chiasmodontidae, ORDER: Perciformes, CLASS: Pisces.

BLACK WIDOW *Gymnocorymbus ternetzi,* a 3 in (8 cm) fish from the Matto Grosso region of South America. It is a most popular species with aquarists, who also refer to it as the Black tetra or the petticoatfish. The dorsal and anal fins are large and dark while the tail is transparent and gives the fish a shortened appearance. Black widows are easy to breed at 80°F (27°C) and the sexes can be determined by the shape of the body cavity when held up to light (rounded posteriorly in the male, pointed in the female) FAMILY: Characidae, ORDER: Cypriniformes, CLASS: Pisces.

BLACK WIDOW SPIDER *Latrodectus mactans,* jet black North American spider with a sinister reputation. Underneath the abdomen is a small hour-glass mark in vivid scarlet which represents warning colouration. The bite of this spider causes intense pain accompanied by symptoms of nausea, partial paralysis and difficulty in breathing and the venom is said to be 15 times as potent as that of a rattlesnake. Fortunately the quantity injected is far less than that of a snake. Death is known but this is not usual. A serum has been prepared in America but in its absence doctors usually give intraven-

ous injections of 10 cc of 10% calcium chloride or gluconate.

The Black widow is not a large spider, being less than $\frac{3}{4}$ in (18 mm). It lives a retiring existence and is not aggressive. Men are likely to be bitten more frequently than women because the cavity beneath the seat of earth privies is often selected by the spider to spin the strong coarse threads of its snare and anything brushing against these threads is apt to be bitten.

Most members of the genus *Latrodectus* share the same evil reputation. These include the malmignatte of southern Europe, the red-back of Australia, the katipo of New Zealand and others in Africa. These can usually be distinguished from the American Black widow by the possession of scarlet

Black widow spider showing its red markings.

spots or bands but some have proved to be only subspecies. All have the globular abdomen typical of the family. FAMILY: Theridiidae, ORDER: Araneae CLASS: Arachnida, PHYLUM: Arthropoda. W.S.B.

BLADDER WORMS, popular name for the larval stage of a tapeworm (Platyhelminthes, Cestoda) found in the muscles of mammals.

BLASTULA, a stage in embryonic development where the embryo typically forms a hollow ball composed of a single layer of cells enclosing a central cavity.

BLEAK *Alburnus alburnus,* a small freshwater carp-like fish found in slow-flowing waters and large lakes in Europe north of the Alps, but which has also been reported from brackish water in the Baltic. Although found over most of England and Wales, it is rare in Scotland and absent from Ireland. The bleak is gregarious and is frequently seen shoaling at the surface and catching insects; it will also browse on the bottom for aquatic larvae. During the breeding season of April to June the males develop a green-blue colouration on the back and the fins become orange. The sticky eggs are laid between stones in shallow running water. Lake-dwelling bleak migrate up feeder streams to breed. In Europe, large numbers of bleak were formerly caught and their silvery scales used in the manufacture of artificial pearls. Since the adults are only about 8 in (20 cm) long and are practically tasteless, bleak are rarely caught for any other purpose. FAMILY: Cyprinidae, ORDER: Cypriniformes, CLASS: Pisces.

BLENNIES, a group of fairly small elongated marine and brackish water fishes comprising 15 families grouped in the suborder Blennioidei. The name blenny comes from the Latin *blennius* (the scientific name used for one of the principal genera) and indicates a worthless sea fish. Blennies have very long dorsal fins and the pelvic fins, when present, are located in front of the pectoral fins under the head. Typically, the head is large, with a steeply rising forehead, and the body tapers evenly to the tail. A fleshy flap, the orbital tentacle, is often present just above the eyes. Blennies are carnivorous, bottom-living fishes, frequently well camouflaged for a life amongst rocks and in shallow waters. They are almost world-wide in their distribution.

The Scaleless blennies (family Blenniidae) are amongst the most common shore fishes of the North Atlantic but are also found in most other seas. The Tompot blenny or gattorugine *Blennius gattorugine* is the largest of the British species of blenny, its range extending southwards to the Mediterranean. It grows to 12 in (30 cm) in

Common blenny or shanny out of water.

length. The Butterfly blenny has a similar range but only reaches 6 in (15 cm) in length. The first part of the dorsal fin is high and bears a black spot with a light border round it. The shanny *Blennius pholis* derives its name from the Cornish branch of the Celtic language. It is probably the most common of the British blennies and is frequently found in rock pools, which may have given rise to the

legend that it basks on rocks in the sunshine. The male shanny exhibits parental care, looking after the eggs until they hatch. Many of the Scaleless blennies pass through a juvenile or ophioblennius stage that is so different from that of the adult that they were at first thought to be distinct species.

The Scaled blennies or klipfishes (family Clinidae) occur mostly in the southern hemisphere. These, often highly coloured, fishes are live-bearers, the male having an intromittent organ, formed from the spines of the anal fin, for introducing sperms into the female. *Heterostichus rostratus* from the Pacific coasts of North America grows to 2 ft (60 cm) in length and is able to change its colour to match its surroundings. *Neoclinus blanchardi* from the American Pacific has a greatly enlarged mouth with the lower jaw elongated resembling what Dr Earl Herald terms a 'vast scoop shovel'. Some of the clinid fishes have fights while defending their territories, the jaws being opened wide and the gill covers extended to display two spots like eyes. After several sessions of display and aggression, one may bite the other or merely give way and swim off.

Tompot blenny *Blennius gattorugine,* of European seas.

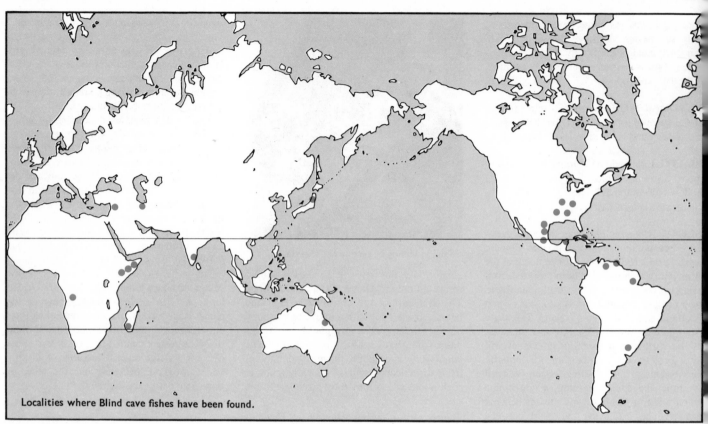

Localities where Blind cave fishes have been found.

The gunnels (family Pholidae) include eel-like species found offshore in the northern hemisphere. One of the best known is the butterfish *Pholis gunnelus* which is described elsewhere. A considerable amount of parental care is shown by members of this family, the female, sometimes the male, wrapping its body around the eggs which lie in a mass on the seabed.

The wolf-fishes (family Anarhichadidae) from the North Atlantic are the giants of the blennioid tribe. As a rule, all teeth in a fish's jaws are approximately the same shape, but in the wolf-fishes the teeth at the front of the jaws are long and pointed while those at the back are flattened, crushing teeth. Two species of wolf-fish are found in the northern Atlantic and both are fished commercially. The wolf-fish *Anarhichas lupus* is the more common in the North Sea and reaches 5 ft (1·5 m) in length. The Spotted wolf-fish *A. minor* grows to about 6 ft (1·8 m) long. Both species are sometimes known as cat-fishes. ORDER: Perciformes, CLASS: Pisces.

BLESBOK, one of the subspecies, the other being the bontebok, of the *hartebeest *Damaliscus dorcas* known as the Bastard hartebeest.

BLIND FISHES, species with degenerate eyes usually found either in caves or in the deep sea. Not all deep-sea fishes are blind, but a large proportion of those that spend their time permanently in the lightless zones lack eyes. Eyes are of use, however, in those species whose prey or mate possess light organs (see Deep-sea fishes).

The cave fishes are distributed throughout the world in the warmer zones. Some inhabit vast caves while others are known from small subterranean springs or wells. A fairly wide range of fish groups have cavernicolous representatives, including families of the sub-orders Cyprinoidei (carp-like fishes), Siluroidei (catfishes), Characoidei (characins), Amblyopsoidei and Ophidioidei.

Blind cave characins of Mexico.

The Blind cave barb *Caecobarbus geertsi* is found in caves near Thysville in the Congo. It resembles its surface-living relatives of the genus *Barbus* in general shape but is flesh-coloured and lacks eyes. A few were imported into Europe in 1956 but the export of these fishes is now rigidly controlled to prevent their extinction. The most common blind fish kept by aquarists is the

Blind cave characin *Astynax jordani,* a species found in caves near San Luis Potosi in Mexico. The species from which it most likely evolved is a Mexican subspecies of *Astynax fasciatus* which is found in surface streams in the same area. Apart from the colouring and the absence of eyes, the cave species is remarkably similar to the surface form. Small eyes are present in the young blind fish but these become covered by skin as the fish grows, even if kept in the light.

Among the catfishes, there are four families containing blind species in wells and subterranean streams in Africa, the United States, Trinidad and Brazil. One of the best known is the Blind cave catfish *Typhlobagrus kronei* from the Caverna das Areias near Sao Paulo in Brazil. There is a very similar catfish, *Pimelodella transitoria,* living in the same area and this may have been the ancestor to the blind species.

The family Amblyopsidae of the United States comprises five small species with reduced eyes and the anus far forward in the region of the throat. *Chologaster cornutus* lives in swamps and small streams in the southeastern part of the United States and is a rather secretive form. The related *C. agassizii* lives in caves in Kentucky and Tennessee. Both species have functional eyes. The two other genera in this family, *Typhlichthys* and *Amblyopsis,* which includes the famous Kentucky blindfish *A. spelaea,* live in limestone caverns and have vestigial eyes covered by skin in the adults. Although it remains blind, *T. subterraneus* slowly develops pigment if kept in the light. The breeding habits of the amblyopsids are not known, but males have been found with eggs under the gill cover.

The Cuban blindfishes of the genera *Lucifuga* and *Stygicola* or pez ciego as they are called are found in underground streams in Cuba and in Yucatan in Mexico. They are the only freshwater members of the brotulid fishes in the family Ophidiidae. Unlike the preceding species, the blind brotulids are often pigmented with shades of pink to dark blue. The eyes are fairly well formed in the juveniles but become covered by skin in the adults.

With the reduction of eyes in the blind fishes, they have become increasingly dependent on other senses. Thus in the surface-living amblyopsids there is a series of sensory papillae on the head and body but in the blind cave-dwelling forms these papillae are greatly enlarged and are highly sensitive to disturbances in the water. The lateral line sensory system is invariably more highly developed in the cave forms than in their surface-living relatives. Curiously enough, the senses of taste, smell and hearing do not seem to be more highly developed, although it should be pointed out that these are often extraordinarily acute in surface-living forms in any case (e.g. smell in salmon). Thus, it can be inferred that it is the lateral line organs in blind fishes that compensate for the lack of sight. The barbels of the cave-dwelling catfishes and carp-like species also appear to be more sensitive than in normal forms.

It is unlikely that the cave-dwelling species have evolved from surface forms that were trapped in caves or that individuals, which through some genetic upset had developed without eyes, then sought the shelter of caves. The relatives and presumed ancestors of most of the cave forms also show a heightened sensitivity of the lateral line sensory system and many live in muddy waters or under stones, the eyes being of little use, often being reduced. One feature of cave fishes which is evident when they are kept in an aquarium is their ceaseless motion. Food is adequate but not overabundant in the cave environment and since these fishes are mainly small they must search for small food particles.

BLIND SNAKES or Worm snakes, are among the most primitive of living snakes. The 300 species are grouped into two families, the Typhlopidae, which contains the vast majority of the species, and the Anomalepididae. Blind snakes occur throughout the tropical and sub-tropical zones and extend also into South Africa and the southern region of Australia, but not Tasmania. They have reached numerous

oceanic islands. All Blind snakes are harmless; most are quite small and worm-like, though a few reach a length of 2 ft (61 cm) or more. Even the longest specimens seldom have a girth greater than finger width, apart from a few African species which may have a diameter of up to 1 in (2·5 cm). Blind snakes have poorly developed teeth, on the mobile upper jaw only. Vestiges of the hindlimbs are sometimes present.

Blind snakes feed on a variety of small soil animals, such as worms, termites, and ants and their eggs and larvae. They are nocturnal and live underground, or under large flat stones, rotting logs or stumps, or in termite nests. The Blind snake is adapted for burrowing. The head is small and narrow, and unlike most snakes, has no movable bones in

Tail end of Blind snake *Typhlops*, showing spine.

the cranial part of the skull. The snout is blunt and projecting, with a tiny mouth on the ventral surface, so the whole head is a most efficient structure for forcing a passage through the soil. There is little change in diameter throughout the length of the body. Blind snakes do not develop broad scales on the ventral surface of the body, which in other land snakes assist in locomotion. Instead their firm, round body is covered with small, smooth, highly polished scales that offer a minimum of resistance to the soil as the animal forces its way through. Further, the tail is very short and ends in a small, sharp spine, which is pushed into the soil and provides a purchase when the animal is moving forward. If a Blind snake is caught it will struggle to escape, and in so doing may press the tail spine into its captor's hand. This will inflict no more than a very mild and perfectly harmless prick, but has given rise to the belief among some peoples that Blind snakes are dangerous and have a sting in the tail.

The eyes of Blind snakes are small and very poorly developed, and each appears as a dark spot covered over by a transparent scale. Probably they can only distinguish between light and darkness. Many Blind snakes, and especially the females, have a pair of large scent glands in the tail from which, when disturbed, they produce an evil-smelling liquid. Its primary purpose is probably to attract members of the opposite sex, though it can also be used as a weapon of defence.

FAMILIES: Typhlopidae, Anomalepididae, ORDER: Squamata, CLASS: Reptilia.   J.R.

BLIND SNAKES. One of the smallest Blind snakes, *Typhlops braminus,* has earned the name of Flowerpot snake. Its habit is to burrow around the roots of plants and consequently it often burrows in flowerpots that have been placed on the ground. One result of this is that it has been spread around the world with potted plants. It has become established in Hawaii and Mexico. Another Blind snake achieved fame when it appeared in the water supply of Calcutta, after large numbers had been washed out of their burrows and into the reservoirs by heavy rain.

BLISTER BEETLES, winged true beetles with characteristically soft bodies and long legs, comprising, with the flightless Oil beetles, the family Meloidae of about 2,000 species.

The Blister beetles are widespread and are particularly notable for the complex and hazardous life-history of many species. For example, in one species the larvae hatch from eggs deposited in autumn near the nests of certain bees (*Anthophora* spp). In spring a few only of these minute larvae out of the 2–10,000 eggs laid by each female, succeed in grasping the hairy bodies of the male bees, later transferring to female bees. The female bee constructs a nest of cells in the ground, each cell being stocked with honey, pollen and a single egg. When the bee deposits the egg the beetle larva drops on to it and is then sealed up by the bee in the cell. The larva feeds first on the bee's egg and then on the food store of honey and pollen and after a complicated development a mature beetle emerges from the cell.

Blister beetles contain the substance cantharidin in many of their tissues and structures. Perhaps the best known in this respect is the 'Spanish fly' *Lytta vesicatoria,* a common insect in parts of southern Europe. In recent times the administration of cantharidin as an aphrodisiac by non-qualified persons has lead to deaths and during the 19th century its use as a blistering agent for many kinds of ailments caused great misery. Cantharidin is used medicinally in the treatment of diseases of the urino-genital system. FAMILY: Meloidae, ORDER: Coleoptera, CLASS: Insecta, PHYLUM: Arthropoda. M.J.P.

BLOOD, a fluid which circulates around the body, usually within tubular vessels forming a closed system and known as the *blood vascular system. Its primary function is the transport of a wide variety of materials from the site where they were obtained or produced to the place where they are required or destroyed, or to the area from which they leave the body. In addition to transport, blood serves a number of subsidiary functions, such as aiding homoiostasis, that is the maintenance within the body of relatively constant conditions, the transport of heat and hormones and, in some animals, the maintenance of a rigid shape through hydrostatic pressure. Blood is found in the majority of invertebrates and in all the vertebrates.

The flow of blood around the body is generally maintained by a specialized muscular pump, the heart.

Not all animals with a vascular system have a well-defined organization of arteries and veins. In insects and crustaceans, in particular, the veins have become enlarged to such an extent that they occlude the true body cavity (coelom) substituting for it another, topologically within the vascular system, known as the haemocoel. Movement of blood through the haemocoel is necessarily rather sluggish, as it is caused by contractions of muscles in the body and only partly by the influx of blood propelled from the arteries by the heart.

The composition of the blood. The blood of vertebrates contains many red cells (erythrocytes) and white cells (leucocytes) suspended in the basic fluid, the plasma. All these cells contain nuclei (and to that extent are typical cells), except the red cells of mammals.

The erythrocytes of a mammal are biconcave discs about $\frac{3}{10,000}$ in (7 μ) in diameter. There are about 5 million in each cubic millimetre or nearly 3 billion in a pint. The erythrocytes contain haemoglobin, a red pigment specialized for oxygen carriage. They are produced in the red bone marrow and live in the circulating blood, for about four months, although they have no nuclei. They eventually die and fragment, the debris being removed largely by the liver and spleen. Breakdown of the haemoglobin in the liver produces the pigments responsible for the green colour of the bile.

The white cells contain no haemoglobin. There are far fewer of them than red cells, sometimes only about $\frac{1}{1,000}$ as many. The white cells, generally somewhat larger than the red cells, take a variety of forms. Some, the phagocytes, can ingest invading bacteria, engulfing them by amoeboid movement; others produce antibodies, substances which neutralize the damaging effects of foreign proteins should these enter the blood in some way. In addition to the red and white corpuscles, the blood of a mammal contains minute bodies known as blood platelets, involved in blood clotting.

The fluid plasma comprises slightly over half the volume of the blood. It is largely water, but contains many important substances. Chief among these are the plasma proteins, known as the albumins and the globulins. Simple sugars and fats, the excretory product urea, fibrinogen (also important in blood clotting), hormones and ions such as sodium, potassium, calcium and chloride are also present. The concentrations of the nutrients and the excretory products are variable. Glucose, for example, will be at a high concentration in the hepatic portal vein linking the intestine to the liver when food is being digested; urea occurs in the greatest quantities in the vessels through which it must travel from the liver, where it is formed, to the kidneys, where it is eliminated from the body. On the other hand, the concentrations of inorganic salts are generally kept within very narrow limits. Their functions are many and demand rather rigidly maintained ionic concentrations. The mechanisms controlling the concentration of the various plasma constituents are described below.

Some animals have unusually high concentrations of particular substances in their blood, as compared with the majority of species. For example, sharks and rays retain a fairly high concentration of urea in the blood which helps in their *osmoregulation. Whales and seals, when in a prolonged dive, accumulate abnormal quantities of lactic acid in the blood (see diving animals). Cows and other ruminants carry an unusually high concentration of fatty acids in their blood, as a result of the activity of micro-organisms in the rumen.

The functions of the blood. One of the principal functions of almost any blood system is the carriage of oxygen from the surface through which it has entered the body (for example, a gill or a lung) to the respiring tissues. Certain cells, e.g. muscle cells, where much respiration takes place require more oxygen than others, but all cells of the body require some oxygen for metabolism. In the larger and more complex animals a blood system is essential in order that these tissues may receive an adequate oxygen supply. Oxygen has rather a low solubility in water, however, so although a little is carried in solution in the plasma, the vast majority is usually temporarily bound to a specialized blood pigment. The most widely occurring of these pigments is haemoglobin, which is present in the blood of most annelid worms, the more primitive crustaceans, some molluscs, and practically all vertebrates. Haemoglobin is a complex molecule composed of a unit called haem, in the centre of which is an atom of iron, and a protein, globin. Oxygen molecules attach readily to the iron atoms especially when the oxygen concentration in the surrounding plasma is high but become detached again when the oxygen concentration falls. Consequently, haemoglobin becomes loaded with oxygen at the lungs or gills and unloaded at the respiring tissues. The amount of haemoglobin in the blood and its oxygen-carrying capacity is very variable, both between individuals and between species. Three other blood pigments are known, which are, however, inferior carriers of oxygen as compared with haemoglobin. These are chlorocruorin, found in some families of polychaete worms; haemocyanin, occurring in the more advanced crustaceans and in some molluscs; and haemerythrin, which has a scattered distribution among some rather obscure invertebrate species.

The blood also serves to carry carbon dioxide, a waste product of cellular respiration, from the tissues to the gills or lungs. Some is carried as carbonic acid (H_2CO_3) in the plasma, but most of it enters the erythrocytes where, under the influence of the enzyme carbonic anhydrase, it forms carbonic acid as part of a series of reactions involving the release of oxygen from haemoglobin. Conversely, at the lungs, the carbon dioxide is released again in the processes also involving the binding of the absorbed oxygen to haemoglobin.

A wide variety of other substances are transported by the blood. Of the digested food materials absorbed in the intestine, simple sugars, such as glucose, and amino acids (the end-products of carbohydrate and protein digestion respectively) are carried to any cells which may need them. Excess blood glucose is withdrawn from the blood by the liver and stored as glycogen. Amino acids are not readily stored by animals, and excess amino acids are withdrawn from the blood by the liver and broken down. The nitrogen freed in this process is formed into urea, which is transported by the blood to the kidneys where it is eliminated in the urine.

The blood is the vehicle whereby hormones are distributed. Hormones are produced in ductless glands, which pass their secretions directly into the blood stream. In this way they are carried to their site of action, which may be quite localized. For example, one of the hormones produced by the pituitary gland (a small but complex organ under the brain) is carried by the blood stream, and on arrival at the thyroid gland, situated in the neck, stimulates it to release its own hormone, thyroxin.

Birds and mammals keep their body temperature constant. This allows the metabolic processes to proceed with greater efficiency, for a change in temperature alters the rate of enzyme action (see Q_{10}). One of the varied mechanisms which maintain this constant temperature, the condition of homoiothermy, concerns the blood. Heat is produced chiefly in the muscles and the liver, and lost predominantly from the skin and lungs and to a smaller extent in the urine and faeces. The blood distributes heat about the body, tending to keep all the body regions at the same temperature. In addition, dilation of the superficial blood vessels near the skin increases blood flow there and so increases loss of heat from the body surface. This is one of the ways in which heat loss is increased at times when it is necessary for the mainten-

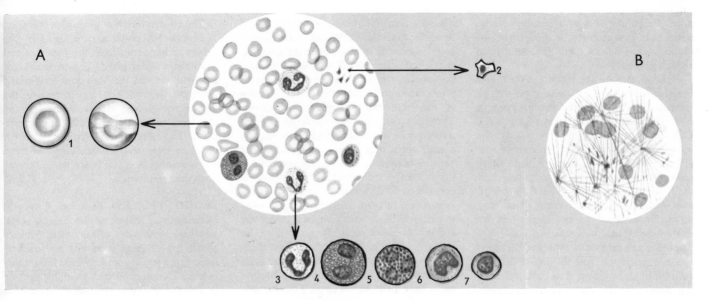

Blood

A **Structure.** 1. Red blood corpuscles (erythrocytes). 1 mm³ of blood contains about 5 million red blood corpuscles, the whole body 25,000,000,000,000, which take up a surface area of 1,300 m². The life-span of each cell is about 100 days. 2. Blood platelet (thrombocyte). 1 mm of blood contains about 250,000 blood platelets each with a life span of a few days. 3–7 white blood corpuscles (leucocytes). 1 mm³ of blood contains 5–9,000 white blood corpuscles, the most important of which are shown. 3. an ordinary granular lencocyte (60%). 4. eosinophil (2%). 5. basophil. 6. monocyte (4–8%) and 7. lymphocyte (30%). The life span varies but is usually about 5 days.

B. **Clotting.** Thromboplastin from white blood cells, converts prothrombin to thrombin. Thrombin then converts soluble fibrinogen to insoluble fibrin fibres which clot the blood.

C **Blood Groups.** The four main blood groups in man, 1.A, 2.B, 3.AB and 4.O, showing which antibodies and antigens are present in each.

D. **Blood Groups.** Bloods of different groups cannot always be mixed (see text), the blood groups which can be mixed are here linked by arrows.

E. and **F.** Different races of man show different proportions of the blood groups. The distribution of blood group B in aboriginal populations is shown in E, and of blood group A in F.

Key: % frequencies, 1. 25–30, 2. 20–25, 3. 15–20, 4. 10–15, 5. 5–10, 6. 0–5, 7. above 40, 8. 35–40, 9. 30–35, 10. 25–30, 11. 20–25, 12. 15–20, 13. 10–15, 14. 5–10, 15. 0–5.

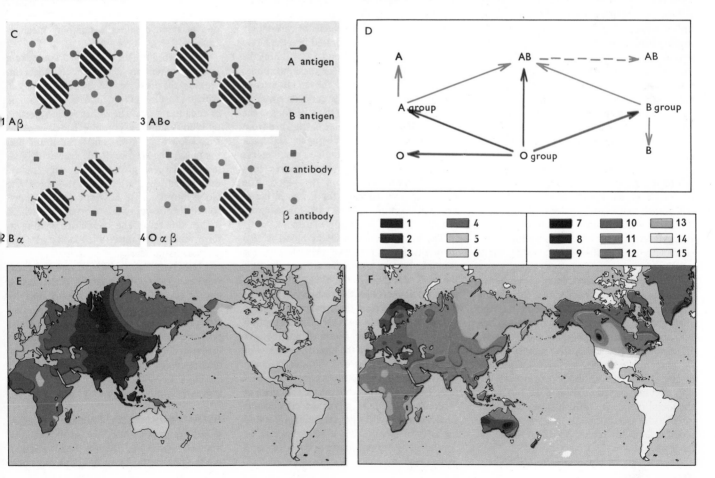

ance of a constant temperature. Conversely, when heat loss needs to be diminished, the blood vessels of the skin are constricted reducing blood flow.

In some animals the blood has the minor function of distending certain organs by increased hydrostatic pressure. An example of this is seen in the erection of the penis. Other instances may be seen among the molluscs, where much of the space around the viscera is filled with venous blood. These blood-filled spaces extend into the head and the foot. Muscle action can generate significant hydrostatic pressure here, which may serve, for example, to extend the foot by dilation during locomotion.

The blood as a defence mechanism. The blood has a considerable role to play in defence, which it fulfils by means of its phagocytes, by the clotting mechanism and by antibodies. The introduction of foreign proteins (antigens), through a cut for example, into the blood induces the formation of antibodies, which neutralize them and so remove their possible threat. The occurrence in humans and other Primates of 'blood groups' is the result of different antigen-antibody reactions. The four chief blood groups in man are termed A, B, AB and O. Blood of group A has an antigen A on the erythrocytes and an antibody β in the serum; B blood has antigen B and antibody α; AB blood has both antigens but no antibodies; O blood no antigens but all antibodies. The transfusion into a person of blood of a group which is incompatible with his own results in agglutination of the donor's antigens by the recipient's antibodies, with disastrous results. It follows that the AB group is a 'universal recipient' since it has no antibodies to agglutinate transfused antigens. On the other hand, group O is a 'universal donor', for it contains no antigens and therefore cannot be agglutinated by the recipient's antibodies, if any. Group A blood can only be given to A or AB recipients, for if transfused into a person of O or B group, the recipient's α antibody will react with the donor's A antigen. Similarly, group B blood can only be given to B or AB recipients, because the B antigen will react with the β antibody possessed by the A and O groups.

The familiar rhesus blood group is so called because it was first found in the Rhesus monkey. A rhesus-positive person has the rhesus antigen, a rhesus-negative person has not, and neither, normally, has the antibody. If, however, a rhesus-negative mother should be carrying a rhesus positive foetus, the mother forms the antibody because of the diffusion into her circulation of the antigen in the foetal blood. On diffusing into the foetal circulation the antibody will destroy the blood cells of the foetus, usually resulting in its death.

The clotting of blood at a freshly opened wound quickly stops loss of blood as well as acting as a valuable defence mechanism. If blood is flowing from a wound the damaged cells and the blood platelets produce thromboplastin, which causes the precursor prothrombin to be converted (in the presence of calcium) into the enzyme thrombin. Thrombin catalyzes the conversion of the soluble substance fibrinogen into the insoluble fibrin, which forms the basic fibrous network of the clot. Prothrombin is formed in the liver under the influence of vitamin K. Its conversion into thrombin is normally prevented by a substance heparin (not, however, in a case of thrombosis), but at a wound the action of the heparin is neutralized by thromboplastin and so the clotting mechanism is initiated. Individuals who suffer from the hereditary condition known as haemophilia have an imperfect clotting mechanism, because they carry a gene which in some way prevents the formation of thromboplastin.

The regulation of the blood contents. The composition of the blood, particularly in a mammal, is remarkably constant. Under normal circumstances the amounts of water, of ions, and of metabolites such as glucose are regulated by elaborate feedback mechanisms. An increase in blood concentration, or a decrease in blood volume, is likely to be an indication that too much water is being lost by way of the kidneys. In such circumstances specialized receptors in the region of the brain known as the hypothalamus are stimulated. The hypothalamus responds by producing hormones, which are liberated into the blood by way of the pituitary gland. On reaching the kidney in the blood stream these hormones cause a constriction of the small arteries serving the kidney tubules and also cause an increased permeability of those regions of the kidney tubules where water is resorbed from the urine, in the process of being formed, back into the blood. Both these effects result in less water leaving the body in the urine, thus stabilizing the amount in the blood. The system is very delicate, for a rise in blood concentration of as little as 1% can lead to a reduction of 90% in the flow of urine.

The balance of salts in the blood is also maintained by hormones. Aldosterone, for example, is produced by the adrenal glands if the level of sodium in the blood is becoming too low. It increases the resorption into the blood of sodium from the urine forming in the kidney tubules, and increases the absorption of sodium into the blood from the gut contents. In this way the appropriate level of blood sodium is restored. Similar mechanisms regulate the blood levels of the other vital ions. Little is known about the mechanism in invertebrates, but in advanced crustaceans such as the crayfish the uptake of water and the level of blood calcium are known to be controlled by hormones secreted from a gland in the eyestalks.

The concentration of glucose in the blood is kept within rather narrow limits by the action of hormones from the pancreas and from the adrenal gland. The pancreas, for example, secretes the hormones insulin and glucagon. Insulin acts by increasing the amount of glucose stored in the liver as glycogen, while glucagon has the reverse effect. The blood glucose level is regulated, therefore, by a variable balance between these two hormones. See also heart, homoiostasis, lymph and respiration.   A.E.B.

BLOOD FLUKES, parasitic flatworms (*Schistosoma*) inhabiting the hepatic portal and mesenteric veins of mammals. Schistosomes are of great economic and medical importance and cause the disease bilharziasis in man. The intermediate host of this parasite is a Water snail and great efforts have been made to exterminate this snail in attempts to control the disease. Bilharziasis is very widespread, being found in Africa, Asia, South America, India and the northernmost parts of Portugal. See also schistosomes, bilharziasis and Water snails. ORDER: Strigeatoidea, CLASS: Trematoda, PHYLUM: Platyhelminthes.

BLOOD VASCULAR SYSTEM, a transport system found in all except the smallest and simplest animals, consisting of a liquid, the blood, a series of tubes or more irregular spaces through which the blood can flow, and one or more contractile pumping mechanisms.

In vertebrates, the single heart acts as a multistage pump, successive chambers increasing the pressure on the contained blood, which is forced out into the arteries at the end of each heartbeat. The rather violent ejection of blood causes a pressure shock-wave to travel down each artery and this can be felt as the pulse. The arteries divide repeatedly and, in the tissues, give rise to very many, thin-walled capillaries through which the blood moves rather slowly, exchanging dissolved substances with the tissue fluid which bathes the cells. The capillaries reunite to form veins which return the blood under low pressure to the heart.

In invertebrates the blood vascular system is generally less well organized. There may be one or several hearts, or pumping may be done mainly by waves of contraction passing along some of the major blood vessels. Blood pressure is much lower than in vertebrates. In the arthropods and molluscs there are few tubular vessels and capillaries are absent, and the blood flows through very large, irregular spaces or sinuses surrounding the organs.

BLOODWORMS, small aquatic worms so called not because they live in the blood of another animal but because they are blood-red in appearance. They are thin worms only about ½ in (1¼ cm) in length. Species of the genus *Tubifex* are typically found burrowing in the soft muds of freshwater lakes and rivers. Millions occur in the intertidal mud of the upper Thames estuary, for example, and in the bottom deposits of deep lakes. They are often extremely abundant, several thousand occurring in 1 sq yd (1 sq m), feeding on particles of organic matter, algae or bacteria.

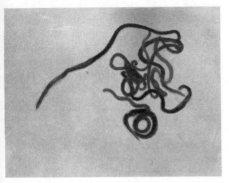

Bloodworms *Tubifex*, freshwater worms.

Tubifex belongs to the Annelida or ringed-worms, of which the two main divisions are the Oligochaeta, the earthworms, and the Polychaeta, or Marine bristle worms. The oligochaetes have a few bristles to each segment of the body: polychaetes have many. *Tubifex* has numerous chaetae or bristles in two bunches on each side of each segment, one above, one below, and so to some extent it resembles a polychaete. In a polychaete, however, the chaetae are usually mounted in flap-like extensions of the body wall called parapodia and these are absent in *Tubifex*.

Bloodworms are usually found in foul conditions, where pollution causes partial de-oxygenation, and are well adapted to tolerate oxygen lack. They can withstand a total absence of oxygen for much longer than most annelids, being able to respire anaerobically when necessary. Such a process involves trapping energy during the breakdown of glycogen in a process called glycolysis, which does not require oxygen. When the oxygen supply is poor, *Tubifex* protrudes the posterior region of the body up into the overlying water and by corkscrew-like undulations of this region draws better oxygenated water down from above. The oxygen-carrying blood pigment haemoglobin is very plentiful, causing the red colouring of the worm, and the blood supply to the skin, through which the respiratory gaseous exchange takes place, is extensive. The haemoglobin itself is specialized in having an unusually high oxygen-carrying capacity.

Tubifex differs anatomically from the earthworm *Lumbricus* (both are oligochaetes) in many respects; for example, *Tubifex* has no gizzard, only one pair of pseudo hearts (*Lumbricus* has five), and only one pair of testes (*Lumbricus* has two).

Other aquatic oligochaetes may be briefly mentioned here, although being transparent or colourless they are not bloodworms. Most burrow in muds of the sort where *Tubifex* is found, or crawl on vegetation, and some make tubes of mud particles, cemented with mucus, which may either be attached or carried about with the worm. *Aulophorus carteri* makes its tube with the spores of aquatic ferns. Some can encyst in mucus, to aid survival of either low temperatures in winter or temporary drying up of the pools in summer. Several (e.g. *Stylaria* and *Chaetogaster*) frequently reproduce asexually, by fragmenting the body into sections each of which becomes an entire worm. There are a variety of aquatic oligochaetes which are marine, generally occurring in the intertidal region, on algae, under stones or in mud (see also oligochaetes).

The name 'bloodworms' can be confusing. In Britain it is also, perhaps more commonly, used for the blood-red aquatic larvae of midges (*Chironomus*). In the United States the name is more often applied to the marine oligochaetes. FAMILY: Tubificidae, ORDER: Plesiopora plesiothecata, CLASS: Oligochaeta, PHYLUM: Annelida. A.E.B.

BLOWFLIES, large-eyed flies, with worldwide distribution, such as the bluebottles *Calliphora* and the greenbottle *Lucilia sericata*. Bluebottles and others lay their eggs in decaying meat and other foodstuffs, hence the expression 'fly-blown', but the greenbottle and *Lucilia cuprina* lay their eggs in living sheep causing a serious condition called sheep-strike. At one time blowflies were used in hospitals to clean wounds as the larvae ate rotting flesh but left healthy tissue. See bluebottle and flies. FAMILY: Calliphoridae, ORDER: Diptera, CLASS: Insecta, PHYLUM: Arthropoda.

BLUEBIRD, a name usually applied to three small North American thrushes of the genus *Sialia*. The male is blue in one species and blue and chestnut in the others. The females and young are brown with some blue on wings and tail. They are mainly insect-feeders and are well-known since they live around farms and orchards and nest in artificial nest-boxes as well as natural holes. The name is also given to the Fairy bluebird *Irena puella,* which is a leafbird of the Oriental region. The male is black and vivid glossy blue, while the female is dull blue. ORDER: Passeriformes, CLASS: Aves.

BLUEBOTTLE, name given to two similar species of true flies, *Calliphora erythrocephala* and *C. vomitoria,* which are a little under ½ in (1¼ cm) long, stoutly built and of a metallic blue colour. They sip sugary liquids and the loud buzzing restless flight of females, which seems so frantic and is so irritating, is characteristic of their unceasing search for a suitable place to lay their eggs. They are often to be found in the kitchen where their sense of smell directs them to any flesh food left unprotected. When no such site is to be found they fly backwards and forwards sometimes into the darkest corners and sometimes to bright lights, Out of doors they are found making their buzzing flight over decaying animal matter and dung, but generally they lay their eggs in the tissues of animals recently dead. Each female lays up to 600 eggs which hatch in about a day. These larvae are the 'gentles' used by anglers as bait but they are commonly also called *maggots. Under favourable conditions the larvae pupate in about a week and emerge as adults a fortnight later.

Several other metallic blue flies occurring in the tropics are commonly called bluebottles. Among these are the Screw worms. Greenbottle refers to a number of metallic green flies, many of them closely related to bluebottles. All of them have larvae which feed on decaying animal matter, but greenbottles are less prone to come indoors. Some of them lay their eggs in the wool of live sheep and the larvae attack the flesh causing a disease known as 'sheep strike' which is often fatal. FAMILY: Calliphoridae, ORDER: Diptera, CLASS: Insecta, PHYLUM: Arthropoda. R.F.C.

Bluebottle fly *Calliphora*.

BLUEFISH *Pomatomus saltatrix,* a marine perch-like species amongst the most savage and bloodthirsty of all fishes. It does not attack humans, however, and never achieved the notoriety of the barracudas. Bluefishes are deep-chested, slender-tailed and derive their name from their colour. They live in fast moving shoals in all tropical and sub-tropical waters except the eastern Pacific. Anglers hunt for bluefishes both for sport and for food and since these fishes reach 30 lb (13 kg) in weight they are a worthy challenge to the sportsman.

The large shoals of bluefishes that move up and down the American Atlantic shores principally feed on the enormous shoals of menhaden *Brevoortia,* species related to the

Bluefish, a large killer fish of the western Atlantic.

shads. The bluefishes have the reputation for being animated chopping machines the sole aim of which appears to be to cut to pieces, or otherwise mutilate, as many fish as possible in a short time. They have been seen to act like a pack of wolves, driving part of a shoal of menhaden into shallow coves from which they cannot escape. The menhaden apparently fling themselves onto the beach in an effort to escape from these savage predators. The sea is bloodstained and littered with pieces of fish after the bluefishes have eaten. Various impressive statistics have been cited to illustrate the destructive powers of the bluefishes. As many as 1,000 million bluefishes may occur each summer season off American coasts and if each eats only ten menhaden a day and the season lasts for 120 days, then the stock of menhaden must be depleted by 1,200,000,000,000 individuals during that time and this does not take into account the juvenile menhaden that fail to live to adulthood from other causes. FAMILY: Pomatomidae, ORDER: Perciformes, CLASS: Pisces.

BLUE SHEEP, not a sheep but a goat with sheep-like characteristics living at high altitudes in Asia, from Kashmir to Mongolia. See Bharal.

BLUE WHALE *Balaenoptera musculus,* the largest animal of all time. Prior to being over-hunted it reached a maximum size of 100 ft (33 m) and a weight of 130 tons. Another name for it is sulphur-bottom because individuals are sometimes tinged yellow on the underside due to a coating of the microscopic plants known as diatoms. See rorquals.

BOARFISH *Capros aper,* an oceanic fish related to the John dory. It has a deep, compressed body, $6\frac{1}{4}$ in (16 cm) long, and a pointed snout. It is found throughout most of the Atlantic Ocean and also occurs in the Pacific. FAMILY: Zeidae, ORDER: Zeiformes, CLASS: Pisces.

BOAS, non-venomous snakes that bear their young alive. See Boidae.

BOATBILL *Cochlearius cochlearius* or Boat-billed heron, a small, grey heron with a black crown and long, black ornamental plumes on the back of the head. The bill is broad and scoop-like. Some ornithologists consider the boatbill to be an aberrant Night heron, while others place it in a family of its own—the Cochlearidae.

The boatbill is confined to Central and northern South America, where it inhabits mangrove swamps. It feeds at night, as its large eyes suggest, and is usually inactive by day. Little is known of its diet or how it uses the oddly-shaped bill. The clutch of two to four pale blue eggs are laid on a platform of dead sticks, built in a mangrove tree. FAMILY: Ardeidae, ORDER: Ciconiiformes, CLASS: Aves.

BOBCAT *Lynx rufus,* the wide-ranging wild cat of America, which probably got its name from its short tail and a lolloping gait rather like that of a rabbit. Its total length is about $2\frac{1}{2}$–3 ft (76–92 cm) with an average weight of 15–20 lb (7–9 kg) but it can be much larger. The colour varies with the race and habitat but in general is brown spotted with grey or white. The short tail has a black bar on the upper side fringed with white hairs and the ears are tipped with pointed tufts of hair which are said to improve the bobcat's hearing. Bobcats are found throughout most of the United States, Mexico and the south of Canada. Because of their small size and the variety of prey they feed on, ranging from small rodents to deer and domestic animals, they have largely survived the spread of agriculture. Usually two kits are born, at any time of the year, in a den or under logs, and are defended fiercely by their mother. FAMILY: Felidae, ORDER: Carnivora, CLASS: Mammalia.

Royal python curled in a ball, its defensive posture.

BOIDAE, a non-venomous family of snakes containing about 80 species of boas, pythons and their relatives. The family is generally considered to be primitive, having retained several features found in lizards but absent in the more advanced snakes such as the colubrids and vipers. A pelvic girdle is nearly always present, although much reduced, and the hindlimbs are usually present, at least in the male, in the form of claw-like cloacal spurs. Boids also retain the coronoid bone in the lower jaw, another lizard feature that is absent in higher snakes. Most boids have two functional lungs of which the right is much larger than the left. In this respect they are intermediate between the lizards, which usually have two lungs of equal size, and the higher snakes in which the left lung has disappeared.

There are four subfamilies: the Loxoceminae, Pythoninae, Boinae and Bolyeriinae.

The Loxoceminae contains a single species, the Loxocemus python *Loxocemus bicolor,* a small semi-burrowing inhabitant of the lowlands of Central America. Earlier zoologists placed this controversial snake either with the Sunbeam snake *Xenopeltis unicolor* or in a family of its own but recent research suggests its affinities lie with the boids.

The seven genera that form the Pythoninae inhabit the warmer regions of the Old World from Africa to Australia. They differ from other boids in having a separate supraorbital bone in the skull, a feature unknown in any other group of snakes. All pythons lay eggs, as many as 100 in a clutch in some species, whereas all boas bring forth their young alive.

The boas, subfamily Boinae, are divided into 15 genera most of which inhabit the warmer regions of the New World. The four genera occurring outside the Americas are the Sand boas *Eryx,* of northern Africa and western Asia, the Pacific boas *Candoia,* of New Guinea and the Pacific islands, and the two genera *Acrantophis* and *Sanzinia* of Madagascar. Because of their disjunct distribution some experts consider the boas to represent three distinct subfamilies of separ-

Sand boa *Eryx jaculus*.

ate origin whose apparent similarity is due to parallelism rather than to a common ancestral stock.

The fourth subfamily, the Bolyeriinae, contains two species, *Bolyeria multocarinata* and *Casarea dussumieri*, both of which are found only on Round Island, a small island near Mauritius in the Indian Ocean. They are the most advanced of the Boidae, having completely lost their pelvic girdle and hindlimbs. In addition their left lung is much more reduced than that of any other member of the family. They are believed by some to be descended from the forerunners of the higher snakes.

Probably the best known boa is the Boa constrictor *Boa constrictor* an inhabitant of Central America, tropical South America and the Lesser Antilles. Primarily a surface dweller, it may be found in a variety of habitats ranging from tropical rain-forest to semi-desert regions. It is divided into eight subspecies, each having its own area of

This python clearly shows the notch in the upper lip through which the tongue is protruded.

distribution. Many stories have been written about the great size and prowess of the Boa constrictor but in reality it is only the fifth largest of living snakes, having a maximum length of a little over 18 ft (5·5 m). Its food consists mainly of small mammals and the occasional bird and lizard. Like most boas its prey is killed by constriction before being swallowed whole.

The habitat of the boids is varied, ranging from arboreal to fossorial and semi-aquatic. Some species, such as the Boa constrictor, the Rainbow boa *Epicrates cenchria* and the Royal python *Python regius,* are surface dwellers. These tend to inhabit scrubland and wooded regions where their blotched or reticulate pattern forms an excellent camouflage. There are seven species of *Epicrates*, six of which inhabit the West Indies. The only mainland member of this genus, the Rainbow boa is primarily a surface dweller feeding on small rodents, but it has been known to climb trees and devour bats. It rarely exceeds 4 ft (122 cm) in length and is called the Rainbow boa because of the bright green and blue iridescent sheen reflected by its scales.

The arboreal species include the South American Tree boas *Corallus,* the Malagasy tree boa *Sanzinia madagascariensis* and the Papuan tree python *Chondropython viridis.* These are often blotched like the surface dwellers but two species, the Emerald tree boa *Corallus caninus,* of South America, and the adult of the Papuan tree python have acquired an effective camouflage in their bright green colour with whitish markings. This is an excellent example of parallelism, where two unrelated species acquire a similar appearance as an adaptation to a similar environment. These two species are also alike inasmuch as the young differ from the adults in being yellow or pinkish brown with darker markings.

Royal python hatching from egg.

All arboreal boids have prehensile tails as do many of the surface dwellers. Some species such as the Asiatic Rock python *Python molurus* appear to be at home in several different habitats, spending much of their time in or near water yet retaining their ability to climb trees.

The Ground boas *Tropidophis* number 15 species most of which inhabit the West Indies. They are ground dwellers, feeding on frogs and lizards. The Cuban ground boa *Tropidophis semicinctus* possesses the defensive habit of voluntarily bleeding at the mouth. At the same time the eyes become ruby red.

The anaconda *Eunectes murinus* is the most aquatic member of the family, inhabiting swamps in the jungles of the northern parts of South America.

Many of the smaller boids are burrowing or semi-burrowing. The Sand boas, the Rosy boas *Lichanura,* the Rubber boa *Charina bottae* and the Calabar ground python *Calabaria reinhardtii* fall into this category. They are all small, rarely exceeding 3 ft (91 cm) in length and all have a short thick tail. They spend their time burrowing in sand, loose earth or forest litter. The Rubber boa inhabits western North America where it preys on small mammals and lizards. When threatened it defends itself by rolling up into a tight ball with its head concealed beneath the coils. Its short, blunt tail, which bears a superficial resemblance to its head, is then raised above the ball and waved about to distract the enemy from the more vulnerable parts of its body.

The five remaining New World genera are all small, burrowing or semi-burrowing, and little is known about their habits. One species, *Exiliboa placata* was not discovered until 1967.

The ten known species of Sand Boa, genus *Eryx*, of North Africa, southern Europe and western Asia, rarely exceed 3 ft (91 cm) in length and inhabit desert and semi-desert regions. They are burrowers with short thick tails and feed mainly on lizards.

Boids prey chiefly on small mammals although most species will also take birds and reptiles. Most pythons and a few boas are provided with special sensory labial pits on the scales bordering the mouth. These are believed to act as heat-detectors, in the same way as the loreal pits of the pit-vipers, enabling the snake to locate prey which is too well camouflaged to be seen. In nocturnal species, such as the Cuban boa *Epicrates angulifer,* which feeds mainly on bats, these pits are particularly advantageous.

The burrowing species are not endowed with labial pits and their eyes which are of little use in a subterranean habitat are reduced in size. In locating their prey they rely more on their modified inner ear which, as in all snakes, is adapted to pick up vibrations passing through the ground. Their prey consists of small mammals and lizards.

The majority of boids rely on their cryptic colouration for protection. The adult Cook's boa *Corallus enydris cookii* bears a superficial resemblance to the deadly fer-de-lance *Bothrops atrox,* thereby probably discouraging some of its predators. Some ground dwellers, such as the Royal python *Python regius* and burrowers, like the Rubber boa, protect themselves from predators by rolling up into a ball with the head concealed by the coils of the body. See anaconda and pythons. FAMILY: Boidae, ORDER: Squamata, CLASS: Reptilia.　　A.F.S.

BOLLWORMS, caterpillars of several species of moths which feed in cotton bolls.

An arborial member of the genus *Boa*, Cook's tree boa *Boa cooki*.

Pectinophora gossypiella is particularly important in the United States and *Heliothis armigera* in Australia and East Africa, but both species, together with *Heliothis zea,* occur in many parts of the world, having been carried from place to place in consignments of cotton seed. In bad years up to 70% of the cotton crop in an area may be damaged by bollworms. They can feed on many different kinds of plants. *Pectinophora* for instance is known to develop on at least 39 species, and may cause damage to economic crops other than cotton. Similarly, as a consequence of this, *Heliothis zea,* as well as being known as a Cotton bollworm is called the Corn earworm or the Tomato fruitworm depending on the crop it attacks.

The caterpillars of *Pectinophora gossypiella* are called Pink bollworms because they turn pink in the later stages of development. They bore into the cotton boll from the eggs, which are laid on the outside, and eat through the lint, finishing up by eating several seeds. Thus, they not only reduce the yield of cotton, they also reduce the number of seeds produced. The fully grown caterpillars are about $\frac{1}{2}$ in ($1\frac{1}{4}$ cm) long and they may pupate in the cotton seeds or bore out of the boll and drop to the ground. In summer the adult moths emerge in a few days so there may be several generations in a year. The caterpillars of *Heliothis* live in a similar way, but grow to a larger size, about $1\frac{1}{2}$ in (3·8 cm) long, and the adult moth is correspondingly larger.

Damage by bollworms can be avoided to some extent by growing varieties of cotton which mature early in the season before bollworms become too abundant and attention to methods of culture in general considerably reduces the losses. Infestation can also be reduced by spraying insecticides from aircraft. ORDER: Lepidoptera, CLASS: Insecta, PHYLUM: Arthropoda.　　R.F.C.

BOMBAY DUCK *Harpodon nehereus,* a marine fish also known as the bummalow which is eaten seasoned and dried in India. The Bombay duck is one of the myctophoid fishes, a group that includes the deep-sea lantern-fishes. It is found in estuaries round the coasts of India, Burma and China. It reaches about 16 in (40 cm) in length, has long pectoral and pelvic fins and a row of enlarged scales along the lateral line. There are several other species of *Harpodon* but only *H. nehereus* is of commercial importance, mainly because of the proximity of large shoals of these fishes to centres of population. It is also eaten fresh as well as dried. FAMILY: Harpodontidae, ORDER: Salmoniformes, CLASS: Pisces.

BOMBAY LOCUST *Patanga succincta,* a pest of rice crops in India but more especially in Thailand. See locust.

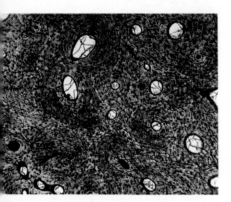

Section of bone with Haversian canals.

BONE, the hard, rigid skeletal material of most vertebrate animals. On the outside of the body it forms the protective scales and plates of the dermal skeleton. Within the body it forms the system of articulating elements to which the muscles are attached, and is thus the means by which the weight of the body is supported and by which the muscles provide movement of part, or all, of the body.

Bone is formed by the activity of cells of the connective tissue, which are called osteoblasts and which surround themselves with an irregular network of fibres. Upon these, the osteoblasts then deposit the hard, opaque mineral which makes up the substance of the bone. This mineral, called apatite, is a complex combination of calcium phosphate and calcium hydroxide. The osteoblasts eventually become almost completely surrounded by the bone substance and are then known as osteocytes. Each osteocyte is connected with neighbouring cells by fine extensions which run through tiny canals in the bone substance. These canals provide the route by which the osteo-

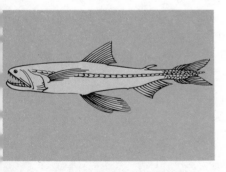

Bombay duck or bummalo or *Harpodon nehereus*, an edible marine fish found in estuaries round the coasts of India, Burma and China.

cytes obtain food materials and oxygen from the blood vessels.

To begin with, the bone is present only as a latticework of 'spongy bone', but a more compact type of bone is laid down around this. Much of the bone is eventually resorbed and re-deposited in a more regular pattern which is characterized by the presence of a system of branching 'Haversian canals',

most of which run parallel to the long axis of the bone. Each of these canals is surrounded by concentric cylinders of bone, the cells of which are supplied by the blood vessels and nerves which run within the Haversian canals.

Bones in the more superficial regions, such as the scales and the outer layers of the skull, are formed as described above, directly in the membranes of the skin. They are therefore known as 'membrane bones' or 'dermal bones'. The deeper-lying bones of the skull, body and limbs appear first in the form of cartilage. They are therefore known as 'cartilage bone' or 'replacement bone', the cartilage being later replaced by bone. The more central regions of the cartilage are the first to be invaded by connective tissue, and much of the cartilage is eroded away, bone being laid down around the remaining fragments of cartilage. Like the other parts of the developing embryo, the cartilages themselves are growing while this is happening. This growth takes place at each end of the cartilage, and the process of replacement by bone does not catch up with the process of formation of new cartilage until the animal is adult; growth then stops. This occurs in most vertebrates when the process of bone formation reaches the ends of the bones. However, in mammals and a few reptiles a separate centre of bone formation or 'ossification' appears at each end of the limb bones. This 'epiphysis' makes it possible for the elongation of the bone to take place without disturbing the joint region between one limb bone and the next. Growth therefore ceases when the epiphyses have become united to the rest of the bone by the ossification of the bands of cartilage between them and the shaft.

Even after growth has finished, bone is not simply an inert, static material but forms a reservoir of calcium and phosphorus which the body can use in case of need, for example, in the formation of egg shell in birds and in the annual growth of bony antlers in stags. Furthermore, the spaces between the bone lattice in spongy bone are filled with the bone marrow, which is one of the main blood-forming regions in the vertebrates. This is especially true of birds and mammals, in which the large limb bones are hollow and filled with marrow.

Except for the cyclostomes (lampreys and hagfishes) and cartilaginous fish, which have secondarily lost the ability to form it, bone is present in all the vertebrates. Since it is hard, it is readily preserved after the death and decay of the animal, and it is fossilized bones which have provided the main evidence of the evolutionary changes which have taken place in the vertebrates. The earliest vertebrates are known from fossil bony scales found in rocks of the Ordovician Period, about 500 million years old.   C.B.C.

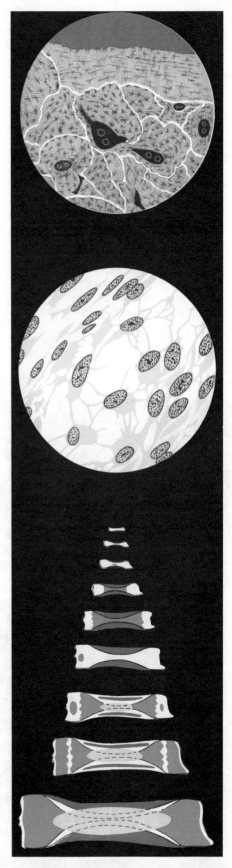

Top: cross section through bone tissue. Centre: formation of dermal bone. Below: formation of endochondral bone. Endochondral bone (blue) and compact perichondral bone (red), replaces cartilage (white) until resorbed by the marrow cavity (yellow).

Bone's many uses

BONE'S MANY USES. Among the first tools used by our ancestors were the long, narrow bones from animals which they had killed. When these were smashed open to expose the marrow, sharp edges and points resulted and these could have been put to a variety of uses. Bones were later used in the manufacture of advanced flint implements and were themselves turned into intricate harpoon heads and needles with eyes. Until modern times bone has been used for domestic and decorative purposes, as knife handles, combs, cups and buttons. Boiled down, it has been turned into glue, gelatine and soap; burnt, it has become 'animal charcoal' for the absorption of gases and dyes and an ingredient in bone china; and crushed it has been used as manure. Within recent years bone has been largely replaced by artificial materials. 'Whalebone' which has been replaced by plastics is not true bone.

BONGO *Boocerus euryceros*, close relative of the eland but lacking the dewlap and the frontal tuft, and with open-spiralled horns more like the kudu group. The average height is 4 ft (120 cm), weight 480 lb (220 kg). There is an erect mane from shoulder to rump. The colour is reddish, with 11–14 transverse white stripes, a white chevron between the eyes, white cheek-spots, throat-band, lips and chin, and a white stripe down the inner side of the limbs. The horns, which resemble those of a sitatunga, may be over 3 ft (1m).

Bongos, essentially forest elands, inhabit the tropical forest belt of Africa from Sierra Leone to Togo. They occur again from Cameroun, south of the Sanaga river, across the Congo into the extreme southern Sudan, but are not found in Nigeria. East of the Congo, bongos are found only in isolated montane forests in Kenya–Mt Kenya, the Aberdares, the Mau forest, Cherangani hills, Ndasegera forest, and perhaps Mts Meru and Kilimanjaro. In these eastern forest 'islands', bongos ascend to 7–10,000 ft (2,100–3,050 m). They live in the densest parts of the forest, where they move about by day. Bulls are often solitary, but some join with the herds of cows and calves, which may number as many as 20. They are fond of wallowing. They can move very fast through the forest, slipping under obstacles with the ease of a limbo dancer, with head held low and horns laid back. Bongos feed on leaves and shoots and can rear on their hindlegs, planting the front hoofs on tree trunks, to browse. The horns are kept sharp by constant rubbing, but bongo appear to be as unaggressive and placid as eland. They bleat, like calves or like elands, rather than barking like bushbucks or kudus.

Female bongos come into their first heat at 20 months, and from then on every 21 days, like cattle and eland. During oestrus, females are nervous, frisky and diarrhoeic. In the wild, calves are born between December and January as a rule. The gestation length is unknown. In Antwerp Zoo two bongo-sitatunga have been born. They resemble the bongo more closely, but have haunch-spots and elongated hoofs. FAMILY: Bovidae, ORDER: Artiodactyla, CLASS: Mammalia. C.P.G.

A young bongo *Boocerus euryceros*. Bongos are probably the most handsome of antelopes.

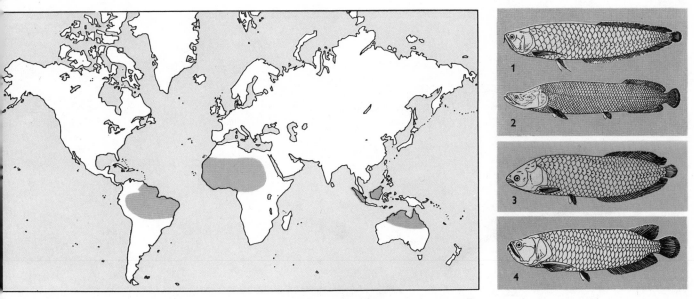

The distribution of the Bony tongues: I. *Osteoglossum bicirrhosum*, 2. *Arapaima gigas*, 3. *Clupisudis niloticus*, 4. *Scleropages leichhardtii*.

BONITOS (sometimes spelt bonitas in the United States), a name used for certain of the smaller tuna-like fishes but not with any consistency, the name being arbitrarily applied to some of the striped fishes of the family Scombridae. In Europe, *Katsuwonus pelamis* is known as the Oceanic bonito, but in the United States this species is referred to as the skipjack. The bonitos, in the broad sense of the term, are found in both the Atlantic and the Indo-Pacific region. They are highly streamlined fishes, often with the fins folding into grooves, and the tail is crescentic. Their bodies are superbly adapted for an oceanic life. The pelamid or Belted bonito *Sarda sarda,* known in the United States as the Atlantic bonito, is found on both sides of the Atlantic as well as in the Mediterranean and sometimes reaches British coasts. It attains 3 ft (10 cm) in length and its high quality white meat is canned in the United States. The Oceanic bonito has a similar distribution and reaches about the same size. It differs from the Belted bonito in having bluish bands running horizontally along the lower part of the body (the bands run obliquely on the upper part of the body in the Belted bonito). It has a remarkable turn of speed, about 25 mph (40 kph) which enables it to chase flying fishes, often leaping clear out of the water to do so. It is also said to circle shoals of fishes and will then charge into the middle of the shoal. Occasionally specimens have been washed onto British coasts (Wales) but the species is essentially one of warm water and 68°F (20°C) seems to be its optimum temperature. FAMILY: Scombridae, ORDER: Perciformes, CLASS: Pisces.

BONTEBOK, common name given to one of the subspecies of the hartebeest *Damaliscus dorcas* and known as the Bastard hartebeest.

The other subspecies is called blesbok. See entry on hartebeest.

BONY TONGUES, a family of freshwater bony fishes found in South America, Africa and Australasia and characterized by the fact that the fishes use the teeth of the tongue and those on the roof of the mouth when biting rather than utilizing the upper and lower jaws. The distribution of the Bony tongues, which parallels that of the lung-fishes is both confirmation of the primitiveness of the group and also evidence for the theory of Continental Drift proposed by Wegener.

The South American Bony tongues are the arapaima *Arapaima gigas* and the arawana *Osteoglossum bicirrhosum,* the former being one of the largest of all freshwater fishes. The arawana swims at the surface and has two leaf-like processes under the chin. These are held in front of it and appear to register any disturbances in the water such as might be caused by a struggling insect, which is then promptly eaten.

The single African Bony tongue *Clupisudis niloticus* lives in central and west Africa, chiefly to the north of the equator. Unlike other members of this family, *Clupisudis* has a small mouth and feeds on tiny organisms. It reaches 3 ft (10 cm) in length and constructs nests up to 4 ft (1·3 m) in diameter with thick walls made from vegetation cleared from the centre of the mass selected, the floor of the nest being the bare bottom of the swamp.

The Australian Bony tongue *Scleropages leichhardtii* is found in Australia and New Guinea, while its close relative *S. formosus* lives in Borneo and Sumatra. Both have shorter dorsal fins than the African and South American species. The mouth is inclined downwards and as in the arawana

there are two small barbels. The two species of *Scleropages* are mouth brooders, as may be the arawana, the eggs being incubated in the mouth of the fish and not in a nest. *Scleropages* reach over 3 ft (10 cm) in length.

The Bony tongues show many primitive anatomical features and are of great interest in tracing the evolution of the more advanced bony fishes. Their closest relatives amongst modern fishes appear to be the Elephant-snout fishes or Mormyriformes. FAMILY: Osteoglossidae, ORDER: Osteoglossiformes, CLASS: Pisces.

Arawana, South American Bony tongue.

BOOBIES, fairly large seabirds of the genus *Sula* closely related to the gannets, with which they form the family Sulidae and which they replace in the tropical waters of the world. They resemble gannets in general appearance, physiology and many details of their life-history, but are smaller and considerably lighter, weighing from 2–4 lb (0·9–2 kg). They also differ from gannets in

Blue faced booby or Masked booby, one of six species of seabirds closely related to gannets. This species is found in the Atlantic, Indian and Pacific Oceans.

some aspects of breeding biology and social behaviour and in a few minor external features, including a more extensive area of bare facial skin which, together with the legs and feet, is more brightly coloured in some species.

There are six species. The Masked booby *Sula dactylatra,* the Red-footed booby *Sula sula* and the Brown booby *Sula leucogaster* are all 'pan-tropical' and occur widely in the three major oceans. The Peruvian booby *Sula variegata* and the Blue-footed booby *Sula nebouxii* are confined to the eastern Pacific, the former occurring in the fish-rich, cold Humboldt current area off Peru and Chile (where it breeds on the famous 'guano islands') and the latter occurring farther north as far as Baja, California. Finally, the Abbott's booby *Sula abbotti* breeds only on Christmas Island in the Indian Ocean.

Four species are gannet-like in plumage, especially the Masked booby and the white phase of the polymorphic Red-footed booby, though the Peruvian and Abbott's boobies are more chequered with black. The Blue-footed booby is somewhat darker, with a brownish, white-flecked head, neck and back. The Brown booby shows white only on its lower breast, belly and underwing, while the brown and grey forms of the Red-footed booby are either wholly dark or have a white tail and, sometimes, a white lower belly. The

sexes of most boobies are alike in plumage but, unlike gannets, the female is larger and heavier than the male and usually differs appreciably in voice.

The Peruvian, Blue-footed and Brown boobies are essentially inshore feeders, but the Masked, Red-footed and Abbott's boobies range far out to sea, even during the

breeding season. The main diet is fish caught by plunge-diving. Only the Peruvian booby nests in large, dense colonies, those of the other species usually being smaller and less crowded. Though breeding is annual and seasonal in some populations, it is more often less than annual and non-seasonal, mainly because food supplies are either con-

A Red-footed booby, at its nest site on the Galapagos islands. The species is pan-tropical.

tant throughout the year or unpredictable. This latter situation, together with recurrent food shortage, usually faces the three pantropical boobies so that at best they rear only single young (even though the Masked and Brown boobies lay two eggs) and many young die of starvation in the nest. Conditions are probably similar for Abbott's booby which has a particularly long breeding-cycle so that, if successful, it can nest only every other year. The Blue-footed booby, on the other hand, often breeds in somewhat better circumstances and may rear two (occasionally three) young, while the Peruvian booby has easily the best feeding conditions of all and rears two or three (occasionally four). The nestling periods of boobies are mostly longer than in gannets, lasting up to 20 weeks or more in the Abbott's booby. Unlike young gannets, the juvenile booby has no surplus fat but returns to the birth-site for several weeks at least after fledging to be fed by its parents. FAMILY: Sulidae, ORDER: Pelicaniformes, CLASS: Aves.   K.E.L.S.

BOOBIES ARE FOOLS. The name booby is derived from the Spanish *bobo*—fool. This is a reference to their landing on the decks of ships and being unable to take off, so falling as easy prey to the sailors. Similar names indicating apparent stupidity have been given to the closely related North Atlantic gannet. This is *Basstölpel* in German (*Tölpel*—clumsy fellow) and *Fou de bassan* in French.

Albatrosses have similar names such as mollymawk from the Dutch for stupid gull, gooney from an old English word for stupid person and the Japanese *bakadori* or 'foolbird'.

BOOKLOUSE, name given to over 1,000 very small to minute insects living in temperate and tropical regions. They have plump bodies, may be winged or wingless, and are characterized by modification of the maxillae of the mouthparts into a pair of chitinous rods or 'picks' which, together with the mandibles enable the animal to bite or rasp food from the surface of bark or leaves. They take their name from one wingless species *Liposcelis divinatorius,* found especially in old books, feeding on the flour, size and glue of the bindings and on the moulds that grow on old paper.

Most species are winged but many are wingless or short-winged and these occur naturally under the bark of trees or in the nests of birds and mammals. Some have established themselves in human dwellings or in warehouses and ships' holds, thereby becoming cosmopolitan, and are classed as minor pests.

Also known as psocids, from their family name, they are among the few insects which spin silk when adult. Some, such as *Reuterella helvimacula* spin only small webs protecting both adults and their eggs and nymphs; others, like *Mesopsocus immunis* only spin a web above an egg cluster; in still others, including *Liposcelis* no silk is produced at all. The psocid life-cycle comprises the large heavily-yolked egg stage, usually six nymphal instars and the sexually mature adult. With each moult during development, the externally visible wing pads enlarge and the genitalia develop. There is no quiescent pupal stage.

Habitats and life-histories are varied but psocids are pre-eminently insects of forest and woodland. A few live permanently in the upper layer of the litter of dead and decaying leaves on the woodland floor. Others, in particular those which lay their eggs on the leaves of deciduous trees, usually produce one generation in the spring in the leaf litter and later generations in the foliage of the trees themselves. The *Liposcelis* species and *Embidopsocus enderleini* live in bark crevices on the trunks of trees or under the bark of dead or dying trees. A few species are much more mobile than most, probably seeking out habitats which are only temporarily favour-

A wingless booklouse (top) and one of the many winged species (below).

Boomslang *Dispholidus typus*, the dreaded large African Tree snake.

able, where they rapidly breed and from which they disperse by flight. One of these species is the small *Lachesilla pedicularia* which often enters houses in late summer and which is the most common psocid represented in the aerial plankton. Finally many species live out their whole life-cycle on the bark of trees, feeding on the unicellular green algae, the Honeydew moulds growing on the bark or on lichens.

The Psocoptera are known as fossils from the Lower Permian, 270 million years ago, when the order represented the stock ancestral to true bugs Hemiptera, Bird lice Mallophaga and the Sucking lice Siphunculata. FAMILY: Psocidae, ORDER: Psocoptera, CLASS: Insecta, PHYLUM: Arthropoda.
E.B.

BOOMSLANG *Dispholidus typus,* large African Tree snake with three enlarged grooved fangs in the upper jaw below the eye. It is the most venomous of the backfanged snakes and its bite can prove fatal to man. 'Boomslang' is Afrikaans for 'Tree snake'.

The boomslang averages $4\frac{1}{2}$ ft (1·4 m) in length. It has a short head with very large eyes and a slender body and tail covered above with narrow, oblique, strongly keeled scales. It is common throughout the well-wooded parts of Africa south of the Sahara but is absent from the rain-forest and semi-desert regions.

Towards the end of the dry season the female boomslang lays 5–16 elongate eggs of about 1 in (25 mm) in length. The newly hatched young are about 15 in (38 cm) in length.

The boomslang hunts by day and may stay in a tree or group of trees for several days if food is plentiful. Its diet consists largely of chamaeleons, but during the nesting season many fledgling birds and eggs are eaten; adult birds are rarely caught. Lizards, frogs and rats are also devoured but other snakes are rarely attacked.

If disturbed, the boomslang will always try to escape at speed, but when cornered it inflates its throat with air, giving the impression of an enormous head, then makes savage lunges at its aggressor with gaping jaws. Its venom is extremely toxic, destroying the fibrinogen in the blood and causing extensive internal bleeding. Because the amount of venom produced by a boomslang is very small, the specific anti-venom is in short supply. FAMILY: Colubridae, ORDER: Squamata, CLASS: Reptilia. D.G.B.

BOT FLY, a fly, the larvae of which are better known than the fly and are parasitic in warm-blooded animals. The larvae of certain blowflies can infest wounds and attack living flesh, as well as living in carrion, and Bot flies represent a further step in evolution, the larvae having become completely parasitic. Since the larvae have a virtually unlimited supply of food, the adult flies have ceased to feed at all, and some have even lost their mouthparts. Adults are rarely seen and some species are known only from specimens bred from larvae, which, in contrast, may be extremely numerous. The larvae are the 'bots' and are generally less pointed than maggots and covered with rows of strong spines which help them to move about in the tissues of their host. The hind spiracles have many small pores, which make them less liable to become clogged.

The Sheep nostril fly *Oestrus ovis* lives in the head sinuses of sheep, feeding mostly on mucus. *Cephenomyia* similarly infests deer, *Tracheomyia* the throats of kangaroos, *Cephalopina titillator* the head-cavities of camels and *Pharyngobolus africanus* the gullet of African elephants. *Hypoderma bovis* and *H. lineatum* are the common Warble flies of cattle in Europe and are more directly parasitic. Their larvae migrate through the body until they come to rest under the skin of the back where they form boils with an opening to the exterior for breathing purposes. *Oedemagena tarandi* is a Warble fly of reindeer. Horses, zebras and rhinoceroses are often heavily infested with stomach bots belonging to the family Gasterophilidae. At one time they were thought to be remote from the other bots, but now they are felt to be closely related. Bots do not normally attack man, but infrequently the eggs of *Oestrus* or *Hypoderma* may get into the eyes of shepherds or herdsmen and the small first-stage larvae can cause irritation or even more serious damage to the eye. See also Warble fly. FAMILY: Oestridae, ORDER: Diptera, CLASS: Insecta, PHYLUM: Arthropoda.
H.O.

BOTRYLLUS, widespread and abundant genus of Sea squirt, common on lower parts of the sea-shore throughout the world. There were once thought to be hundreds of species, but most are now known to be mere colour variants of a few. *Botryllus* perhaps represents the acme amongst the Ascidiacea of the development of asexual reproduction by budding.

The individuals (zooids) of which the colony is formed have lost much of their separate identity, sharing a common blood supply and other features. The zooids lie embedded in a common test or tunic and reproduction, both sexual and asexual, is synchronized throughout the colony. *Botryllus* is, thus, a compound ascidian. The zooids are only about $\frac{1}{25}$ in (1 mm) long, but a colony may consist of so many members that it may cover an area 1 ft (30 cm) across as a brilliantly coloured sheet. See also Sea squirt and Ascidiacea. FAMILY: Botryllidae, ORDER: Pleurogona, CLASS: Ascidiacea, SUBPHYLUM: Urochordata, PHYLUM: Chordata.

BOTTLENOSED DOLPHIN *Tursiops truncatus,* also known in North America as the Common porpoise, is famous as the

Ankole or Watussi cattle, of Uganda, a savannah breed of the zebu, members of the Bovidae family.

'porpoises' which perform before visitors to seaquaria. It was study of these animals in captivity which led to a better understanding of dolphins and porpoises in general, and especially of their intelligence. See dolphins.

BOTTLENOSED WHALE, two species of *Hyperoodon* are so called because the head has a prominent beak and a rounded dome

containing a reservoir of oil. See Beaked whales.

BOVIDAE, the largest and most successful family of the mammalian order Artiodactyla, usually described as cattle, sheep, goats and antelopes. The term 'antelope' however, is such a vague one as to be almost meaningless: it implies any bovid with a rather slender

build and largely upwardly-directed horns—which is the same thing as saying that they are bovids which are not cattle, sheep or goats. Certain forms, such as chamois and goral, are often called 'goat-antelopes', implying that they are very goat-like, but are less stockily built and so perhaps more like the gazelles, which are the most 'typical' antelopes. Bovidae belong to the true ruminants, suborder Pecora, with four stomachs including a rumen or paunch. They are unguligrade and have fusion of radius and ulna, tibia and fibula, and the respective metapodials; lateral hoofs are generally present. Many species have glands between the toes (interdigital or pedal), below the eyes (pre- or anteorbital, or facial), in the groin (inguinal) or on the 'knees'.

Like most other Pecora, the Bovidae have horns on the head above the eyes. Each consists of a bony core, which is part of the skull, and a keratinized sheath which covers the core and is derived from the skin. The horny sheath is composed of hair-like filaments arising from follicles in the skin; they differ from true hairs in being hollow. Over the core is a germinal layer of epidermis which secretes the filaments and so provides for the horn's growth. This type of horn differs considerably from that seen in deer, family Cervidae, in which the 'horn' or antler is a bony outgrowth from the skull and is shed and regrown every year, being nourished as it grows by an external covering of highly vascular skin known as velvet, which peels off in the summer.

Indian humped cattle, or zebu, members of the Bovidae family.

A bull nyala *Tragelaphus angasi*, of southeast Africa.

More closely allied to the Bovidae is the pronghorn, the sole living member of the family Antilocapridae. In this family the horn has the same structure as in the Bovidae, but is shed annually. It is not generally known that the Bovidae themselves shed their horns: this happens only once during the animal's life-time, however, during adolescence, instead of once a year as in pronghorn. The new horn develops inside the old one. The border between them is quite sharp and the new horn cuts the old one off from its nutrient vessels so that it dries up. The old horn is either raised up by the new one, appearing to form the new one's tip and finally falling off (as has been recorded in blackbuck), or the old horn is pierced by the new one and so forms a kind of sleeve, fraying at the juncture of the two (as happens in the kouprey). Alternatively the whole process may be quite gradual and unnoticeable, the dead outer horn being rubbed off against trees and bushes.

The dental formula in Bovidae is regularly $\frac{0 \cdot 0 \cdot 3 \cdot 3}{3 \cdot 1 \cdot 3 \cdot 3} = 32$. Some forms tend to lack the anterior lower premolar. There is a long gap, the diastema, between the lower canine and the premolars. Upper incisors and canines are never present except as an anomaly: this is in strict contrast to deer, in which upper canines are often not only present but long and dagger-like. Bovidae have no gall-bladder, unlike both Cervidae and Giraffidae.

Scientifically, the Bovidae are a very difficult family to classify. A number of very distinctive types are included, and in the view of various experts they should be classed in several subfamilies. Different classifications, into subfamilies, tribes and even subtribes, have been offered by such authorities as Pocock, Schwarz, Simpson, Sokolov and Haltenorth, each relying on a slightly different array of characters. It seems clear from the sum of all the information offered, especially the extensive behavioural data which has recently been collected, due almost entirely to the researches of Fritz Walther, that there are two polar types within the Bovidae, represented by the cattle on the one hand, and the sheep and goats on the other. Sorting out the heterogeneous collection of antelopes, one finds that some must be aligned with one polar type, some with the other. Only the duikers remain virtually unclassifiable, they retain some very primitive characters and it seems that their ancestors must have separated from those of the other Bovidae at a very early period. Probably they are rather closer to the cattle group, but the evidence is still incomplete.

The classification that follows is in outline similar to that made by Ernst Schwarz in 1936, but is modified in accordance with other authors' opinions and the behavioural data. (The number of species is given in brackets after each genus.)

Subfamily Cephalophinae Tribe Cephalophini Genera: *Cephalophus* (11) *Sylvicapra* (1)	Forest duikers Plains duiker
Subfamily Bovinae Tribe Bovini Genera: *Bos* (5) *Bison* (2) *Syncerus* (1) *Bubalus* (4)	Cattle, yak, gaur, banteng Bison, wisent African buffalo Indian buffalo, anoa
Tribe Boselaphini Genera: *Tetracerus* (1) *Boselaphus* (1)	Four-horned antelope Nilgai
Tribe Tragelaphini Genera: *Tragelaphus* (6) *Boocercus* (1) *Taurotragus* (2)	Kudu, nyala, bushbuck Bongo Eland
Subfamily Caprinae Tribe Neotragini Genera: *Neotragus* (3) *Raphicerus* (3) *Ourebia* (1) *Oreotragus* (1) *Dorcatragus* (1) *Madoqua* (5) *Pelea* (1)	Royal antelope, suni Steinbok, grysbok Oribi Klipspringer Beira Dikdiks Rhebok
Tribe Antilopini Genera: *Antilope* (1) *Gazella* (10) *Procapra* (3) *Antidorcas* (1) *Litocranius* (1) *Saiga* (2)	Blackbuck Gazelles Goa, dzeren Springbok Gerenuk Saiga
Tribe Reduncini Genera: *Redunca* (3) *Kobus* (5) *Ammodorcas* (1)	Reedbuck Waterbuck Dibatag
Tribe Hippotragini Genera: *Hippotragus* (3) *Oryx* (3) *Addax* (1)	Sable, Roan antelope Oryx Addax
Tribe Alcelaphini Genera: *Alcelaphus* (3) *Damaliscus* (3) *Aepyceros* (2) *Connochaetes* (2)	Hartebeest Bastard hartebeest Impala Gnu

Topi, local name applied to subspecies of one of the Bastard hartebeestes *Damaliscus korrigum*, in East Africa.

Tribe Caprini	
Genera: *Pantholops* (1)	Chiru
Nemorhaedus (6)	Goral, serow
Rupicapra (1)	Chamois
Oreamnos (1)	Rocky mountain goat
Hemitragus (3)	Tahr
Capra (9)	Goat, ibex, markhor
Ammotragus (1)	Barbary sheep
Pseudois (1)	Bharal
Ovis (2)	Sheep
Budorcas (1)	Takin
Ovibos (1)	Muskox

Most of these are dealt with in independant articles under the common names of the animals concerned, but all the Neotragini (except the somewhat aberrant *Pelea*) are treated under the heading 'Dwarf antelope'.

In the Bovinae, the horns are smooth except for keels, which may be either light or strong and which travel up the length of the horn and give it a certain angularity. The horn-cores are themselves keeled, with either one or two keels. The Caprinae have no keels on their horn-cores and only rarely any on their horns–the horns are instead ringed for most of their length. The horns are placed further back on the head in the Bovinae than in the Caprinae. The face is less bent down on the braincase in the Bovinae and the muzzle is distinctly broader, the distance between the nostrils being greater than the height of the upper lip.

The colour-pattern also differs very markedly between the Bovinae and Caprinae. In the former, there is usually a row of spots on the haunches, sometimes vertical white body-stripes, a white band between the eyes, two white spots on either cheek, a white mark on the throat and the lower segments of the limbs (shanks) are often white except for a dark line down the front. These markings are the kind one might expect to find in forest-living animals as they provide good camouflage there, blending with the light falling irregularly through the leaves. On the other hand, the Caprinae colour-pattern typically consists of white stripes down the face, from the eyes to the muzzle, with a darker nose, and blackish stripes bordering them below; the white face-stripes may be reduced, just leaving white rings round the eyes. The Caprinae also have a light underside and darker flanks, the two tones often being divided by a longitudinal black stripe. This type of colouration is an open-country type, which compensates for the light coming down strongly from above.

The behaviour of the Bovinae and Caprinae also differs markedly; their flight reactions, for instance are quite distinct. The Caprinae immediately run off, but after about 100 yd (90 m) they stop and turn to see what was the cause of the trouble. When running, many species 'spronk' or 'stott' that is they jump vertically into the air with the back arched, all four legs coming straight down together. This action probably serves to alert other members of the social group and also perhaps gives the animal a better view, The Bovinae tend not to flee immediately, typically freezing in mid-stride, and then proceeding very cautiously until the cause of the disturbance has been discovered. This is a very typical forest reaction.

Walther's studies of courtship and mating patterns has revealed very sharp differences between the two main subfamilies. In the Caprinae the courtship ceremony includes an element known as 'laufshlag', in which the male extends a foreleg stiffly and either places it between the female's hindlegs or under her belly, or strokes one of her hindlegs with it. All the time the male's head is held up, with the neck stretched out, and mating takes place in this position. In the Bovinae there is no laufschlag, the male laying his neck along the

Male Defassa waterbuck *Kobus defassa* in Uganda. It is like the Common waterbuck in size and habits and is distinguished by the white round the eyes. ▶

Below: Rocky mountain goat *Oreamnos americanus*, of North America. Its shaggy coat is white all the year round. It can run up almost perpendicular cliff faces.

female's neck or back and mounting with his head in this position. The courtship often includes a phase during which the male walks or runs in front of the female barring her path; sometimes he even ploughs the ground in front of her with his horns.

The duikers have been little studied. A courtship ceremony has, however, been described, but seems to bear little resemblance to that of either Bovinae or Caprinae. There is an exchange of secretions, the partners pressing their preorbital glands against one another and the male is very aggressive, butting the female hard in the belly and flanks. The colouration of duikers is unlike that of other antelopes, and shows widely divergent types. They do, however, have keeled horn-cores like the Bovinae. Another similarity to the Bovinae is the presence of a little cornified or cartilaginous 'tooth' in the lower jaw behind the canines: this is not preserved in macerated specimens, but can be identified in freshly dead animals. The 'pseudo-tooth' has been identified so far only in duikers, bushbuck, kudu, sitatunga and eland. It seems, therefore that the duikers, when more is known about them will come to be included in the Bovinae; meanwhile, they should stand as a separate subfamily.

In fact, only two bovid tribes, Bovini and Antilopini, are extensively represented in both subsaharan Africa (the Ethiopian faunal region) and Eurasia (the Palearctic faunal region); all others are either essentially Ethiopian or essentially Palearctic (mostly the former). In both cases, the tribes concerned are sharply split between their Ethiopian and Palearctic representatives. In the Antilopini, the blackbuck of India and its fossil relatives are distinct, with their corkscrew horns, from the African springbok and gerenuk. The primitive genus *Gazella* is widespread in both continents and forms an exception to the rule. It has given rise, apparently fairly recently, to two similar genera, *Procapra* and *Saiga*. In the case of the Bovini, Gentry could not trace any fossil connections within the Pleistocene between the African buffalo and its Asiatic relatives, so here too there is a rather sharp separation.

Only four genera of bovids *(Bos, Bubalus, Capra, Ovis)* are kept widely as domestic animals today, but it is thought that the Ancient Egyptians kept and force-fed oryx and addax for the table. Recently several people have pointed out the potential value of the eland as a domestic animal, and it is possible that *Taurotragus* will become the fifth truly domestic bovid genus. ORDER: Artiodactyla, CLASS: Mammalia. C.P.G.

BOWERBIRDS, a family, Ptilonorhynchidae, of 18 species of perching birds noted for the very elaborate sexual displays. They are found in New Guinea and the surrounding islands, and in north and east Australia.

The bowerbirds are very closely related to the Birds of paradise, the latest opinion being that they have evolved from a number of separate stocks of Birds of paradise to produce a group of birds that are of rather uniform appearance and lacking the showy display plumes of their ancestors. In view of this it seems probable that ornithologists will cease to recognize the family Ptilonorhynchidae and unite them with the family Paradisaeidae (Birds of paradise).

Bowerbirds vary from 9–15 in (23–38 cm) long and show a wide range of colours and patterns in their plumage. Bold patterns of green, orange, lavender, and yellow with grey or black are found in many species; some have a plain grey or brown plumage and a few are spotted. In the more brightly coloured species the male bird is much brighter than the female, but the sexes are alike in the dull-coloured forms. Some of the species have a crest of elongated feathers, the crest often being brilliantly coloured. In a few species it forms an elaborate ruff or a mane hanging over the upper back. The bill is slightly hooked at the tip in all of the bowerbirds, but in some it is slightly down-curved, in others straight, in some it is thin and weak, in others again rather heavy, and in a few species the upper mandible has some small tooth-like notches along its cutting edge.

Bowerbirds are most numerous in New Guinea, where five of the eight genera are found. The other three genera only contain one species each and are confined to Australia. There is now good evidence that the bowerbirds evolved from the plumed Birds of paradise in the jungles of New Guinea and then spread to Australia where these three genera evolved.

The genus *Ailuroedus* has three dull-

Four-horned, Piebald or Jacob's sheep, a breed found in England and Wales, now disappearing.

coloured species known as catbirds. One of these is confined to New Guinea, one is found in Australia and New Guinea and one is confined to Australia. They are bright green above and pale brown or pinkish brown below, boldly patterned with black.

The stagemaker or Tooth-billed bowerbird *Scenopoeetes dentirostris* is found only in Australia. It is an olive-brown bird, about 11 in (28 cm) long, with prominent pale stripes on the underparts.

In another monotypic genus is Archbold's bowerbird *Archboldia papuensis* of the mountains of New Guinea. This is a rather large species that varies from 12–15 in (30–38 cm) long. The male is black or sooty grey with a crest of golden yellow feathers; the female is dull grey with pale brown markings on the wings.

The genus *Amblyornis* contains four species that are again confined to the mountains of New Guinea. They are 9 or 10 in (23–25 cm) long, rather short-billed, with red-brown plumage. The females lack crests but the males of all but the Vogelkop gardener bowerbird *A. inornatus* have brightly coloured crests; red, orange or yellow according to the species.

The genus *Prionodura* has only one species, the Golden bowerbird *P. newtoniana*, which is found only in the mountain forests of northern Queensland, Australia. It is about 9 in (23 cm) long, rather short-billed, with different plumages in the male and female birds. The male is bright olive-green with yellow underparts, head, neck and tail, while the female is dull yellow-green with grey underparts.

The three species of the genus *Sericulus* vary from 9–11 in (23–28 cm) long and are found in both Australia (one species) and New Guinea (two species). The males have large areas of orange, red or bright chrome yellow in their plumage, and an erectile cape of brightly coloured feathers; the females are brown or pale yellow above with grey or olive-brown underparts marked with a dark, scaly pattern. The bill is rather long and nearly straight.

The Satin bowerbird *Ptilonorhynchus violaceus* is the only member of its genus and is confined to eastern Australia. About 1 ft (30 cm) long, it is rather long-billed, the bill also being heavy and straight. The plumage is glossy black in the male and grey-green in the female.

The last genus, *Chlamydera*, has four species. Two of these are confined to Australia, one is found in New Guinea and in the Cape York area of Australia, and the other is restricted to New Guinea. In two species the sexes differ in plumage, the male being grey-brown or yellow-brown with a spotted or scaly pattern on the underparts and a glossy violet-pink crest on the back of the neck. The females of these species are duller and only

Male Satin bowerbird of the coastal area of eastern Australia, best-known of the bowerbirds, decorating its bower with pebbles, shells and blue feathers.

occasionally have a crest. In the other two species both the male and female are dull grey-brown or olive-brown with a salmon-pink wash on the body plumage.

The bowerbirds are so-called because of the complicated, and often highly decorated, structures that the males of some species use when they are displaying. These sometimes take the form of cleared areas the size of a table-top, containing a domed tunnel of sticks, decorated with brightly coloured stones, fresh flowers, spiders' webs and coloured insects' skeletons. Some of these bowers are so impressive that, when they were first discovered, the explorers believed that they could only be the product of human skill and artistry. The degree to which the bower-building habit is developed varies in the different genera of bowerbirds, in general becoming progressively more advanced in the birds that have diverged further from their Bird of paradise ancestors.

In the genus *Ailuroedus* no bower is built, though the males appear to defend a territory near to the forest floor. In display the male rustles its wings, jumps spasmodically upwards on slender, leaning saplings, chases

the female and gives a head-jerking display in which the head is jerked upwards, then lowered as a rasping call is given. Both male and female of this species have been seen at the nest, pretending to be injured in an endeavour to lure the intruding human from the nest area.

In the genus *Scenopoeetes* the male defends a perch from which it sings, above a cleared patch of ground amongst slender young trees. It decorates its private lawn with large leaves laid upside down and a few snail shells. In display the male flicks its wings open, bobs its head from side to side with its bill gaping, hops about erratically, fluffs its breast feathers and holds a leaf in the bill for long periods. The males only see the females at mating time and take no part in rearing the young.

In the genus *Archboldia* the male has one, or sometimes more, perches on which it sits waiting for females to approach. The perches are usually about 10–20 ft (3–6 m) up on a tree branch above a cleared ground court which is decorated with pieces of vegetation, snail shells, pieces of insects and chips of tree resin. In display the male crawls about

in front of the female for up to 20 min or more, pausing occasionally to make short hops towards or away from her. He faces the female for most of the time as she moves around the edges of the cleared area. Whilst doing this the male carries a small twig held crosswise in the bill.

The males of the genus *Amblyornis* defend perches that are often closer together than they are in the three preceding genera. The perch is usually from 15-30 ft (4½-9 m) up in a tree near to a cleared ground court. The court surrounds a moss-covered stage which is built around a sapling that is ringed with sticks carefully placed there by the male. In two of the three species the stage is roofed and ornamented with coloured fruits and berries, jungi and charcoal; in the other species the stage is not roofed and has few ornaments. In display the male has a strange song, ventriloquial and imitative of many sounds of the forest, as well as whistling, crackling and rattling noises. When singing the male stretches its neck towards the base of the tower built around the sapling and hops from side to side, jerking its head from side to side the whole time. The female remains at the edge of the ground court and also sings. In these three species the sexes meet only for mating, the nesting and rearing of the young being carried out entirely by the female.

In the genus *Prionodura* the males defend territories that are grouped together, each male's territory being a fairly large area surrounding the private court and bower. The male sits for most of the time on a stick or creeper above the bower structure. The bower itself is remarkable; it may be up to 7 ft (2 m) tall, surrounded by smaller towers and decorated with moss, berries and flowers. In display the male bird hovers around the bower, jerks its head from side to side, flutters the wings and carries sticks and flowers to the bower. The male and female meet only for mating, the female building the nest and rearing the young unaided.

Little is known of the behaviour of the species of the genus *Sericulus,* but two of them are known to build a walled bower.

In the genus *Ptilonorhynchus* each adult male defends a separate court and bower inside a traditional courtship area. The bower consists of a solid mat of small sticks with a wall of sticks on each side. The whole structure is painted with a paint made of vegetable juices and is brilliantly decorated by the male with shells, flowers, leaves and dead insects. In display the male spends most of its time at the bower, uttering scraping, grating, cackling, churring and squeaking notes. It dances about with its tail raised over its back, jumps right over the bower, points the bill to the ground and becomes so excited that its eyes bulge outwards. The female bird enters the bower and may crouch down as a signal to the male that she is ready to mate. The females appear to remain at the bower with the male for several days, but after this they separate and the female builds a nest and raises the young alone.

In the four species of the genus *Chlamydera* the males have bowers in groups in the forests, but they are widely spaced within these groups. Each male defends a private bower consisting of two walls of sticks that are built up parallel to one another and decorated with fruit, flowers, snail shells, fungi, insect skeletons and a wide range of other brightly coloured objects. In display the males spend most of their time at the bower giving a variety of strange calls, including popping notes, cat-like mewings, rhythmically repeated mechanical noises and imitations of the calls of other forest birds. When a female bird appears the male shakes objects held in its bill, crouches, leaps jerkily to one side then the other, raises the tail vertically over the back, droops the wings and runs around its bower. Mating occurs in or near the bower and the female bird may remain near the bower with the male for

Bowfin, of North America, sole surviving species of a family that was once widespread.

several days. After this she moves away and nests without any aid from the male.

It seems that the complexity of bowerbirds' plumage patterns bears a fairly close relationship to the complexity of the bower that is built. In the species that build no bowers, or only clear a ground court, the plumage is often coloured with red, orange, yellow, green or black in varying combinations of brilliance, but in the species that build the most elaborate and brilliantly decorated bowers the birds are disappointingly dull in colour, with the exception sometimes of the crest. As the bower seems to function as a signal from the male bird to attract a mate, it is apparent that the species that do not have elaborate bowers need to 'make up for' this lack by having colourful plumage. On the other hand in those species with large and brilliantly decorated bowers, the bright plumage-patterns have become superfluous to some extent, and have thus tended to disappear in favour of a cryptic pattern.

Many of the Birds of paradise show off their grotesquely shaped and vividly coloured display plumes on special perches in the tree-tops. A few Birds of paradise have changed their display areas from the tree-tops to thin saplings lower down in the forests and these are probably the forms that are most closely related to the more primitive of the bowerbirds. Many Birds of paradise clear leaves from the twigs near to their display perches so that shafts of sunlight fall through the forest roof and help to show off their gaudy display plumes. Other Birds of paradise clear leaves from the perch itself so that the displaying male bird is visible from farther afield. It seems likely that the habit of clearing a ground court of vegetation, that is shown by many bowerbirds, developed from this habit of leaf-clearing performed by their Bird of paradise ancestors.

Some of the Birds of paradise display

from a thin sapling low down in the forest. As these species developed the habit of clearing a ground court beneath their display perch on the sapling it seems likely that some of the cleared material would often lodge against the base of the sapling itself. As this may have made the ground court appear more conspicuous it could well have been followed by the deliberate deposition of sticks, followed eventually by the building of elaborate bowers. Several species of bowerbirds place ornaments on their cleared ground courts, so that it is not surprising that the species that build bowers ornament them to a varying degree, the best decorated being a vivid mass of fresh red or yellow flowers, with shiny snail shells and iridescent insect skeletons adding to the effect.

So far as is known all of the bowerbirds live mainly on the fruits of trees and bushes, supplementing this diet with insects, larvae, spiders, and sometimes small snakes and lizards, tree frogs and seeds. It is this predominantly frugivorous diet that enables the males to have the time necessary for bower building, as tree fruits are abundant for most of the year. This abundance of food also enables them to nest polygamously, the female bird carrying out all of the nesting duties without encountering any difficulty in feeding herself and her offspring.

Bowerbird nests vary from bulky cups in *Ailuroedus, Amblyornis* and *Chlamydera* that are built in bushes, to a bulky cup in a tree-hole in *Prionodura*, and a frail, shallow cup built in a bush in *Scenopoeetes, Sericulus* and *Ptilonorhynchus*. In *Prionodura,* as in many other hole-nesting birds, the eggs are pale in colour (cream) without markings. In *Ailuroedus* the eggs are a deep rich cream, but they are fairly well hidden from predators, being inside a deep nest-cup. In the other species the eggs are cream, white or light blue or grey, variously spotted, mottled and streaked with grey, lavender or brown to hide them from predators, as they rest in the open cup of the nest.

Except perhaps in the genus *Ailuroedus*, the female bird builds the nest alone, lays the clutch of from two to five eggs, incubates them and then feeds the young until they fledge and for a week or two afterwards. Incubation periods of between 12–15 days have been recorded and approximate fledging periods of from 13–20 days, though some of these were probably inaccurately recorded. Females of several species attempt to lure predators, away from the nest by flopping into the undergrowth and giving a distraction display with trailing wings, appearing to be injured and therefore an easy victim for the predator.

Males of the brightly coloured bowerbirds, and of the species that construct large bowers do not attain adult plumage until they are several years old. Until then they resemble females and feed either alone or in small groups in the forests. After they moult into adult plumage they take up a territory within one of the spaced out groups of bower or court defending males and proceed to build a bower, a court, or both. FAMILY: Ptilonorhynchidae, ORDER: Passeriformes, CLASS: Aves.   D.T.H.

BOWFIN *Amia calva,* a member of one of the two surviving groups of Holostei, primitive ray-finned fishes that gave rise to all the modern bony fishes (see fishes and Fossil fishes). Fossil bowfins have been found in Europe but the only surviving species is now confined to the eastern side of North America. It is a cylindrical, solid-looking fish with a long dorsal fin and a heavy armour of scales. The body is dull brownish-green in colour, lighter underneath, with several dark vertical stripes. A black spot is found near the base of the tail, margined in males with yellow.

There are certain anatomical features which are of interest in the bowfin. Underneath the lower jaw is a bony plate, the gular plate, a relict from its more primitive ancestors. In the intestine there are remnants of a spiral valve, a device that is found in many primitive fishes increasing considerably the digestive surface of the intestine. A spiral valve is also found in sharks. The swimbladder has a cellular structure that enables the bowfin to breathe atmospheric oxygen. Whereas most fishes swim by undulations of the body, the bowfin cruises majestically by a series of waves passing along its long dorsal fin. The normal method is adopted, however, for faster swimming.

Bowfins live in warm sluggish waters, especially in shallow and weedy areas. In the breeding season in early summer the males make a round nest on sandy or gravelly bottoms or in clearings in weed patches. They then mate with several females and after the eggs are laid guard them until the fry hatch and can swim well. They are carnivorous and seem to have a particular liking for game fishes. A large bowfin may reach almost 3 ft (10 cm) in length.

Bowfins are of little economic importance. They are eaten in the southern parts of the United States but are elsewhere regarded more as pests. Throughout the United States there is only a single species but it has received a variety of common names such as dogfish, mudfish, lawyer, grindle, choupique, Speckled cat and spot-fin. FAMILY: Amiidae, ORDER: Holostei, CLASS: Pisces.

BOXFISHES or trunkfishes, fishes belonging to the genus *Ostracion,* the head and body of which are enclosed in a solid box of bony plates with only the fins, jaws and the end of the tail projecting and free to move. In cross-section the box-like body is triangular, rectangular or pentagonal, the underside being flat. There are several species, growing

The boxfish or trunkfish *Ostracion cornutus*, encased in bony armour, indulges in chemical warfare by secreting poison into the water when attacked.

Another species of the boxfishes or trunkfishes, *Ostracion lentiginosus.*

BRAIN CORAL *Meandrina,* colonial *polyps belonging to the true or stony corals. The surface of the massive, calcareous skeleton is marked by long curved depressions and bears a striking resemblance to the human brain. Each colony generally arises from a single planula larva which settles onto a suitable object, such as a shell, and grows into a coral polyp. The polyp then starts to bud off other polyps. At an early stage in colony formation, each polyp is partly enclosed in a calcareous cup or theca, which bears ridges or sclerosepta radiating from the margin. But the budding of new polyps occurs very rapidly and in a manner termed intra-tentacular, a new mouth arising on the oral disc of the older polyp and inside the same ring of tentacles. In many corals, the skeleton becomes partitioned off into two cups to accommodate the old and new polyps. In Brain corals new mouths arise at a rate faster than the rate at which the skeleton is laid down, so that polyps share common walls of the cups. The polyps never become separated and share tentacles and internal mesenteries. The skeleton, which is the only part of the animal normally seen, shows these valleys which are lined with polyps in the living animal. ORDER: Scleractinia, CLASS: Anthozoa, PHYLUM: Cnidaria.

to 20 in (50 cm) found around the coral reefs and coasts of the Indo-Pacific area. Since the body is rigid, swimming can only be accomplished by sculling movements of the unpaired fins, with the pectoral fins helping to stabilize what would otherwise be highly erratic movements. Many of the boxfishes are brightly coloured with patterns and spots of red and blue, yellow and blue, blue with a red band, and so on. These bright colours probably serve to warn predatory fishes that the owner is not edible. When boxfishes are attacked they secrete a virulent poison into the water which can kill other fishes. FAMILY: Ostraciontidae, ORDER: Tetraodontiformes, CLASS: Pisces.

BOX TURTLE *Terrapene,* an animal like a European garden tortoise living in the eastern United States, where it is native, from New England to Florida and Texas. Its peculiarity is that the shell on the underside is hinged across the middle and the two halves can be brought up in front and behind to completely close the shell after the head and legs have been withdrawn.

It is reported that some hounds used in deer hunting and gundogs used for quail become addicted to Box turtles. A hound may find a Box turtle and carry it around instead of tracking deer, or a gundog may 'point' a Box turtle instead of a bird. Some dogs will habitually seek out the turtles, bring them home and bury them, but without doing them harm. FAMILY: Emydidae, ORDER: Testudines, CLASS: Reptilia.

BRACHYURA, the true crabs, decapod crustaceans in which the abdomen is greatly shortened and held permanently under the body. A few of the Anomura, relatives of the Hermit crab, have independently undergone the same modification and have come to resemble the true crabs. See crabs.

BRACONID WASPS, minute parasitic wasps resembling the Ichneumon flies in certain ways. They can be distinguished from true wasps by the absence of a 'waist' between the thorax and the abdomen. They are parasites, laying their eggs in various insect larvae of economic importance, notably the plant-feeding larvae of certain lepidopterans and flies. In some cases, several hundred wasp larvae may be found within the body of a single host. FAMILY: Braconidae, ORDER: Hymenoptera, CLASS: Insecta, PHYLUM: Arthropoda.

BRAIN, in most animals there are nerve cords, which control all the reflexes, running the length of the body. Most animals travel predominantly in one direction, that is, head first. We therefore find that this anterior region contains the most sense organs, to detect the environmental changes ahead of the animal. These sense organs have large amounts of nervous tissue associated with them, to analyze the complex information that they receive. Since the animal's reactions

Brain coral, named for the slight resemblance to the convolutions of the human brain.

to external stimuli are dependent on these sense organs, the nervous apparatus for the overall control of movement also comes to lie in the head. Thus we find that (at a low level of organization) a cockroach with the anterior nervous tissue removed will keep walking, due to local reflex interaction, whilst a frog *Rana* in a similar condition is incapable of doing so. Throughout the animal kingdom there is a gradual development of the dominance of the anterior 'brain' over the rest of the nervous system and this is especially true in the vertebrates.

In vertebrate animals the simpler types, such as fish, have brains divided into discrete lobes each of which serves mainly one sense, such as smell, sight or taste. As more complex vertebrates evolved one part of the brain came gradually to control all these functions, so we find an increase in the importance of the cerebral cortex (the grey folded tissue on top of our brains). In mammals, this cerebral cortex is mainly concerned with analyzing information being received from the environment and organizing the necessary movements.

The brain is not, however, concerned wholly with the outside world. It is very much involved in preserving the constant internal state of the animal. In mammals, a very slight rise in temperature of the blood flowing through the brain sets off sweating, and a fall in temperature causes the converse responses of shivering and the erection of hair. The brain thus acts as a thermostat, keeping the body temperature constant. It is helped in this by other temperature receptors throughout the body. Similarly, the brain maintains the blood sugar, water and carbon dioxide content, and changes the rate of eating, drinking and breathing to keep the body at its optimum efficiency. Such changes in willingness to eat and drink, also to reproduce, are considered to indicate *'drive'. An animal in a state of drive is lacking some essential such as food or a mate, and is kept stimulated until it has found the desired thing. Drives and instinctive behaviour are closely related. As the level of the drive changes, so some instinctive behaviour becomes more or less apparent. See instinct.

Not only is the brain concerned with short-term internal changes, it can affect much longer-term changes. Under the brain lies the pituitary gland, the 'master gland' of the hormone system. Nerves run from the brain to the pituitary (which is itself partially formed of nervous tissue) and control the level of secretion of hormones. For example, birds have a 'clock' in the brain which measures the changes in the length of the day. When the length of the day has increased to a certain value, the pituitary is stimulated to produce hormones which cause changes in the reproductive organs and the spring courtship and mating occurs. The brain can also initiate

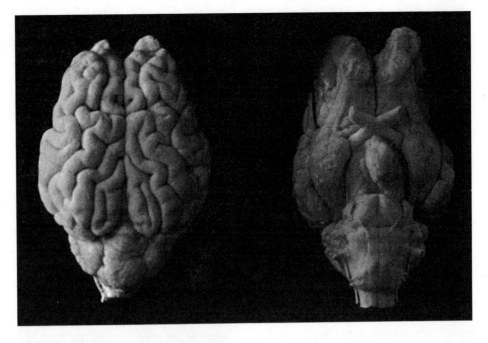

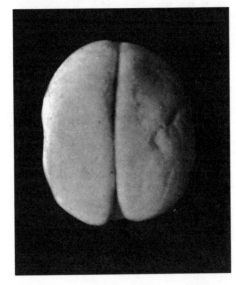

changes which occupy days rather than minutes.

The brain serves to control the animal's reactions to outside and inside changes, but in more advanced animals, such as mammals, it also decides to which of many outside stimuli the animal shall respond, that is, it controls the attention of the animal. We have all experienced the sensation of concentrating upon, for example, a book, and having little idea of what is going on around us. The loss of information about the room is real, for the brain actually inhibits activity in the sense organs that we do not need, so that we can better attend to the book. Thus it selects what to attend to and maintains our attention on this despite other happenings around us—assuming, of course, that we are determined to maintain such attention! This aspect of the brain's activity has been shown in the cat. Electrical impulses were recorded from the ear nerve of a cat in response to a series of

Brain of domestic sheep, upper surface to left, underside to right. If the convolutions of the brain were the only guide sheep would be rated of high intelligence.

Left: brain of marmoset *Midas aedipus*.

clicks made near the ear. When the animal lay quietly, each click caused a pulse in the ear nerve. When fish (surely a meaningful stimulus for a cat) was presented, the number of pulses in the ear nerve dropped rapidly, that is, the cat's attention mechanism was focused on the fish and had shut down the inflow of information from the ear.

Man is characterized by the large size of his brain compared with that of other animals, and it is the presence of a large, folded surface at the front of the human brain, the cerebral cortex, which has lead to the evolution of intelligence and the ability to think. In lower vertebrates, the cerebral cortex is not present and in most mammals a large part of the cortex is concerned with either sense organs or muscles. However, in more intelligent mammals, there are large areas which do neither of these things. These are the so-called 'silent areas' and are concerned with more complex behaviour such as learning.

Much the same applies to the brains of invertebrates as to vertebrates. For example, the central nervous system of a primitive mollusc consists of a series of masses of nerve cells, performing various specialized activities, amounting to little more than a simple reflex system. The most developed molluscs, the octopus and the cuttlefish, have complex brains with special motor and sense areas and with silent areas similar to those of higher mammals.

The less complex invertebrate and lower

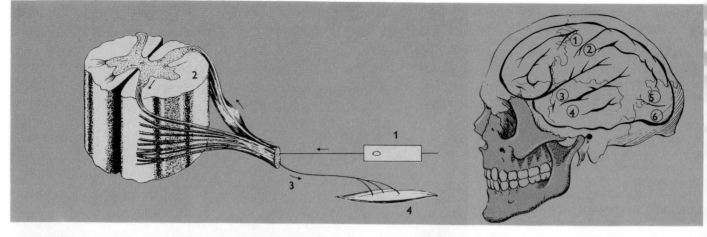

Left. Diagram illustrating a simple reflex tract: the sense-organ cell (1) receives a stimulus; this causes a change in the cell which is passed on through a nerve to the spinal cord (2) and at that point is switched over to a movement or motor tract (3); when the stimulus reaches the muscle (4) the muscle contracts; the reflex is therefore an automatic response to a stimulus.

Right. The fore-brain or cerebrum is amongst other things the centre for voluntary movements and sensory perception; 1. motor and 2. sensory centre for arms, legs, head, etc.; 3. primary and 4. secondary auditory centre; 5. primary and 6. secondary optical centre.

Right: The size and weight of the brain related to the surface of the body. In proportion to his body surface man has the breatest brain weight; he stands at the highest level of cephalization. Man-like apes are at a lower level, dogs and other beasts of prey even lower, while bats and insectivores occupy the lowest positions amongst mammals. Nevertheless it would be misguided to consider this relation as a measure of intelligence. A great number of other factors play a part in this.

Left: The development of the brain in man and some vertebrate animals. The fore-brain (telencephalon) is coloured grey; the upper part of this is very strongly developed in the higher vertebrates and finally exceeds in size the whole of the rest of the brain. At the highest levels of development the cortex is enlarged even more. The mammals show great differences in this development. 1. man, 2. chimpanzee, 3. dog, 4. rabbit, 5. pigeon, 6. crocodile, 7. frog.

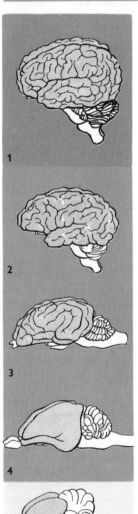

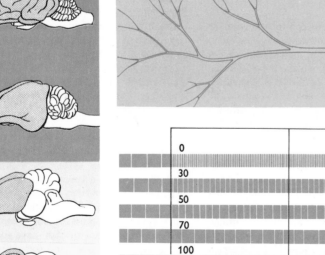

Schematic diagram of a single nerve cell. Schematic diagram of a single nerve cell. Note that part of the axon has been omitted, on account of its length.

Nerve impulses in the ear nerve of a cat *Felis*. Each "spike" is one nerve impulse. As the loudness of the sound increases, so more and more impulses travel along the ear nerve. All impulses are the same size.

0			
30			
50			
70			
100			
start of sound			
0	½	1	1½ seconds

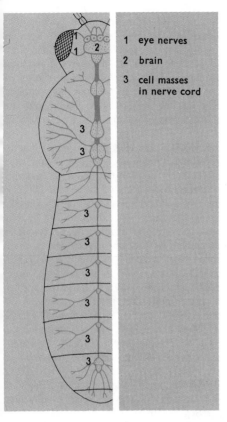

1 eye nerves

2 brain

3 cell masses in nerve cord

Drawing of the nervous system of the midge *Chironomus* to show the insect nerve cord, and the large brain at the anterior end. Note the large eyes and nerves associated with them.

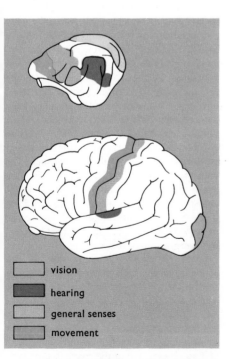

☐ vision

■ hearing

☐ general senses

■ movement

Drawings of the brains of cat and man. Only the cerebral cortex is shown. In both, the parts of the cerebral cortex concerned with sensing objects, and moving, have been shaded in. Man has large areas of brain which are "silent"; they are not directly concerned with either detecting objects or responding to them.

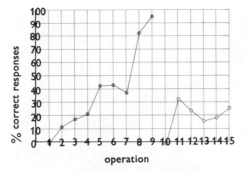

The effect of brain damage on memory in the octopus *Octopus*. The animal was trained to attack a crab. After 8 days, part of its brain was removed and it was unable to remember what to do – it was otherwise normal.

vertebrate nerve systems are by no means incapable of learning. For example, the octopus and the fish, two widely separate forms, can both learn well but removal of certain parts of the brain causes the animal to forget, although its behaviour is otherwise unimpaired.

Brain surgery of this sort has led to the production of 'maps' of various areas of brain which are involved in learning and memory, but many other methods are also used. Electrodes, placed either on or in the brain, allow the study of the electrical changes accompanying learning. There have been attempts to examine brain function by electrical stimulation. Thus, rats, which received electrical stimulation at a certain point in the brain, responded as if it was pleasant. If allowed to press a pedal to deliver short low voltage electrical pulses to their own brains, they pressed many thousands of times without exhaustion. Such areas may be concerned with allowing the animal to perceive 'pleasant' sensations.

Other work has shown that there are cells in the visual areas of the cat's cerebral cortex that respond to visual stimuli such as rectangles, but only in certain orientations. For instance, a vertical rectangle will cause the nerve cell to discharge fully, but if the rectangle is rotated through 45°, the discharge is much less and a horizontal rectangle produces no discharge in this particular cell. Another cell will discharge maximally for a horizontal rectangle but will not respond at all for a vertical rectangle. In this way, we can start to see how shapes are converted into information meaningful to the brain.

It is, of course, very difficult to investigate man's brain, since only when some injury occurs as the result of an accident can the effects of damage to one part of the brain be seen. For instance, certain damage to man's brain renders his memory of recent events almost non-existent but he can remember more distant events quite well. Thus it seems that we have more than one type of memory in the brain. Incoming information is kept in one form, rather susceptible to destruction

by, for instance, a blow on the head, then it is changed into a more permanent form. We call these short- and long-term memory. The short-term memory may exist as a series of electrical pulses travelling round the brain for a short period, to be changed, if useful, into a more permanent structural memory.

Only a few patients have such damage so, therefore, animals are used in experiments to find out how learning and memory occur. Such experiments often help in suggesting new cures for brain diseases in man and also lead to fundamental advances in the study of how the brain stores information.

We have little idea as yet as to exactly how the information is permanently stored. It may be that the synapses change in size, so that one pathway is more easily followed than another, or it may be that one pathway is closed by special inhibitory cells. Recently, it has been suggested that the brain stores information as a chemical code, so that perhaps one molecule would be equivalent to a piece of memory. This has been partially substantiated by scientists who have trained rats to do simple problems, removed certain chemicals from their brains, and injected them into the brains of untrained rats. The second group of rats showed signs of having acquired the learning. Despite this, we have little idea of how information is put into this form, or used, but it provides a fascinating problem for future study. See cephalization, memory, nervous system and spinal cord.

G.E.S.

BRAIN PROPORTIONS. During the last 30 years, since dolphins and porpoises have been kept alive in seaquaria, and carefully studied, it has been realized that they are highly intelligent animals. Some scientists even go so far as to suggest that they are second only to man in intelligence. Earlier than 30 years ago, anatomists dissecting the carcases of these animals stranded on the beaches noted that the brain of a dolphin or porpoise was large proportionally to the size of the body. They also noted that the surface of this brain was highly convoluted. As a result, they suspected that these marine mammals might be highly intelligent. They refrained from laying too much emphasis on this because the relationship between brain and body size can be deceptive. It is a rough guide to intelligence and no more.

Non-scientists interested in animals and noting their behaviour are often struck by seemingly intelligent behaviour in an animal, for example a bird, with a relatively small head. The broad answer is that most birds have as large a brain relatively to the weight of the body as mammals. Weight must be used because the volume occupied by a bird is often far greater than that occupied by the actual carcase. An owl, for example, stripped of its feathers, is surprisingly small. Both

Bream *Abramis brama*, valued as a sport fish. It favours the lower reaches of large rivers.

birds and mammals have larger brains than reptiles, amphibians and fishes, so in gross consideration brain size is linked with degree of intelligence. There are, however, many qualifying factors.

The first difficulty in examining this question is that surprisingly few records are available. The *Handbook of Biological Data* published in 1956 gives figures for only 29 bird species out of the total of 9000 known species of birds, or 0·3 per cent. What conclusions we draw from these can only be based on a very small sample of the whole.

In this *Handbook* the weight of the brain is expressed in grams per 100 grams of body weight, both measurements having been taken while the carcase was fresh. The ostrich is at the bottom of the list with 0·03, the canary heads the list with 4·72. Relatively, therefore, a canary has 150 times as much brain as an ostrich. This may explain why canaries given tests in problem-solving in experimental laboratories have shown astonishing performances. It conflicts with the idea, generally accepted by ornithologists, that members of the crow family are among the most intelligent of birds. Their index is only 2·76 for the crow *Corvus brachyrhynchos* and 2·81 for the raven *C. corax*. It is noticeable also that all long-legged, long-necked birds, such as storks, herons and cranes, have a low index but not so low as that of the ostrich, round about the 0·40 mark, and that plump-bodied birds, such as domestic chicken, partridges and pheasants, have much the same index.

In general, the smaller the bird the higher the index—for a hummingbird it is 4·16—and the figure drops fairly regularly as the body weight increases. In default of evidence to the contrary, it would seem that the proportion of brain to body in birds reflects something other than the degree of intelligence.

This is more clearly shown in mammals. The indexes for the African elephant and the shrew are 0·08 and 1·99 respectively. It would take especially cogent arguments to convince that a shrew is more than twice as intelligent as an elephant.

In these tables weights are given for 95 species of mammals out of the 3700 known species, or 27 per cent. Even so, there are the same anomalies. The index for a gorilla is 0·41, for a domestic cat 0·77, for a dog 0·59 and for the wily red fox no more than 1·15. The giraffe, with long legs and long neck, is awarded 0·38 and the camel, of comparable build, only 0·02. Those who have charge of camels would probably argue that even this is far too high for such a refractory beast.

One factor is that the relative proportions of the various parts of the brain differ in different animals. In the insectivores, the most primitive of living mammals, a large part of the cerebral hemispheres is given over to dealing with the sense of smell. In higher mammals, including probably the elephant, much more of the cerebral hemispheres is devoted to the higher nervous activities such as we normally include under the heading of intelligence.

Another factor, especially in mammalian brains, is the increase in surface area by folding, giving rise to the convolutions of the brain. The elephant has highly convoluted cerebral hemispheres and those of a shrew are almost entirely without convolutions. The folding would have little significant effect on the weight of the brain.   M.B.

BRAMBLE SHARK *Echinorhinus brucus,* sometimes known as the Alligator dogfish, a large shark found in tropical and temperate waters in most parts of the world. This fish has two dorsal fins, set rather far back on the body, and there is no anal fin. The body is covered with the usual denticles found in sharks but each one bears one or two sharp spines to give the fish its prickly appearance. Bramble sharks grow to about 10 ft (3 m) in length and although very rare in the western North Atlantic they are fairly common off the Atlantic coasts of Africa and Europe reaching as far north as the British Isles. FAMILY: Echinorhinidae, ORDER: Pleurotremata, CLASS: Chondrichthyes.

BREAMS, deep-bodied carp-like fishes of European freshwaters. They are unrelated to the Sea breams (family Sparidae). In England there are two species, the Common bream *Abramis brama* and the Silver bream *Blicca bjoerkna* which has been described elsewhere. The Common bream has a compressed body with a very high back and short head. The upper parts are grey to black, the sides lighter, the belly silvery and the fins grey or blue-black. It is found chiefly in sluggish weedy waters throughout most of Europe north of the Pyrenees. Bream normally swim in shoals, each shoal made up of individuals of about the same size, usually near the bottom except in hot weather when they tend to lie still near the surface. They grow to over 12 lb (5·4 kg) in weight and are cunning and difficult to catch. They feed on insect larvae, molluscs and worms which they extract from great mouthfuls of mud sucked up from the bottom. The Common bream often shoal with Silver bream and when small the two species are difficult to distinguish. The pharyngeal or throat teeth of the Silver bream are in two rows whereas those of the Common bream are in a single row.

From the angler's point of view, the relative ease with which the bream will hybridize with the roach is a source of considerable annoyance. The hybrids strongly resemble the roach but grow to a much larger size, so that potentially record roach have, on closer examination, proved to be merely hybrids of the two species. From the roach, the hybrids can be distinguished fairly easily, having 15–19 branched rays in the anal fin (9–12 in the roach, but 23–29 in the bream). FAMILY: Cyprinidae, ORDER: Cypriniformes, CLASS: Pisces.

BREEDING. In the wild state animals choose their partners, mate and produce offspring. Some of the offspring survive, the majority die soon after birth or within a few months of it, leaving only a small proportion to reach sexual maturity to reproduce their kind. Which shall survive is largely a matter of random selection. Therefore, provided the conditions of the environment remain relatively unchanged the characters of the species are little altered.

In selective breeding change can be speeded up. The breeder decides which animals shall be the parents of the next generation. His aim is to change the characters of his stock, to improve it along certain desirable lines. In doing so he speeds up the evolution, producing changes in a few years that in nature might take thousands of years. He can even produce changes that would never occur in nature. For example, the wild jungle fowl lays only a few eggs each year. Its descendant, the domesticated chicken, will lay eggs almost continuously throughout the year.

Whether it is a matter of breeding cattle for beef production or for milk, sheep for wool or meat, dogs to win at shows, cats to start a fashion or aquarium fishes to satisfy a hobby, there are rules to be followed. The breeder's object must be to settle first what his aim is to be. He will then select the animals showing the greatest potentialities towards this goal, rejecting those that are faulty or inferior according to the standard he has set. The male must be perfect in those features in which the female is deficient, and vice versa. Even in the present advanced state of the science of *genetics there is bound to be some trial and error which will be largely minimized by the judgement of the breeder. Having produced the next generation there will be a selective weeding out, so that the following generation develops the desired characteristics. M.B.

BREEDING BEHAVIOUR, is primarily concerned with mating and the care of the young but it can also be taken to include subsidiaries such as the laying down of scent trails to attract a mate, as in certain insects and mammals, the building and maintenance of a nest for the protection of the young, and the establishment and defence of a harem as in many mammals. In a wider sense it includes the physiological background to the visible aspects of such behaviour.

For reproduction to take place, the *gametes from the opposite sexes must come together closely enough for the eggs to be fertilized by the sperm. This naturally means that the two mating partners cannot be far apart and indeed in many animals male and female must come into physical contact in an act of copulation. Therefore synchronization of gamete production and *courtship behaviour is essential. But in addition the fertilized egg must either be retained to develop in the female's body, as it does in mammals, or must be laid with protective coverings on it such as the shell and membranes of the bird's egg. These activities must in their turn be timed to occur in the correct sequences. Even after the young have hatched or been born, *parental care may be essential for their survival; this behaviour must take its correct turn. From the production of the gametes to the time the offspring are independent involves a time-table largely governed by the parent's physiology.

Types of mating behaviour: invertebrates. In the simplest kind of mating, in some unicellular animals, the whole organism acts as the gamete and fuses with another to form a zygote. This occurs, for example, in a number of species of *Chlamydomonas*, single-celled flagellates which swim in water. In some species of *Chlamydomonas* all gametes are of the same size. In other species some individuals first divide producing different sizes of gamete. When a zygote is formed from the fusion of two different sizes of gametes, we have the beginnings of sex—the larger gamete representing the ovum of higher animals, the smaller representing the spermatozoon.

In some of the more advanced Protozoa, such as *Paramecium*, a process of mating takes place which, although the organisms are unicellular, is very similar to the hermaphroditic mating seen in snails, for example. In this, known as conjugation, two paramecia come together by their oral surfaces and each exchanges nuclear material with the other. That is, a male nucleus from each moves into and fuses with the female nucleus of the other. Thus, cross-fertilization takes place.

In the Metazoa or true multicellular animals the gametes, ova and spermatozoa, are produced in special sex organs or gonads, the ovaries or female gonads and the testes or male gonads, usually in different individuals. When both kinds of gonads are present in one individual it is said to be *hermaphrodite. In the lower Metazoa, such as Sea anemones, corals and jellyfishes, which are aquatic the sperms leave one individual and swim through the water to the body of another individual, enter it and make their way to the ovary. So mating proper does not take place.

In the next highest group, the Platyhelminthes, including the flatworms, tapeworms, and flukes, almost all species are hermaphrodite and true mating, or copulation, takes place. The male has an intromittent organ, or penis, which when inserted into

Breeding behaviour in the Arctic tern *Sterna paradisaea*. The female (left) solicits copulation, the consummation is shown in the picture on the next page.

Arctic tern, copulation. The male balances on the female's back, then thrusts his tail down to bring the cloacas together.

the genital opening of the female facilitates the transfer of sperm. This is less wasteful than releasing them into water, but since the two individuals must come into physical contact this necessitates some kind of attraction between individuals, often a chemical given out by the female, so that sperm can be transferred. The more complex the organism the more important are these attractant processes and the more complex the breeding behaviour as a consequence.

In the parasitic platyhelminths that are hermaphrodite cross-fertilization is relatively straightforward as the two individuals are likely to be lying close together anyway; or if they are tapeworms, the two segments from different parts of the tape will be near each other. The same is true for the parasitic nematode worms, which are unisexual and copulate.

In the more primitive of the annelid worms, the marine Bristle worms, the gametes are released into the water, as they are in many other aquatic animals, and fertilization is external, the zygote developing into a plank-tonic larva. Such spawning is said to be random, but in many of the Bristle worms simple but unusual breeding behaviours have been developed which increase the chances of sperms finding the ova. For example, when sexually mature the worms may leave the sea

bottom all together in a swarm and swim up through the water, discharging their gametes as they go or even casting off the hind end of the body which has become full of the ripe gametes. In many species this occurs inter-mittently throughout the summer, but in a few it has achieved an amazingly accurate peri-odicity, for example in the *Palolo worm, in which it is governed by the lunar cycle.

Such regularity of breeding behaviour must depend on accurate internal timing mechanisms which, in turn, will be dependent on seasonally changing environmental influ-ences. In many Bristle worms, however, a chemical is released by the swarming females that stimulates the discharge of sperm by the males. In species of *Odontosyllis* breeding individuals become luminescent, so exchang-ing light signals which help to synchronize the discharge of their gametes.

Earthworms are hermaphrodite and copu-lation takes place but with cross-fertilization. Two worms from adjacent burrows come together head-to-tail and sperm are passed from each worm to the other.

Most Crustacea are aquatic and the sexes usually separate; but their sperms are typi-cally incapable of movement so copulation must occur. In crabs, lobsters, and shrimps certain of their many abdominal appendages are modified for the transfer of sperm.

During mating the male releases sperm at the moment the female extrudes her eggs, these being retained by the female attached to her paddle-like swimmerets until they hatch. She is then said to be 'in berry'. Some crustaceans have special breeding displays that bring the sexes together. The male Fiddler crab *Uca* sits at the entrance to his burrow and signals with his one greatly enlarged pincer. Other Fiddler crabs have sound-producing organs for bringing the sexes together. Various lobsters produce sounds by rubbing a special pad on the base of the antenna against a projection on the head. Shrimps of the genera *Alpheus* and *Synalpheus* are known as 'Snapping shrimps' because they produce snapping sounds by clapping together the fixed and the moveable sections of their specially-enlarged pincers. Sound production for sexual signal-ling is probably as widespread in Crustacea as it appears to be in other aquatic groups, for sound travels particularly well through water while visibility is often poor.

Barnacles, crustaceans that do not move once they have settled, are hermaphrodite and usually live in colonies; and fertilization commonly takes place by the long extensible penis of one individual being inserted into the shell of a neighbour. Parasitic Crustacea show varying degrees of degeneration of the principal organs. In *Sacculina* which is parasitic on crabs, the adult is simply a hermaphrodite bag of reproductive tissue. In others, such as *Lernaea,* the sexes are separate and one stage at least is free-swimming, with the male smaller than and attached to the female.

The vast majority of insects are unisexual and copulate. As they are also usually very active animals they use displays and other means to bring the sexes together. Male bumblebees, for example, lay scent trails by biting leaves and twigs along their daily path, depositing scent from special glands in the mouth. The trails of different species are laid at different levels above the ground, and each male stays on his own trail until a female following the scent in search of a mate comes along. Many female moths give out a scent attracting males from a mile or more. Scent is also important in the breeding behaviour of a number of butterflies. In the grayling *Eumenis semele,* mating begins with a sexual chase. If the female is virgin she responds by alighting. The male then settles in front of her and bows so that special scent glands on his forewings touch the sense-organs on her antennae.

Son et lumière. Visual signals are used by many insects. Fireflies use a flashing light, different species having distinctive flash patterns, so although a dozen species may be active at the same time and in the same place, they respond only to the appropriate flash pattern. For example, at breeding time the male *Photinus pyralis* flies around giving a short flash every 5·8 secs. The response of the female, sitting on a plant, is to flash back after exactly 2 secs, and the male approaches any kind of light which appears after this interval. In other insects the visual displays may be rather more complex, as in the wing displays of certain butterflies and the dancing displays of flies, such as midges and mosquitoes.

Sounds are produced by insects for breeding purposes with a variety of mechanisms. Certain wood-boring beetles, for example, the Death watch beetle, produce sounds by striking parts of themselves against the walls of their tunnels. Others, such as mosquitoes, do so by wing vibration. Grasshoppers, locusts and crickets rub wings or legs, or wings and legs together. In all such insects there are sound-receiving as well as sound-producing organs. These friction-produced sounds, or stridulations, may even be produced by aquatic insects, such as certain waterboatmen which stridulate by rubbing the middle pair of legs together. In the majority it is the male which produces the sounds, though both sexes have 'ears'.

Praying mantis courtship: this time the pairing is successful and the male avoids being eaten by the female; this happens all too often. All photographs are of the species *Mantis religiosa.*

Praying mantis courtship commences with the male stroking the female with his antennae.

Praying mantis courtship: the male climbs carefully onto the back of the female.

Male and female Indian rhinoceroses *Rhinoceros unicornis* mating.

care of the eggs or young. The Three-spined stickleback *Gasterosteus aculeatus,* with its elaborate nest-building and zigzag dance, is a well-known example. Even more complex is the breeding behaviour of the male Siamese fighting fish *Betta splendens.* His breeding dress of brilliant iridescent colours is shown to full advantage by ritualized postures and spreading of the fins. He builds a nest of bubbles at the water surface, coating them and sticking them together with saliva. Should another male enter his territory his posturing is aggressive but if the newcomer is a female in mating condition his display becomes a courtship dance which, when successful, culminates in the simultaneous shedding of sperm and eggs by male and female respectively. As the eggs fall through the water the male collects them in his mouth and spits them up to the bubble nest at the surface—if the female sees them she simply eats them. In other fishes, such as the cichlids, both sexes take part in the care of eggs and young, some of them carrying eggs and, later, the baby fishes in their mouths to protect them.

Fishes, like many other aquatic animals, make sounds. Some grind their teeth together, others their neck bones, while others use their swimbladder as a sort of drum. At times the sea can be very noisy.

Well-known among aquatic sound-producers are the frogs and toads, with their churring or whistling breeding songs. In some species both sexes have vocal sacs but those of the male are usually the larger. The breeding songs, some of them very musical, bring the sexes together in the same pond at the appropriate time. Fertilization is external, the male mounting the female and clasping his forelimbs round her middle. A male frog or toad will clasp any object he meets but only remains clasped for any length of time around a mature unmated female. When she sheds her eggs he releases his sperm so fertilization occurs before the protective coating of albumen swells up around the egg.

In other Amphibia, such as newts, more elaborate courtship displays are used. Bright colours in the male may be shown to advantage, or he may give out chemicals from glands in his skin and waft these towards the female by undulations of his tail, by what is called tail-beating. Fertilization is external.

All reptiles lay their eggs on land, even those which, like turtles, live in water. The males have an intromittent organ to facilitate

The sense of touch also plays a part in the breeding behaviour of insects, particularly during copulation, but it may be important in display also. Pond skaters are sensitive to vibrations transmitted across the surface of the water, and almost certainly respond to vibrations set up by members of the opposite sex, as well as to those from prey. Empid flies show particularly well how a complex of sensory stimuli may enter into breeding behaviour. These flies are carnivorous and before mating the male captures and kills some small insect. He then presents it to the female and, while she is devouring it, he mates with her. In the empid *Hilara* the offering is wrapped up in strands of silk; as this takes the female some time to unravel, the males have developed the habit of using non-food objects such as flower petals instead of real prey.

Male spiders belonging to species with poor vision vibrate the female's web in a special way or carefully stroke the female herself to bring her into a responsive mood. In some species the male locks her fangs in his own, which are specially modified for the purpose. Hunting spiders, on the other hand, have good vision and the males perform elaborate displays before closing with the females, dancing from side to side, waving the forelegs or signalling with the pedipalps—the second pair of head appendages, which male

spiders also use for collecting their own sperm and transferring it to the female.

The famous mating dance of scorpions is not because the female may kill the male, as is sometimes said. The male drops his sperm on the ground, in a capsule or spermatophore, and in the dance he is manoeuvring her over this so that she can lower her body to pick it up.

Some molluscs are hermaphrodite, in others the sexes are separate. Cross-fertilization is, however, the rule. In the Garden snail *Helix,* an unusual preliminary to copulation is the exchange of a pair of hard, calcareous darts which are forcibly ejected into the partner's tissues. On dissolving, these darts seem to release a chemical which brings the snail into breeding condition. In squids and octopuses, mating displays may involve changes of colour or colour pattern.

Types of mating behaviour: vertebrates. In the simpler vertebrates breeding behaviour may be less complex than in the more advanced invertebrates. Some fish, for example, do little more than shed their gametes at random into the water at the same time and place, as in the lowest animals such as anemones and jellyfishes. In other cases the male performs an elaborate courtship display, and in a few species plays a leading role in

Although Land snails are hermaphrodite they copulate, each individual acting as male and female, and fertilizing each other. The picture shows the Garden snail *Helix pomatia* with a calcareous love-dart being driven into the skin of the partner, releasing a chemical which brings the snail into breeding condition.

During the period of heat the male impala licks the genitalia of the female, rises to his hindlegs and mounts. After copulation he becomes aggressive and chases the female.

sperm transfer during copulation, and the eggs have a soft, though tough shell. The eggs are laid in holes in the ground, or on sandy beaches, or in piles of vegetation, and hatch by the heat of the sun, sometimes with the assistance of the heat generated by decaying vegetation. In some species, some snakes and crocodiles, for example, the female guards the clutch of eggs.

Breeding behaviour reaches its most advanced form in the two most highly developed groups of animals, the birds and mammals. In birds particularly, song and visual displays have been elaborated to an extent which sometimes seems bizarre, like the Bird of paradise which, after showing off his magnificent feathers, then hangs upside-down. Birds are amongst the most mobile of animals and their displays must therefore be conspicuous to ensure attraction of a mate. But they must also be clearly and specifically recognizable, hence the great diversification of breeding displays in different species. Such a system works so well that several species of closely-related ducks, for example, all capable of producing hybrids with the others, will breed successfully and separately in the same area.

The song of male birds has a multiple function, including the establishment and maintenance of the pair-bond. In a number of species, particularly in tropical forests where visibility is poor, male and female indulge in antiphonal singing, or 'duetting', the timing of the joint song being so accurate that it sounds like one bird.

In many birds, such as the ducks already mentioned, the display is primarily visual, and involves a number of 'competing' males. A male will display to a female if they are alone, but his display also plays a part in establishing his position in the general 'pool' of males. In a number of species, particularly in the game birds, these communal displays, or 'leks', are regular daily activities during much of the breeding season.

Some birds use a variety of plumes, pennants, trains, crests, and ruffs of all shapes sizes and colours, as in the Birds of paradise, pheasants and hummingbirds. Others have brightly coloured wattles, as in turkeys, bills as in puffins, or casques, as in hornbills. In the bowerbirds the breeding behaviour is excessively elaborate, even for a bird. Many of them are outstanding vocal mimics, but a number of them also build a very elaborate display ground, in the form of a tent, avenue or platform, decorated with bright or coloured objects such as leaves or shells.

In most mammals the visual and vocal displays, though often highly significant, are less elaborate than in birds. The sense of smell, however, plays a very important role in mating and in inter-sexual recognition. The males of many species of mammal find their mates by smell, though in some families, for example the cats and dogs, vocalizations also play their part. The mammals thus use scent for general orientation as birds use song, after which, vision is important in both groups. It is clear that most mammals can distinguish between other individuals of their own species by sight as well as by smell, and simple visual recognition of individual characteristics plays a part in their breeding. But additional visual features are developed in some species as a kind of supernormal stimulus. A number of male primates have brightly coloured areas of skin on the face or buttocks, and in many primates the females periodically develop a gross enlargement of the external genitalia. These features are powerful signals to members of the opposite sex.

In several mammal groups the breeding males have harems of females, as in Fur seals and some deer and monkeys. They are commonly challenged by other males and are only able to maintain their position by natural superiority, physical or psychological, so the 'best' males produce the most offspring. Most mammals, unlike man, will not mate at any time of year, but have a periodicity regulated by the physiological cycle of the female. From time to time during the period of heat, or oestrus, as it is called, the female becomes sexually active and only then will accept the male. This is the time when ova are shed from the ovary. At oestrus, attraction between the sexes may result in unusually vigorous, even violent behaviour. In man, however, the attraction is at a lower but more persistent level. In domestic dogs and cats there are two or three periods of oestrus per year, separated by long periods of anoestrus, when the female is not in season. In other mammals the oestrus periods occur in cycles. These may be regularly throughout the year, as in the 28 day cycle of man and Old World monkeys, or in short cycles of a few days during a restricted breeding season, as in many rodents.

In man, the persistent attraction between the sexes is of great biological importance, for without this strong pair-bond the optimal conditions for the rearing of young cannot obtain. This would seem to be the primary reason for the monogamous human relationship: we have the longest and most complex

Rasbora, a well known tropical aquarium fish, during copulation. With many fishes a brief courtship precedes copulation during which the males particularly show their breeding dress to great advantage. In egg-laying fishes copulation is accompanied by the release of the reproductive cells into the water, where the eggs are fertilized.

period of adolescence of any animals, during which the young must receive a vast amount of information and training if it is to take its place properly in the human environment. the most efficient method of achieving this is by means of a stable, long-lasting 'marriage' between the parents.

Man has also inherited, and developed, a super-sexual social structure, as recent work has made clear. The general persistence of sexual interest, the elaboration of sexual rituals, the accentuation of sexual characteristics, particularly in female dress and cosmetics, together with the fertile inventiveness and intelligence of the human mind, have resulted in a sexual behaviour structure far richer and more complex than in any other animal. This is directly and functionally connected with the unique breeding requirements of the species. It is not generally realized that human hypersexuality, in the monogamous context, is a positive biological adaptation which has contributed greatly to the success of the species. Any departure from the heterosexual monogamous state must be regarded as a biological malfunction.

Physiological control of breeding. The great majority of animals breed only once a year, though looking at the animal kingdom as a whole some species can be found to be breeding at any time during the 12 months. The breeding period of some species lasts months, while that of others is limited to a few days. Some species have two or more periods a year: domestic dogs have two, while Old World monkeys and apes have about 12 (as does man). During these periods the gonads of some animals enlarge by as much as 100 times. But after successful fertilization, the gonads regress, at least for a short time. Development of the young does not necessarily follow immediately after fertilization. In mammals, for example, it does so in the species which mate in the spring but in those that mate in the summer or autumn, like the badger, the fertilized egg does not implant immediately, but is delayed until the late winter so that the offspring is born and develops in the spring. *Diapause in insects is similarly a hold-up of development, resulting in the new generation of insect passing through an adverse period (such as winter conditions) in the relatively protected form of the egg or pupa.

The physiological background to breeding is best illustrated by that of a typical mammalian breeding cycle. The hormone which initiates the change is the follicle-stimulating hormone (FSH) from the anterior pituitary. This causes the ripening of follicles in the ovary, the Graafian follicles as they are called, the number affected being related to the number of young usually born since each follicle will produce one egg. As another hormone, oestrogen from the ovaries, builds up in concentration, it affects the pituitary and FSH production is reduced. The main function of the oestrogen is to bring about the thickening of the uterus walls and changes in the behaviour of the animal. The pituitary also commences producing the luteinizing hormone (LH) which prepares the way for the events which occur after the egg has been ejected from the Graafian follicle. The remains of the follicle will become the corpus luteum which is itself a source for the important hormone progesterone. The activity of the corpus is maintained by luteotropin (LTH) produced from the pituitary. All these events cease if the egg is not fertilized; the corpus regresses and the progesterone level drops while LTH production also tails off. But if the egg is fertilized, both these hormones continue to be produced and their effect is first to prepare the uterus for the implantation of the embryo and then also to bring about the enlargement of the mammary glands ready for nursing the young animal. After birth takes place progesterone, which by then is coming from both the ovary and the placenta, drops in level. Additional LTH is produced by the placenta during pregnancy.

The hormonal changes in birds are not unlike those in mammals. Maturation of the follicles is stimulated by FSH. The response to this hormone is slow early in the season, but it is accelerated when egg-laying is near. In Ring doves, nest-building and the stimuli from the nest itself seems to bring about the release of LH from the pituitary, progesterone causes a burst of LH production and the first egg is laid. Whenever an egg is in the oviduct LH production is temporarily inhibited but minutes after laying, more LH is released and ovulation of the next egg occurs to be followed by the same sequence of events.

These normal events and the changes they bring about are known in mammals as the oestrus cycle and in a female rat they last three to four days. Those species which have one cycle per year are known as monoestrus; the other species with numerous cycles are polyoestrus. The cycles may be brought to an end if the egg is not fertilized and whether an embryo is formed or not, each cycle is usually followed by a period of anoestrus. The changes which the uterus undergoes in Old World monkeys, apes and man are so extensive that if fertilization does not happen, progesterone production ceases and much of the inner lining of the uterus sloughs off to appear as menstrual flow. The whole menstrual cycle lasts about 28 days, with the follicle maturing during this period after the 10th day and up to ovulation on about the 14th day.

In man and the apes, like many other mammals, eggs are produced spontaneously about once a month. But the eggs of rabbits, cats and squirrels, to take a few examples, are retained in the ovary to be released when the females copulate. If mating does not take place, the eggs degenerate in the ovary.

The hormonal background of the changes in a male mammal is not unlike that of the female. FSH and LH (here an interstitial cell stimulating hormone) are released into the blood by the pituitary. FSH stimulates the production of sperm and LH the activity of the interstitial cells, which in their turn produce testosterene which prepares the seminal vesicles and activates the prostate gland. The LH hormone causes the appearance of secondary sexual characters, for

Poplar hawkmoths *Laothoe populi*, mating, produce almost a puzzle picture.

Common bush-babies *Galago senegalensis* are arboreal which shows in their mating position.

Scorpion flies *Panorpa communis* mating. Note how the female wing is held by the fold in the abdomen of the male.

European Midwife toad *Alytes obstetricans* with eggs. Male carries eggs on his back.

example, the mane and antlers of the stag or the thickened neck of the bull. In castrated animals these characters do not appear.

Control of breeding season. The act of breeding is brought about by a number of factors. Spring breeding is common in temperate and subtropical latitudes. It is an advantageous time, for the young animal will have to face less severe climatic conditions and will have a greater supply of food than in winter. The lengthening period of daylight which comes at this time of year seems to be an important stimulus to breeding behaviour. This brings about the growth of the gonads, the length of daylight perceived through the eyes stimulating the pituitary to produce the hormones which cause the recrudescence of ovaries and testes. Fine warm spring days will bring about earlier breeding than cold ones. Autumn-breeding animals seem to respond to shortening days, though the young, for example of some ruminants, are not born until the warmth of the following spring. But this spring onset is not solely controlled by external conditions, there seems to be an annual cycle in birds, at least, which, as it were, readies the system to respond to changes in the length of the day. Also in birds, there may be a refractory period after the previous year's breeding which will last through to the following spring. Such an effect must be important in those birds which fly across the Equator when they migrate southwards in autumn. In their winter homes they will encounter the same external conditions which would have brought about breeding in the northern spring, that is, lengthening days and rising temperature.

There is also a social effect in birds. One of the advantages of the great colonies of gannets and other seabirds is that they tend to begin to lay eggs earlier, and because it is a highly stimulating situation they seem to get it over more quickly. This has the advantage that there are young, vulnerable to the attacks of predators, present in the colony for a shorter total period, thus possibly reducing losses.

In temperate areas much of the breeding is seasonal and regular, but there are arid regions in the world where breeding is opportunist and highly irregular. Rains in these areas create conditions which are good for breeding since plant life temporarily revives, flowers appear and seeds are formed, all potential food for a bird. In the place of the dry brittle grasses, which are to be found during the rest of the year, supple green grass springs up and provides excellent nesting material. The gonads of a number of species from such regions remain enlarged for long periods, the reproductive systems of males and females being kept in readiness, as it were, to respond rapidly to favourable conditions. It is the green grass which appears after the rains that triggers off queleas into breeding and older birds even respond to the sound and feel of the falling rain. If there are no rains one year, then there will be no reproduction.

The behaviour of other members of the species is often important in bringing both partners in courtship to the same physiological state. An isolated female pigeon can be induced to lay eggs by the sight of her own reflection in a mirror, but it is usually mutual behaviour with another bird which has this effect. Courtship movements in Ring doves have the effect of evoking the release of oestrogens from the ovary and indeed the sight of courting males stimulates more hormone production than does the sight of a non-courting bird.   J.D.C. & P.M.D.

Bird-eating spiders *Dugesiella hentzi,* of California, mating.

BRENT GOOSE *Branta bernicla,* a small dark goose with an arctic circumpolar distri-

bution, breeding in the tundra. There are three recognizable races: the Russian or Dark-bellied brent *B. b. bernicla,* which has a black head, neck and breast, dark grey upper-parts, a white rear and an incomplete white collar; the Atlantic or Light-bellied brent *B. b. hrota,* which is much paler beneath; and the Pacific brent or Black brant *B. b. orientalis,* which has a dark belly but light flanks. The Russian brent breeds in arctic Europe and Asia; the Atlantic brent on the islands and coasts of eastern Canada, northern Greenland, Spitzbergen and Franz Joseph Land; and the Black brant on the islands and coasts of western Canada, northern Alaska and Siberia.

Brent geese are on the breeding grounds for some three months of the year from about mid-June. They nest on the ground in large colonies, often with Eider ducks. Three to five eggs are laid and incubated by the female, with the male standing guard close by. The parents share in the care of the young, which are active soon after hatching and accompany the parents over the tundra, feeding on the tundra plants and any invertebrate animal food they can obtain.

After the breeding season, Brent geese migrate south and winter on the shallow coastlines of the more temperate regions of the Atlantic and Pacific Oceans. During this period they take a wide variety of food, mostly plant material and including some algae, but on both the European and North American coasts of the Atlantic the preferred food has long been the Greater eel-

grass *Zostera maxima.* Around 1930 this plant was almost destroyed by disease and the Brent geese suffered drastic losses as a result. However, they were successful in adapting to other foods and after 1940 their numbers built up again and the populations are now quite restored. FAMILY: Anatidae, ORDER: Anseriformes, CLASS: Aves. P.M.D.

BRILL *Scophthalmus rhombus,* a flatfish from the Mediterranean and eastern North Atlantic. It lies on its right side and is similar to the turbot, but is more oval in shape and has smooth scales with no tubercles. The general colour is grey, brown or greenish with darker patches or mottlings and usually speckled with white spots. The brill, which is common round British coasts, lives on sandy bottoms at depths of 180–240 ft (54–72 m) and is often caught on the same grounds as the turbot. It grows to about 2 ft (60 cm) in length and the flesh is considered most delicately flavoured. In the North Sea spawning takes place in spring and summer, the adult female producing about 800,000 eggs. After hatching, the young come inshore, but move back into deeper water after they have completed their metamorphosis and have attained the flat form of the adult. FAMILY: Pleuronectidae, ORDER: Pleuronectiformes, CLASS: Pisces.

BRINE SHRIMP *Artemia salina,* similar in form to other *Fairy shrimps but remarkable for its ability to live in strong brine. Laboratory studies have shown that *Artemia* can live

Brent geese seldom come far inland. They normally feed in the beds of eel-grass, in estuaries, and they usually roost at sea.

in salinities ranging from $\frac{1}{10}$ that of sea water up to five times the concentration of sea water, at which level salts begin to crystallize out of solution. Although it is physiologically capable of living in the sea *Artemia* is a relatively slow swimmer, and is conspicuous, so that it could not survive in the presence of predators such as fishes. The natural habitat of *Artemia* is in salt lakes or saline lagoons, where the salinity rises well above that of sea water and there are few or no predators.

There are differences in the reproductive cycles of *Artemia* in different localities. In the South of France the populations reproduce by *parthenogenesis and males are extremely rare. In California the populations are bisexual and the eggs need to be fertilized before they will develop. In addition *Artemia* may be viviparous, carrying its eggs in the brood pouch until they hatch, or it may be oviparous, laying eggs with a very tough shell. Strictly speaking by the time it has been liberated from the maternal brood pouch it is no longer an egg, but a partly developed embryo, so that it is sometimes called a cyst. The embryos in the cysts will still develop and emerge as nauplius larvae after such treatments as being subjected to desiccation, heated to 212°F (100°C) for a few hours, frozen with liquid air, or stored dry in a jar on a laboratory shelf for several years. The hatching of the embryos from these cysts is a remarkable process. When placed in sea water at 68°F (20°C) the cysts swell, and after 50 hours a split appears in the shell, then the embryo appears enclosed in a thin membrane. The nauplius larva breaks out of the membrane about 90 hours after the cyst has been put into sea water. At this stage the nauplius still has some yolk, and does not begin to feed until it has been free swimming for about 30 hours. During the first stages of development the embryo manufactures glycerol, which increases the internal osmotic pressure, so that the embryo can swell and burst out of its tough shell. The amount of glycerol that is made is proportional to the salinity of the water in which the embryo finds itself. There is a feedback from the environment to the embryo, which then adjusts its internal chemistry to ensure that it can burst out of its cyst in a range of salinities.

Another feature of *Artemia* that varies with the salinity of its environment is the shape of the body. In general the abdomen tends to be longer and narrower in higher salinities, but there are also differences between populations from different areas. Brine shrimps from Algeria have longer abdomens than Californian specimens reared in the same salinity.

The amount of time taken for *Artemia* to reach maturity varies with temperature and food. At 77°F (25°C) maturity is reached in 15 to 17 days when food is abundant, but under poorer feeding conditions maturity

Brine shrimp *Artemia salina*, female, in side view.

may be delayed until the animals are 30 days old. The size at maturity varies with salinity, so that animals growing in very strong brine are somewhat smaller than those growing in sea water. ORDER: Anostraca, CLASS: Crustacea, PHYLUM: Arthropoda. Ja.G.

BRISTLEMOUTHS, a name for small deep-sea fishes with thin fragile bodies, rarely more than 3 in (7·5 cm) long, of the family Gonostomatidae. Although very abundant they are rarely seen except by fish specialists. Their alternative name, lightfishes, expresses the fact that they have luminous organs which in some genera are grouped together in glands whilst in others they are separate.

The genus *Cyclothone* has species all over the world and many authors have voiced the opinion that they are amongst the most numerous fishes in the seas but because of their unsubstantial bodies and the depths at which they live they are not likely ever to be of any economic importance. Some species take five years to reach 2 in (5 cm) in length. Little is known of their breeding but at least one species of the genus *Vinciguerra* has floating eggs and larvae that are difficult to distinguish from those of sardines. FAMILY: Gonostomatidae, ORDER: Salmoniformes, CLASS: Pisces.

BRISTLES, modified hairs distinguished by their thickness and strength, which are found on some mammals. The bristle-like structures on the bodies of annelid worms, crustaceans and a few other invertebrates are sometimes loosely called bristles but should be called setae. The bristles used in the manufacture of some brushes are from the backs of domestic pigs. The hair used in other brushes, which is less elastic than bristles, is usually taken from cattle. 'Camel hair' brushes are, in fact, made from the hair of squirrels' tails, while the finest shaving brushes are made from badger hair.

BRISTLETAILS, wingless insects believed to be closest to the ancestral type from which all present-day insects have evolved. About 400 species are known. Although they are found in all parts of the world they are rarely seen because with few exceptions they are less than 1 cm long. With the springtails and a few other primitive wingless types of insects they make up the subclass Apterygota ('without wings'), the rest of the insects being placed in a subclass Pterygota ('winged').

Bristletails are the only apterygote insects with compound eyes, like those found in the Pterygota. In most of them the mouthparts are of a rather unmodified type suitable only

Another view of the Brine shrimp, seen from above in the natural habitat, a salt lake.

Bristletail *Petrobius*, showing the three moveable appendages which give it its name.

for biting and chewing living or dead plant material. The antennae are long and multi-segmented. The abdominal segments carry a series of leg-like appendages of unknown functions. At the end of the abdomen are three long, movable, antenna-like appendages which give them their popular name. These are believed to be sense-organs. The genital organs of the bristletails are of a type from which it is believed those of most other insects have been derived. Fertilization is internal. The young are like miniature adults in appearance and although they undergo several moults with increase in size before reaching adulthood they show no metamorphosis. Many species become darker in colour and develop a covering of scales on the body as they mature. Unlike pterygote insects, the bristletails, like other apterygote insects, continue to moult at intervals after becoming adult, although with little or no increase in size. This ability to renew the body covering that may have become damaged or worn is probably a characteristic that has been retained by the apterygotes but lost by their more highly evolved relatives. The presence of wings, which are complicated outgrowths of the body covering itself and have complex muscular attachments, in the adults of the pterygote insects probably makes renewal of the cuticle impossible. Some species have been shown to undergo as many as 60 or more moults after becoming adult and, at least in captivity, may live a very long time for an insect, perhaps up to seven years. Several species are known to take two years to reach sexual maturity.

What little is known of their feeding habits suggests that most bristletails feed on decomposing plant and animal material. Perhaps the best known species is the silverfish *Lepisma saccharina* which is common in buildings all over the world, especially in damp places like kitchens and bathrooms. Its bright metallic colour is due to a covering of shiny scales. The silverfish probably feeds on any sort of damp or decaying organic material and on the bacteria and fungi growing on it and is quite harmless. The gut contains symbiotic bacteria

which enable the silverfish to digest cellulose and experiments on related species have shown that adults can survive indefinitely on a diet of paper. The silverfish probably cannot tolerate the conditions found out-of-doors in temperate countries but is found out-of-doors in the tropics.

A species of bristletail that used to be much more common than it is now is the firebrat *Thermobia domestica*. This is found in bake-houses and kitchens and other humid places where the exceptionally high temperatures the firebrat needs for the development of its young—up to 104°F (40°C)—are found. The firebrat probably feeds on food scraps dropped during cooking and, since in recent years bakeries have become much cleaner places, the species has become quite rare. The species of the genus *Petrobius* live on rocky shores in cracks in the rocks around high water mark and are not really marine animals since at high tide they retreat into pockets of air in crevices of the rock and are not immersed. *Petrobius* feeds on marine detritus washed up by the tide and on green algae which it scrapes from rocks. Many species of bristletail, especially in tropical regions, live as 'guests' in the nests of ants and termites and probably act as scavengers tolerated by their hosts. ORDER: Thysanura, SUBCLASS: Apterygota, CLASS: Insecta, PHYLUM: Arthropoda. I.N.H.

BRISTLY-MILLIPEDES, the common European species of which was, in 1758, named by Linnaeus *Scolopendra lagura* along with 11 other centipedes. It is now recognised as a millipede and called *Polyxenus lagurus*. It walks like a centipede, has a cuticle like a centipede and a method of transferring sperm between males and females rather like centipedes, but it has no poison claws, has two pairs of legs under each of the last five tergites and the genital openings are on the third segment at the bases of the second pair of legs. Thus it is certainly a millipede but a very peculiar one and with its relatives is placed in a separate subclass to distinguish them from the more typical millipedes.

Polyxenus is short, with only 11 rings and 13 pairs of legs and about $\frac{1}{6}$ in (4 mm) long when fully grown. The skeletal plates are separate and arranged like those of a centipede—dorsal tergite, lateral pleurites and ventral sternite; they are not calcified as are the hard parts of a typical millipede. The tergites and pleurites carry curious blunt, angular and toothed bristles and the tail-piece or telson carries two long tufts of bristles serrated at their extremities. Another peculiarity of the subclass is that the breathing tubes or tracheae are branched and are strengthened by annular thickenings as in centipedes. Sixty species of this and other genera have been recorded from all over the world.

Polyxenus lagurus occurs all over Europe in a variety of places; at the roots of seapink on the coast, under the bark of trees, on brick walls, sometimes walking about during the day. A similar species, perhaps identical with *P. lagurus,* occurs in the eastern United States and has been found quite commonly in woodland sites in North Carolina. Nevertheless, it is still something of a 'find'. *P. lagurus* is usually parthenogenetic, that is, there are very rarely males; females lay eggs which develop without being fertilized by sperm from a male. But sometimes males do occur and their sperm is transferred to the female by a method quite unlike that in typical millipedes but recalling the condition in centipedes and some primitive insects. The male spins a web on which he lays a spermatophore. The female is guided towards this by two parallel lines of 'silk' secreted by paired sacs at the bases of the legs of the male's seventh segment. These are the legs adapted as intromittent organs in typical millipedes. The eggs are laid together in a mass and are protected by pieces broken-off from the tail bristles. SUB-CLASS: Pselaphognatha, CLASS: Diplopoda, PHYLUM: Arthropoda.   J.G.B.

BRITTLESTARS, mobile, star-shaped marine animals with the five-fold radial symmetry, endoskeleton of calcite plates and water vascular system characteristic of Sea urchins, Sea lilies, Sea cucumbers and starfishes, to which they are related. They resemble the starfish in appearance but may be distinguished from them in details of structure, biochemistry, larval development and mode of life. The most obvious difference is that in brittlestars there is a clear distinction between the central disc which houses the vital organs and the flexible arms, whereas in starfishes this distinction is seldom marked.

The arms are long relative to the diameter of the central disc, narrow from base to tip, and somewhat bony in appearance since they are formed of little more than plates (ossicles) of calcite. Their snake-like form has given rise to the alternative popular name of 'Serpent stars' for the class Ophiuroidea (Gk *ophis*—snake). The arms break easily when handled, hence the name brittlestar.

The 2,000 species are divided into two main groups. The first is the Ophiurae or brittlestars proper. Their unbranched arms have a series of calcite plates embedded in the upper, lower and both side surfaces, with a central series of vertebra-like ossicles that articulate by ball-and-socket joints, permitting lateral (sideways) movements only. The second, smaller group, is the Euryalae, including the basketstars. In these, disc and arms are covered with thick skin, sometimes with granules or tubercles. There is a central series of vertebral ossicles in each arm, and these articulate with broad hourglass-shaped surfaces, permitting all round movement of the arms which may actually coil vertically. The arms may branch and in some genera do so repeatedly. Those in which the arms branch right from the base are known as basketstars, for when the animals are alive and feeding the arms extend upwards and outwards to form an open mesh basket in which they catch their prey.

Morphology. The body is a flat disc, usually $\frac{2}{5}$–1 in (10–30 mm) diameter, from which radiate five (rarely more) thin, flexible arms, 4–7 in (10–18 cm) long, well marked off from the body. Some species, however, have small discs and very long arms. Basketstars have discs up to 4 in (10 cm) across and long, branching coiling arms. The colour varies from cream, yellow, green, grey and brown to purple and black, often in spots and bands.

The body wall is strengthened with a skeleton of calcite plates. The basic pattern for these on the upper surface is of a central plate surrounded by a ring of five radial plates, then further cycles of plates, usually multiples of five, to cover the disc. Two conspicuous plates, the radial shields, lie close to the origin of each arm; their variation in form is much used in classification. In some forms the upper surface is covered with granules or small spines, or a thick naked skin. Unlike starfishes there is no anus, neither are there any pedicellariae (pincer-like spines).

On the lower surface, five plates, the oral shields, lie on the disc at the angles of the arms. One of them is the madreporite, where a single pore, rarely more than this, pierces the plate and leads into the water vascular system within the body. The mouth is central, star-shaped, surrounded by a ring of plates: a pair of jaw plates and aboral shields lie at the base of each arm, corresponding to the ambulacral and adambulacral plates of starfishes. The arms continue inside the disc on the lower surface, and have on each side near their base a slit leading to a genital bursa, a sac which bulges up into the disc: its function is both reproductive and respiratory.

The arms have a central series of vertebra-

like calcite ossicles formed by the fusion of two smaller plates. These are generally covered by series of regularly arranged plates, four to each arm segment, above, below and on each side. The lateral plates correspond to the adambulacrals of starfishes, and like them bear spines: two or three to about 15 in number, and of very variable form. They seem to be used to get a better grip when the animal pushes itself over the ground. A tentacle-like tube-foot emerges through a pore at the junction of each lateral and ventral plate, a pair of tube-feet thus corresponding to each segment. The tube-feet are slender and

pointed, lacking the terminal suckers and the sac-like ampullae generally found in star-fishes. They are used in respiration, loco-motion, feeding, and burrowing, and are usually protected by one or more modified spines, known as tentacle scales. Within the arm they connect with a radial water vessel as in starfishes, but since this is covered by the ventral plates there is no open ambulacral groove as in that group: the brittlestars are thus said to possess a closed ambulacrum.

As in the starfishes, the radial water vessel connects within the disc to a circumoral water ring, and this in turn is connected via a canal

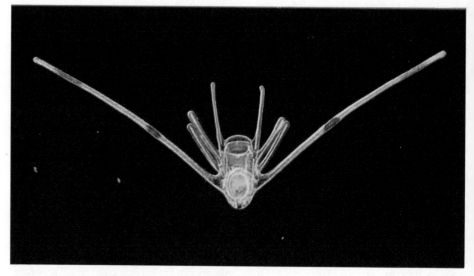

Ophiopluteus larva of Common brittlestar in ventral view.

Anatomy of a brittlestar: lower and upper surfaces of the central disc (top left and top right), with (bottom left) a section through an arm and (bottom right) vertical section through the central disc with (to the left of the picture) a portion of one of the arms showing some of vertebrae (in vertical section) and part of a radial nerve.

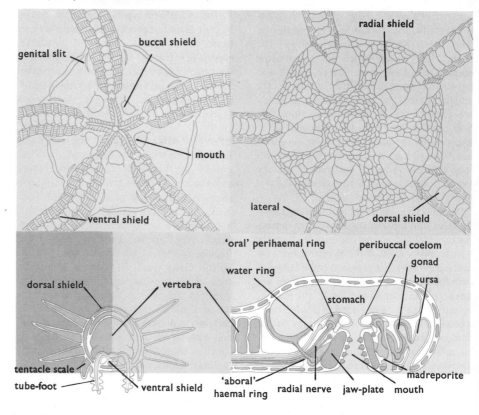

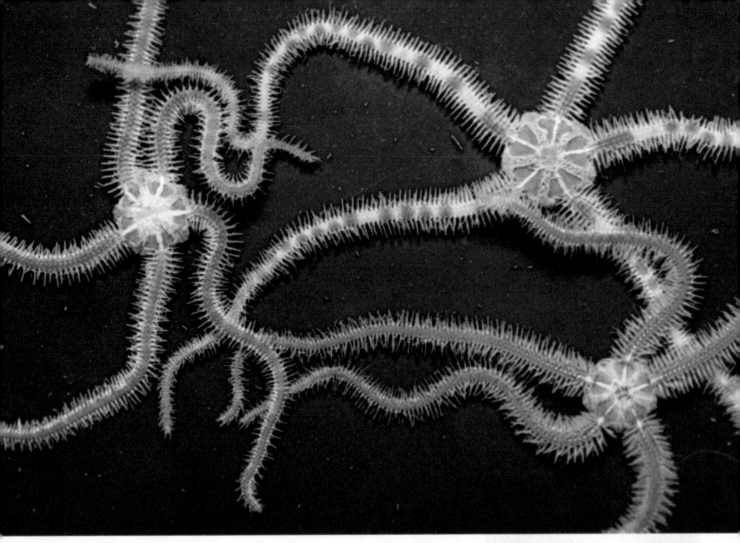

Close-up of a few Common brittlestars, which live in patches of hundreds on the seabed, as shown by the photograph on page 270.

to the madreporic plate, here situated on the lower, not as in starfishes on the upper, surface of the disc. Other systems are very similar in the two groups: a haemal system carries blood from a ring encircling the gut near the mouth radially along tubular extensions below the vertebral arm ossicles; a perihaemal system follows the same pattern; nerves too radiate from the central ring along each arm. But the alimentary canal differs: the mouth opens into a sac-like stomach from which there is no exit to an anus for the discharge of indigestible material, this being ejected instead via the mouth. Moreover, the stomach typically has 10 side pouches, but they are confined to the disc and do not continue into the arms, except in *Ophiocanops*. There is no intestine as such, and there are no hepatic caeca.

Distribution. Brittlestars are the most successful of living echinoderms, the number of living species being greater than that for any other class and the number of individuals reaching a very high density in some areas (over 3,000 individuals of *Ophiothrix fragilis* per square metre on the shallow sea floor near Plymouth, England), where they form up to 90% of the animals present. They are found in all seas, at all latitudes, on all types of bottom,

and at all depths from the intertidal zone to the abyssal region (down to 19,000 ft/6,000 m). This widespread occurrence together with their great abundance has led frequently to their use as characteristic species in the naming and definition of marine communities by oceanographers.

In shallow waters brittlestars lie hidden in the bottom sand or mud, under stones, seaweeds or dead coral fragments, or in nooks and crannies. Some are very widely distributed. *Amphipholus squamata* is found all over the world and is the only cosmopolitan littoral echinoderm. Another species *Ophiomusium lymani* of practically world-wide occurrence outside the polar regions, ranges from 2,100–12,000 ft (700–4,000 m) depth.

Breeding. In many brittlestars the sexes are separate. The females shedding large numbers of eggs into the sea stimulate the males to eject spermatozoa and so bring about fertilization. This spawning is seasonal, usually lasting only 1–3 months for a given species, and varying in time of year with the species concerned, but in the tropical and subtropical forms taking place in the spring and summer and so possibly related to water temperature.

The fertilized egg subsequently develops into an ophiopluteus larva quite unlike the

adults. It has bilateral symmetry, with a mouth at the front and an anus at the rear, bears long projecting skeletal rods which are not retained in the adult, and propels itself by the action of countless cilia arranged in bands around the body. The larvae are planktonic, feeding on the microscopic plant life and so may be distributed far more widely than their slower-moving parents. After a time, which varies with the species, the larvae settle on the sea bottom and develop their adult structure.

Some brittlestars are hermaphrodite, combining both male and female characteristics. They probably avoid self-fertilization by different timing in the ripening and shedding of the two kinds of sexual products. At least one genus, *Ophioceres*, is even reported to alternate its sex, changing from male to female, then female to male again.

The sexual products are discharged from the gonads where they originate via the genital bursae and bursal slits. Sometimes the eggs are retained in the bursae and a brood of young is reared there. Such forms generally produce large, yolky eggs that undergo a modified, shortened form of development. They are especially prevalent in antarctic and sub-antarctic waters, but not entirely restricted to them.

The sexes are normally difficult to distinguish, but in at least four species the males and females are quite distinct, the males being dwarfed and commonly riding upon the females, as in *Amphilycus androphorus,* where the male lies continually across the mouth of the female, his arms entwined with hers. *Ophiodaphne materna* is another example, the small male having been originally mistaken for a young specimen and the larger female for its mother.

Yet other, generally rather small, species reproduce asexually, like some starfishes. Several species of *Ophiactis* propagate by dividing in two across the disc, each half then regenerating the missing parts. Such species tend to have six or seven arms, rather than the usual five. The brittle arms are readily regenerated when broken, but though a disc may regenerate new arms, an arm cannot regenerate a disc.

Habits. Most brittlestars are active, moving over the sea bottom using their flexible arms

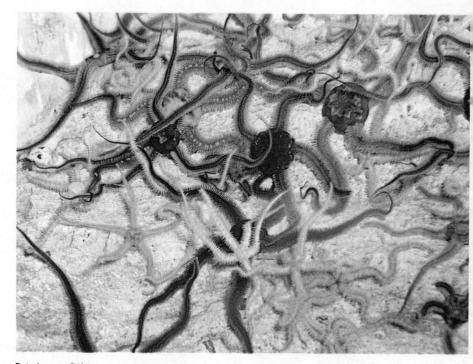

Brittlestars *Ophiocomina nigra* and Common brittlestars, an underwater close-up.

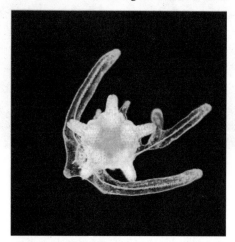

Ophiopluteus larva of brittlestar *Ophiura albida* in very late stage of metamorphosis.

in a sort of rowing action: one arm leads or trails unused, and the others work in pairs to move the body forward in successive bounds. Up to 2 yd (1·8 m) per minute can be reached by this method, which makes relatively little use of the tube-feet, in contrast to the starfishes who move on their many, generally suckered tube-feet with a more uniform gliding motion. There is no preferred direction for movement: any arm may lead or trail.

Brittlestars may feed on almost anything: grazing on detritus on the sea floor; preying on small animals such as polychaete worms and small crustaceans; eating, rather more rarely, algae; or otherwise gathering small particles of edible matter from suspension in the water. Large food particles are carried to the mouth by an arm, but smaller ones are passed along by the tube-feet, sometimes trapped first in sticky mucus secreted by glands associated with the tube-feet or lateral spines. The basketstars, such as *Gorgono-*

cephalus, are particularly well adapted as suspension feeders, catching plankton and detritus on their branching arms which are often equipped with tiny hooks. The burrowing amphiurids too may use this method, though most of the body and arms except for the tips lies buried in sand or mud, and detritus is gathered from the surface or filtered from suspension at the arm tips alone and passed by the tube-feet to the mouth.

Because they function as scavengers, brittlestars play an important role in the economy of the sea. They are also of indirect economic importance to man, in that they form part of the diet of commercially significant bottom-feeding fishes such as the cod and plaice. One unusual character of several species, the fact that they are luminescent, leads to their predation by attracting the fish at night, *Icalia filiformis* being an example of such a phosphorescent species.

If fossil forms are taken into account a total of four orders need to be recognized each ranging from Paleozoic times:
1. Stenurida, an extinct, Paleozoic order in which the ambulacral groove on the lower surface of the arms, which contains the radial water vessel, is not covered by skeletal plates and the arm ossicles are not fused to form vertebrae.
2. Oegophiurida, an order extinct but for the surviving genus *Ophiocanops,* of which only a few specimens are known, from Indonesian seas. The ambulacral groove and body are covered with a soft skin, and the arm ossicles are fused to form vertebrae; extensions of the body (gut, genital organs) are found in the arms.

3. Phrynophiurida, an order which includes the Euryalae. The ambulacral groove is covered by ventral arm plates and body organs are confined to the disc.
4. Ophiurida, modern brittlestars.
CLASS: Ophiuroidea, PHYLUM: Echinodermata. E.P.F.R.

BROADBILLS, 14 species of small, squat tropical birds with short wings, outsize heads, short legs and strong feet. The bill is short and very broad, so that it appears triangular when viewed from above; the upper mandible overlaps the lower and terminates in a small hook. Broadbills are peculiar in a number of anatomical features, such as the number of neck vertebrae, 15 instead of the usual 14, and the musculature of the syrinx. In consequence they are regarded as the most primitive of the passerines possibly allied to other primitive families like the Old World pittas and the New World cotingas. Many of the broadbills are brilliantly coloured and even the more sombre of them with brown plumage, usually have bright patches of colour. In addition, several species have brightly-hued eyes, bills or naked face patches. One species *Eurylaimus steerii* of the Philippines has wattles. Whitehead's broadbill *Calyptomena whiteheadi* is one of the most splendid members of the family. It is relatively large, 10 in (25 cm) long, with brilliant green plumage marked boldly with black streaks and patches which serve to break up the bird's outline and make it most inconspicuous as it sits among the dense evergreen vegetation in the mountain forests of Borneo. Like other members of the genus

Calyptomena, Whitehead's broadbill has a tuft of short green feathers on the head which extends so far forward over the bill as to cover it almost to the tip. Perhaps the best known of the Asian broadbills is the Black and red broadbill *Cymbirhynchus macrorhynchus* which lives along the forest waterways. Its plumage is boldly patterned with black, white and crimson, while the large bill is a lovely soft blue on top and yellow beneath.

The broadbills are restricted to areas of dense vegetation and most are found only in lowland rain-forest or mountain cloud forests. Their centre of distribution is in the dense jungles of tropical Southeast Asia – Malaya, Indonesia and Borneo. Eight of the 14 species are found in Borneo and two of these are restricted to that island. A few small broadbills occur in the African forests, including the very rare Grauer's broadbill *Pseudocalyptomena graueri*, known only from a small montane area in the eastern Congo.

Broadbills construct exquisite pendant nests usually slung from a branch overhanging a stream. The main body of the nest, below the suspending 'rope', is pear-shaped, with an entrance hole at one side. A wide variety of fibrous nesting materials, roots, leaf midribs, lianas, etc. are used by different species. In many cases the outside is covered with moss or lichen and strands of these materials are left hanging below the nest as a 'beard'. This undoubtedly helps to make the nest even more inconspicuous and confuses the nest robbers such as snakes, birds of prey, monkeys and other small mammals, which abound in the humid forests. The eggs are pale in colour, usually two to four.

For the most part, broadbills are inactive birds, spending much of the time sitting quietly on branches among the dense vegetation. They are thus very difficult to see, though many species have distinctive calls which may reveal their whereabouts. There is little precise information regarding their feeding habits, but the majority are probably insectivorous in the main. Some of the small broadbills, such as the African *Smithornis* species, catch little insects in the manner of a flycatcher, darting out from a perch to catch a flying insect and returning immediately with it to the perch. Some of the other members of the family feed on large insects found among the foliage. The *Calyptomena* broadbills are apparently fruit-eaters, while the riverine Black and red broadbill is said to eat a wide range of animal and plant foods, including insects, crabs and fish, which it probably obtains by scavenging along river banks. FAMILY: Eurylaimidae, ORDER: Passeriformes, CLASS: Aves. P.W.

BRONTOSAURUS, well known and much figured gigantic dinosaur. Complete skeletons of *Brontosaurus* have been excavated from the Upper Jurassic of the western United States. This huge quadrupedal herbivore had a total length of some 68 ft (21 m) and a calculated live weight in excess of 35 tons (36 tons). Its head was disproportionately small, its vertebral column massive, for supporting the huge body, and the limbs pillar-like. Recent evidence suggests that *Brontosaurus* and its allies spent much of their life on dry land and were not the lagoon dwelling monsters so often figured. ORDER: Saurischia, CLASS: Reptilia.

BROOD PARASITISM, the utilization of the nest and parental care of one species by another for the rearing of its young. Also known as 'nest parasitism' or 'social parasitism', this habit is particularly well-developed in birds and in ants, bees and wasps.

Among birds, brood parasitism is most highly-developed in the cuckoo family, in which the whole of one subfamily, Cuculinae, and part of another, Neomorphinae, are parasitic. In the European cuckoo *Cuculus canorus* the adaptations developed to promote the success of brood parasitism include a well-developed egg mimicry, with the species divided into different clans, or gentes, each of which parasitizes a specific host. Another outstanding adaptation is the behaviour of the newly-hatched cuckoo which ejects any host eggs or young from the nest by pushing upwards and heaving them over the side on its back, because the young cuckoo grows very much larger than a host nestling. In other cuckoo species which parasitize larger hosts this does not occur. On the other hand, their plumage may tend to match that of the host young, which is not the case with *C. canorus*.

A similar range of habit is seen in the American family of troupials, Icteridae. In this, the Bay-winged cowbird *Molothrus badius* rears its young in the nest of another species; the parasitic Screaming cowbird *M. rufoaxillaris* lays only in the nest of the Bay-winged cowbird, while the Brown-headed cowbird *M. ater* will lay in the nest of almost any other species.

The tropical honeyguides are also parasitic. The young are no larger than those of the host, yet they have hooks on their beaks with which they attack their nest-mates.

In the social hymenopterous insects the behaviour of the nest parasites is essentially the same as in birds in that the parasite young are reared entirely by another species of host, but the context is a social one. It may not involve the total elimination of the host young. In most cases of ant parasitism, for

Green broadbill *Calyptomena viridis*, of Malaya.

Top: cuckoo's egg in the nest of a dunnock or hedgesparrow *Prunella modularis.*

Right top: young European cuckoo ejecting an egg from a Tree pipit's nest.

Right bottom: young European cuckoo in Tree pipit's (*Anthus trivialis*) nest having ejected foster parent's eggs.

example, the host queen is eliminated by the parasites and the host workers thus come to have the parasitic brood to care for rather than their own, for the producer of their own eggs has been removed. However, the queen of the ant *Strongylognathus testaceus* enters the nest of another ant *Tetramorium aespitum* but does not kill the host queen. Both continue to lay eggs, but those of the host queen become workers, and the parasite thus has a continual supply of host workers to care for its young, and any fertile queens which result are only those of the parasite.

Bumblebees *Psithyrus* lay their eggs in the nests of the bumblebee *Bombus,* leaving them to be reared by the *Bombus* workers. Cuckoo wasps of the family Chrysididae lay their eggs in the nests of social bees and wasps, leaving the host workers to look after them.   P.M.D.

BROTULID, one of a family of fishes related to cods. The family contains the Cusk eels, which are dealt with elsewhere, and the brotulids. The latter show a wide range of body forms and adaptations to particular environments, although most are marine fishes from deep waters. There are about 175 species of brotulids placed in about 60 genera. These can be divided into two groups. The oviparous or egg-laying forms (about 100 species) are found only at depths of 450 ft (135 m) or more and half of these are known to occur in the deep abyssal waters. *Bassigigas,* for example, is known from 23,400 ft (nearly 7,000 m). The viviparous species, which bring forth live young that develop in a tough egg case within the mother, comprise about 70 species mostly found along the shore, on coral reefs, in midwater and in freshwaters, although a few are deeper water species. The few freshwater species are Blind cave fishes from Cuba and Mexico. The Cuban species *Stygicola dentatus* and *Lucifuga subterranea*

have been discussed under Cave fishes. They exhibit the general brotulid features of long bodies, long dorsal and anal fins and reduced pelvic fins. Most brotulids are small fishes, usually less than 20 in (50 cm) in length (the largest reaching 4 ft or 1·2 m) and they are secretive in their habits. The species that live in fairly shallow water hide away in crevices in rocks and this habit may well have led to the evolution of the blind cave forms.

The deep-sea brotulids have large heads and thin tapering bodies, with the dorsal and anal fins often confluent with the tail. Most have large eyes but the eyes are smaller in the deeper living forms. The body is very

fragile. *Acanthonus armatus* from 8,000 ft (2,400 m) has small eyes and a soft body with spines on the gill cover, while *Typhlonus nasus* from 16,000 ft (4,800 m) is completely blind and the skeleton is soft and greatly reduced. *Typhlonus* bears a striking resemblance to the Cuban blind fishes. Brotulids are not known to have light organs, limiting their ability to recognize the members of their own species or of the opposite sex. Many of the egg-laying species have prominent drumming muscles and the anterior ribs are expanded and associated with the swimbladder. This suggests that the fishes are able to make drumming sounds and possibly this

is the method used to locate mates and identify themselves to members of their own species. FAMILY: Ophidiidae, ORDER: Gadiformes, CLASS: Pisces.

BROWN LOCUST *Locustana paradalina*, the South African locust which breeds in the dry Karroo area.

BRYOZOA, a phylum of quite common, though often inconspicuous, aquatic animals, alternatively known as moss-animals, which are present in freshwater but are especially numerous in the sea. There are nearly 4,000 living species of Bryozoa and perhaps four times as many preserved as fossils. This number corresponds fairly closely to that of the echinoderms, for example; but whereas a starfish or Sea urchin can be readily seen and admired, the beauty of bryozoans can generally be appreciated only by the use of a microscope.

They are colonial animals constructed from repeated units called zooids. While the zooids in a colony may be few, in the Membranipora which forms lacy patterns over the fronds of large seaweeds, they may number up to 2 million. Such a colony spreads over many square inches, but bryozoans are usually smaller than this. Incrusting species rarely cover more than 1 sq in (6 cm²), although the tufted and coralline types may be a little larger, reaching 2–3 in (5–7½ cm) in height. One of these, the Foliaceous coralline *Pentopora foliacea* of European waters, was once found in a clump 7 ft (2¼ m) in circumference.

Two other distinctive species are hornwrack *Flustra foliacea* and *Alcyonidium gelatinosum*. The coriaceous, buff-grey, citron-smelling fronds of hornwrack are frequently encountered in the flotsam along

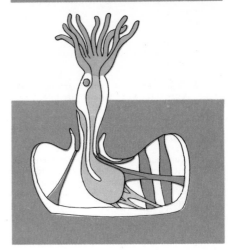

A single zooid of a colony of Bryozoa. (Above) The zooid is entirely withdrawn and the operculum closed. (Below) The lophophore, with its crown of tentacles is extended; the muscles controlling it can be seen in the 'box' and, inside the body, the U-shaped gut and the nerve ganglia (small circle near base of tentacles).

A distinctive species of bryozoan is hornwrack, which although not a shore animal, is not infrequently cast up on beaches.

Bryozoan colonies.

1. *Flustrellidra hispida*, forming a purplish incrustation on the intertidal alga *Fucus serratus*.

2. *Bugula flabellata*, which grows as buff-grey tufts on rocks and pier piles.

3. *Cellaria fistulosa*, a white, jointed-stemmed coralline common below tide-marks.

4. *Cupuladria guineensis*, a disciform non-attached species in section and from above. The little colonies may occur abundantly in the tropics and subtropics where the sea bed is sandy.

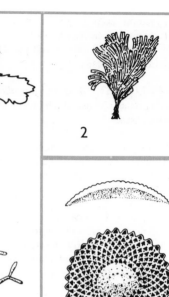

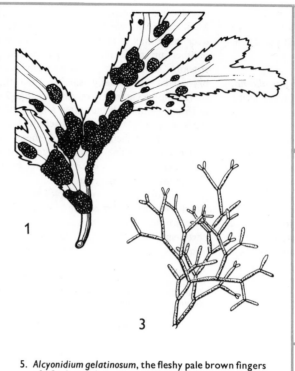

1

3

2

4

5. *Alcyonidium gelatinosum*, the fleshy pale brown fingers of which may be common sublittorally.

6. *Bugula turbinata*, which grows as yellowish spiralling tufts hanging from cave roofs and large intertidal boulders.

7. *Flustra foliacea*, which has buff-grey flexible fronds and lives in rocky regions of the shallow sea where the water currents are strong. Torn-off fronds are familiar objects along a strand line.

8. *Pentapora foliacea*, a shallow sea species having a rigid calcified colony constructed of interlinked flat fronds.

9. *Sertella septentrionalis*, attached to a frond of the Mediterranean eel-grass *Posidonia oceanica*. The colony has the form of a rigid, white, funnel-shaped net.

10. *Myriapora truncata*, a red coralline from the Mediterranean.

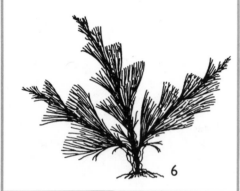

6

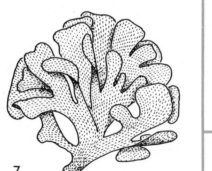

5

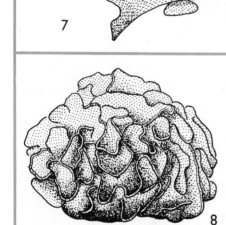

7

8

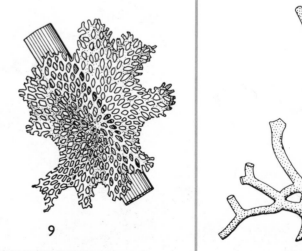

9

10

Diagram showing the structure of *Bowerbankia*. A. Three zooids arranged along a section of stolon, with the tentacles expanded for feeding (left), partially withdrawn (centre) and fully retracted (right). Gonads are indicated, and transverse parietal muscles omitted, in the right-hand zooid. The collar, found only in *Bowerbankia* and its allies, surrounds the everted tentacle sheath but forms a one-way valve in the atrium when the tentacles are fully withdrawn. The constricted sphincter muscle then also protects the interior of the zooid. B. Transverse section through the distal region of the left-hand zooid.

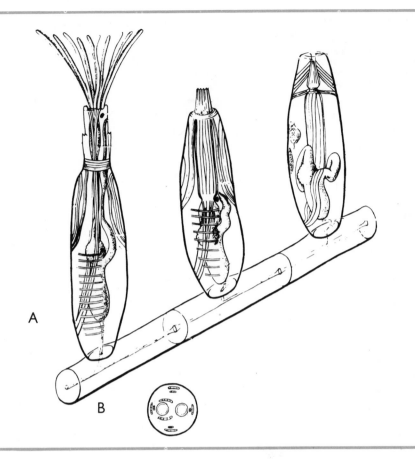

the tide line and *Alcyonidium* may also be found washed up. Its colonies form pale brown fingers, 4–8 in (10–20 cm) long, with the texture of gristly jelly. It is common in parts of the North Sea and huge quantities may sometimes be emptied out of trawlers' nets. *Alcyonidium* is not merely a nuisance, but also a danger, for repeated handling of it can induce severe allergic dermatitis with a painful rash and large blisters.

If freshly collected specimens are examined in water with a strong lens, after being left undisturbed, the surface of the colony will display many tiny bells of tentacles each with a mouth at the centre. These tentacles bear tracts of long *cilia and as we watch iridescent patterns flicker up and down the tentacles as the cilia beat, creating the water current which carries food particles towards the mouth.

Bryozoans must have arisen from worm-like ancestors, for each zooid has an internal organization strikingly similar to that of a marine (sipunculid) worm. Each zooid of a freshwater bryozoan is more or less a cylinder enclosed by a body wall laid down by the epidermis, beneath which is first a layer of circular muscle fibres and below this is a layer of longitudinal fibres, as in an earthworm. The musculature, lined by a peritoneum, encloses a coelomic cavity containing the gut. The mouth is at the end of an introvert (a region of the body capable of being drawn in) and is surrounded by tentacles arranged

along a more or less horseshoe-shaped ridge, the lophophore. This is the 'bell' already referred to. It leads into the pharynx, which passes to the stomach. The intestine leads upwards again, alongside the pharynx, so that the anus is situated close to the mouth but outside the lophophore.

Two other phyla share with the Bryozoa most of the characters just outlined. They are the Phoronida and the Brachipoda, or Lamp shells.

Typical marine Bryozoa are often found on the seaweeds clothing rocky shores. In one of these, *Bowerbankia*, each colony consists of a loose tangle of stolons, from which the zooids arise at intervals. A stolon is a kind of horizontal stem joining the zooids. Each cylindrical zooid attains a height of about $\frac{1}{25}$ in (1 mm) from its point of origin on the stolon. Live zooids in water will display a ring of slender, outward-curving tentacles at their free end. The shape of each zooid is maintained by the turgidity of the fluid-filled coelom acting against the body wall. The latter consists only of the epidermis, which secretes a cuticle, and the peritoneum. The muscle layers present in freshwater bryozoans are lacking. Another difference is that the lophophore in *Bowerbankia* is circular.

If the surrounding water be disturbed, the zooids rapidly withdraw their tentacles, the introvert rolling inwards like a cuff being pulled up inside its sleeve. When completely contracted the introvert ensheaths the ten-

tacles. Looked at now there is nothing of the zooid outside the cuticularized wall, which is broken only by an opening, known as the orifice—not to be confused with the mouth.

The most conspicuous muscle in the zooid is the retractor, which arises low down on the lower part of the body wall and divides into two bands which insert in a ring around the base of the lophophore. It is largely the contraction of this muscle that withdraws the tentacles. Also important are the transverse parietal muscles which replace the layer of circular fibres in freshwater bryozoans. These muscles form a series of short horizontal strands down each lateral wall of the zooid. When they contract they pull in the walls, so raising the internal pressure, and the tentacles are everted.

Running down from the wall of the stomach is a cord of connective tissue, the funiculus, which passes through the base of the zooid and joins a similar strand running along the stolon. The zooids, then, as in all colonial animals, are not isolated individuals, but are inter-connected throughout the colony by the funiculus.

Zooids in *Bowerbankia* are hermaphrodite. How fertilization is achieved is not known, for the egg does not leave the zooid. The embryo develops into a larva which, after liberation and a short free-swimming life, settles and gives rise to the first or primary zooid. The colony develops from this by the continuing process of asexual budding.

Zooids of some Bryozoa cheilostomata.
1. *Callopora lineata*. This is one of the most generalized species in the order. The zooids, which make up a crust, are flattened and largely roofed by the frontal membrane, through which the viscera can be discerned.

2. *Callopora rylandi*. Differs from *C. lineata* in that most of the spines are flattened and bridge the frontal membrane like ribs.

3. *Cribrilina cryptooscium*. The spines or ribs of *Callopora* have fused at intervals with their neighbours. The result is a perforated shield covering the frontal membrane.

4. *Bugula fulva*. Essentially similar to *Callopora* except that the zooids are arranged biserially in free-standing branches. The genus *Bugula* is remarkable for the development of stalked avicularia.

5. *Escharoides coccineus*. The frontal membrane is covered by a solid wall except in the region of the operculum. The perforations around the margin of the frontal wall are not true pores (as found in *Cribrilina*) but pseudopores or spaces in the calcification, and are filled with living tissue.

6. *Hippothoa hyalina*. The zooids are of three types, ordinary feeding zooids, smaller male zooids, and tiny female zooids bearing broodchambers. All zooids have a solid frontal wall containing an orifice (shown black), which is closed in life by a lid-like operculum.

7. *Schizoporella unicornis*. Zooids are constructed as in *Hippothoa*, but avicularia are present and the calcification contains pseudopores.

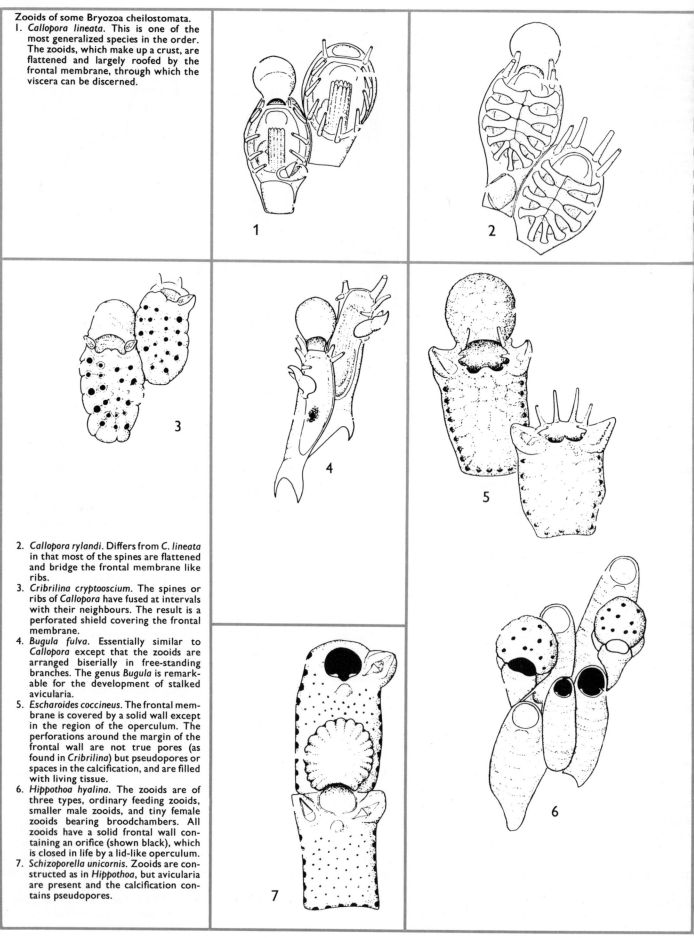

The phylum Bryozoa is classified as follows:-

Class Phylactolaemata. Zooids basically cylindrical, with horseshoe-shaped lophophore and epistome over mouth. Body wall incorporates muscle fibres arranged circularly and longitudinally. Mechanism for everting lophophore dependent upon deformation of wall by its intrinsic musculature. Dividing walls or septa between zooids incomplete, so that coeloms communicate.

The class, confined to freshwater, is widely distributed, though inconspicuous and colonies can seldom be located without careful search. They may, however, be found during summer in almost every lake, pond and river especially in clear, quiet water containing plants. They adhere to tree roots and to the shaded sides of floating logs and foliage and are especially common on the undersides of water-lily leaves.

In more primitive species the zooids are budded off in single file along repeatedly dividing lines. The more advanced forms have compact, gelatinous colonies. One of the most remarkable of these is *Cristatella* which, unlike almost all other bryozoans, can move about. Each colony is an elongated mass of greenish gelatinous substance which may reach or exceed 8 in (20 cm) long and $\frac{1}{8}$ in (1 cm) wide. It crawls on a flattened sole, with the crowns of tentacles projecting from the upper surface.

Like most freshwater animals, phylactolaematous bryozoans have a dormant stage, or statoblast, which helps them survive the winter and resist freezing and desiccation. Statoblasts are asexually produced buds which arise inside the zooids and secrete about themselves a hard protective capsule. They serve both to perpetuate and to distribute the species. In most species there is a raised crest or annulus around the equator of the capsule, which may become filled with air and act as a float. Any zooid may contain one or several statoblasts, and these are mainly liberated when the colonies die down at the onset of winter. The total number produced may be enormous. One American writer has

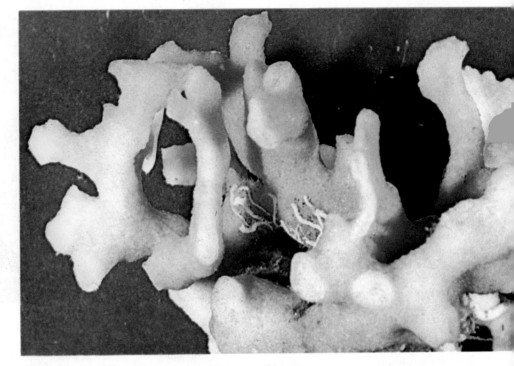

Porella compressa, a coral-like bryozoan, of the coasts of Europe.

described a drift of statoblasts 1–4 ft (30–120 cm) in width extending along half a mile of lake shore. He estimated that the colonies of *Plumatella* living in each square yard of the plant zone could produce about three-quarters of a million statoblasts.

Freshwater bryozoans also multiply sexually, by highly modified larvae which are little more than motile zooids.

Bryozoans used formerly to constitute a very great nuisance in water supply pipes. Today sand-filtration of water from reservoirs not only prevents statoblasts and larvae from colonizing the pipes but removes all the tiny organisms on which bryozoans would feed.

Class Stenolaemata. Zooids basically cylindrical. Body wall calcified and lacks muscular layers. Mechanism for everting lophophore hydraulic, not dependent upon muscular deformation of wall. Coeloms of adjacent zooids separated by dividing walls or septa, which may contain interzooidal communication pores. All marine.

Of the four orders, the Cystoporata, Trepostomata and Cryptosomata flourished during the Paleozoic era and have long been extinct. The special interest of the present day Cyclostomata, which lack diversity and, apart from the tufts of *Crisia* at low water mark, are rarely common, lies in their being the sole survivors of a once great invertebrate group.

The Cyclostomata, of little importance during the Paleozoic, as compared with the other three orders, enjoyed spectacular expansion and diversification during the Mesozoic. They have long tubular skeletons, annular in section. Adjacent zooids communicate through open pores, which presumably permit a pooling of resources throughout the colony. The lophophore, in contrast to that of phylactolaemate bryozoans, is circular; there is no epistome. Reproduction involves polyembryony, a process whereby a sexually produced primary embryo buds off numerous secondary embryos. The Cyclostomata reached their zenith during the Cretaceous period; thereafter their numbers have dwindled and relatively few survive today.

Class Gymnolaemata. Zooids cylindrical or squat, with circular lophophore and no epistome. Body wall lacks muscular layers but often incorporates calcification. Mechanism for everting lophophore basically dependent on deformation of wall by extrinsic muscles. Adjacent zooids separated by septa or by double walls, but communicate through pores plugged by funiculus. Almost exclusively marine.

Gymnolaematous bryozoans abound on many shores and in the shallow sea, where they cover seaweeds, incrust stones and shells, and hang under boulders or from cave roofs. Some tolerate or prefer brackish conditions and *Paludicella* has invaded freshwater.

There are two orders: Ctenostomata and Cheilostomata. In the former the zooids lack calcified walls, and the orifice is blocked by a pleated collar when the tentacles are withdrawn. In the latter the walls are generally calcified, and the orifice is closed by a hinged flap, the operculum.

The Ctenostomata is a small order, though some of its species may be very common on the shore. It is divided into two suborders:

Stolonifera and Carnosa. *Bowerbankia,* described earlier, belongs to the Stolonifera, in which cylindrical zooids arise from slender stolons. Carnosan zooids are often squat and they do not arise from stolons.

The Cheilostomata are believed to have arisen from a ctenostomatous ancestor early in the Cretaceous period. They evolved rapidly, soon deposing the Cyclostomata from their position of dominance; adaptive radiation continued in an impressive manner through the Tertiary period, and cheilostomes are by far the most abundant bryozoans in today's seas. A recent classification recognizes four suborders: Anasca, Cribrimorpha, Gymnocystidea and Ascophora.

The Anasca comprise the oldest and most generalized cheilostomes: the remaining suborders have clearly evolved from them. The anascan zooid is squat and appears rather box-like from the outside. The sides are calcified, the base is either calcified or attached to the substratum (or both), but the front is membranous, with the orifice near the end which is termed distal. When in water, the tentacles spread out above the orifice; when the tide is out, or if the animal has been disturbed, the operculum will be shut and the retracted tentacles are inside the zooid with the viscera and can be discerned only through the transparent frontal membrane. This non-calcified front is very important, for the hydraulic mechanism for everting the tentacles depends upon its downwards flexion under the pull of a series of parietal muscles. The frontal membrane is often surrounded by a circle of upright or inclined spines: occasionally the spines on each side of the zooid lean towards each other so much that they meet, like rafters in an untiled roof.

The zooids in the Cribrimorpha, which enjoyed spectacular success during the Cretaceous period, exploit a development of the ribbed roof. The spines of the two series are flattened and fuse together along the midline. Moreover, each is joined at intervals to its immediate neighbours, so that the gap between them is reduced to a line of pores. The frontal membrane thus remains intact but is shielded by a mesh-like cage.

The frontal membrane in the Gymnocystidea has been protected in another way. The side and rear walls appear to have risen and overarched the membrane until it became covered by an impervious vaulted roof. The space thereby enclosed communicates with the sea by an opening situated just above the operculum, so that the membrane continues to operate unhindered.

The Ascophora are rather different. The frontal surface itself is calcified but underlain

The Foliaceous coralline, a bryozoan commonly seen on European shores growing on rocks or on seaweeds.

by a thin-walled sac, the ascus, which opens narrowly to the exterior. Whether the ascus is really homologous with the original membrane is not clear: its development is quite different, yet the transverse parietal muscles insert on it exactly as they do on the frontal membrane. The ascus is a hydrostatic device: its dilation under muscular action simultaneously everts the tentacles and initiates through its opening an inflow of water which compensates for the decrease in coelomic volume.

Two important characteristics of the Cheilostomata remain to be mentioned. Firstly, the embryos, which are thin yolky and brightly pigmented, usually develop in ooecia—special globular chambers attached to the distal ends of zooids. Secondly, *polymorphism is highly developed. This means that certain zooids have become

Siamese fighting fish *Betta splendens* at bubble nest, shown at the top of the picture.

modified to perform special functions. The two most striking examples are known as vibracula and avicularia.

The body of a vibraculum is rather small, but its operculum has lengthened into a whip-like seta which can be swept vigorously over neighbouring zooids, perhaps keeping them free of debris.

An avicularium likewise has a small body, but the operculum is relatively much enlarged and, like a jaw, repeatedly opens and snaps shut. Avicularia seem analogous to the pedicellariae of echinoderms, and the larger ones at least may fulfil a protective role. Most remarkable of all are the stalked avicularia found in *Bugula,* which, in the words of Charles Darwin, so 'curiously resemble the head and beak of a vulture in miniature, seated on a neck and capable of movement, as is likewise the lower jaw or mandible.' Certainly the Cheilostomata are the most remarkable of all the Bryozoa.   J.S.R.

BUBBLE NEST, a very distinctive type of nest made by some of the labyrinth fishes. The nest is formed by blowing bubbles of air and sticky mucus at the surface of the water, resulting in a small heap of foam that is sufficiently firm to keep its shape in still waters until the eggs have hatched. The adult fishes mate below the nest and if the eggs are heavier than water, as in the Siamese fighting fish, the male takes them in its mouth once they have been fertilized and blows them onto the underside of the nest. The eggs become coated with mucus while in the mouth of the male and this helps them to adhere to the nest. The male then guards the nest and the young until they can fend for themselves. In some of the gouramis, strands of algae may be woven into the nest. The eggs of some gouramis and also some Paradise fishes (*Macropodus* species) contain oil droplets so that they are lighter than water and as they are laid they float up into the nest. If any go astray, the male will retrieve them.

Although these bubble nests are made in still waters, usually amongst floating plants, they are not permanent enough to withstand a long incubation period. In most species, therefore, the young hatch in only 24–36 hours and are able to swim in three days. After this period, the female (if she has not already been driven away by the male) appears to lose her maternal instincts and will eat any young that escape from the guardianship of the male.

BUBBLE SHELLS, marine snails in which the shell is usually reduced to a thin bubble-like structure, but unlike the more advanced members of the subclass Opisthobranchia, the so-called Sea slugs it is not lost entirely. The term Bubble shells is probably best applied to members of the family Bullidae, a

Akera bullata, one of the Bubble shells, in an aquarium. Two individuals are on the bottom. The other two are swimming, using ballet-movements of the mantle flaps.

widespread largely tropical group but with some species in British waters. The shells are large and oval, extremely thin and brittle, with a short spire sunk into the top of the last whorl. One example is the Atlantic bubble shell *Bulla striata,* which has a widespread distribution centred on the West Indies. The fleshy body and large foot, provided with lateral outgrowths (the parapodia), can be almost completely withdrawn into the shell. This species also feeds on whole bivalves, crushing the shells in the gizzard. The Sea hares are closely related to the Bubble shells.

One of the most primitive Bubble shells is the European Acteon shell *Acteon tornatalis.* This has a large, rather solid shell into which

the animal can withdraw completely and its nervous system still shows signs of torsion. It can be found near low tide, and below, on sandy beaches where it burrows. How it feeds is not known but the gut is generally full of sand so probably it digests organic material in the surface film of sand grains. Another Bubble shell found in the same habitat is *Philine.* This has a much more reduced shell which is completely covered by the mantle and extensions of the foot. It digs through sand in search of small bivalve molluscs which are swallowed whole and crushed by powerful calcareous plates in the gizzard. The Boat shell *Scaphander* behaves in the same way, but is found in slightly deeper water.

Bubble shells are the most primitive

opisthobranch molluscs and probably evolved from primitive mesogastropod prosobranchs. A number of characteristics mark them off from the prosobranchs. In most cases the twisting of the visceral mass on the head and foot, known as torsion, which occurs at some stage in all other gastropod molluscs has been reversed, either partially, so that the mantle cavity opens at right angles to the head, or completely, so that it faces posteriorly. There may be a single gill, like that of the prosobranchs, but this is also often reduced and in slugs is replaced by dorsal outgrowths from the mantle. Unlike prosobranchs the heart always has an auricle which lies behind the ventricle and the snail is hermaphrodite. See Gastropoda. ORDER: Pleurocoela, SUBCLASS: Opisthobranchia, CLASS: Gastropoda, PHYLUM: Mollusca.

E.M.D.

Detail of the famous Shwe Dagon pagoda in Rangoon, Burma.

BUDDHA LION, one of the many symbolic, mythical creatures which appear in Chinese art. The lion was not indigenous to China and the Chinese only became acquainted with it by way of the auspicious objects of Indian Buddhism. These stylized representations of the lion, in the hands of the Chinese, developed into something very far from a lion. Tail and mane were both drastically reduced, and the face became flattened, almost pug-like. Symbolically, the Buddha lion came to represent wisdom and guardianship.

BUDGERIGAR *Melopsittacus undulatus*, small Australian parrot commonly kept as a cage-bird. Wild budgerigars are small, $5\frac{1}{2}$ in (14 cm), long-tailed parrots with green underparts, a yellow back with closely-spaced black barring, a bright yellow head with blue

Budgerigars usurped the popularity rating formerly held by canaries.

and black stripes on the cheeks, and a row of black spots on each side of the upper neck. Selective breeding in captivity has produced all-blue, all-white, all-yellow and all-green budgerigars, as well as patterned forms. Besides producing colour variations, selective breeding has favoured those with large heads and distinct face markings and because of this many captive budgerigars bear little resemblance to the neatly proportioned wild ones.

Since budgerigars were first introduced into Britain in 1840 by John Gould, the famous bird artist, they have steadily increased in popularity, and are now the commonest cage-bird, considerably outnumbering the canary which was formerly the favourite.

In Australia budgerigars live in flocks throughout the arid interior regions and in dry coastal areas. They are most numerous in open country that is interspersed with belts of timber or patches of scrub. In prolonged droughts the flocks roam widely in search of food and water and are often seen in very large numbers, sometimes tens of thousands, at isolated water holes. Experiments on captive birds have, however, shown that they can live without water for up to 20 days, eating only dry seeds. This hardiness has probably been a key factor in the budgerigar's success as a household pet. Wild budgerigars feed mainly on small seeds from low-growing plants, running actively on the ground in search of food.

Like many other gregarious birds, budgerigars breed in colonies. No nest is built, and the clutches of 5–8 eggs are laid on the detritus in the bottom of a hole in a gnarled old tree. Several pairs often breed in one tree, so that large areas of old acacia trees are often occupied by breeding colonies. The oval or rounded eggs are incubated by the female alone, but the male helps to feed the nestlings, regurgitating partly digested seeds into their open bills. The young birds remain in the nest-hole for about 20 days and they are fed

by the parents for a week or so after they fledge.

Although the budgerigar is undoubtedly a parrot, its relationships to other parrots have puzzled ornithologists for many years. Some have suggested that it might be closely related to the much larger cockatoos, but the current opinion is that it shows the greatest affinity with the Australian Broad-tailed, or platycercine, parrots. These larger, long-tailed parrots resemble the budgerigar in a number of important anatomical features as well as in some aspects of their behaviour.

The name budgerigar is derived from the name used for this bird by the Australian aborigines. They frequently ate budgerigars and their name for them meant 'good bird' or 'good food'. The name is now spelt in a number of ways, for example boojerrgaa, budgerygah, although budgerigar is the most commonly used spelling. FAMILY: Psittacidae, ORDER: Psittaciformes, CLASS: Aves.

D.T.H.

Cape buffalo, probably the most feared of African game.

BUFFALO, a name which in the original Greek was used for any large cloven-hoofed animal and especially for the Water buffalo *Bubalus bubalis* of southern Asia. It was later used for the Cape buffalo *Syncerus caffer* and also for the North American *bison Bison bison*. See bovidae.

BUFFON G. L. L. de, 1707–1788. French naturalist, savant and stylist. Famous for his epic work *Histoire naturelle,* published in 44 volumes between 1749 and 1804, he was the only 'modern' to attempt a complete survey of natural history. Having interested Louis XV in science he was made keeper of the Jardin du Roi in his early 30s, and became an important member of the Académie Française. Trained in law before taking up natural history and having considerable presence and ability as well as a fortune, Buffon became a leading French intellectual. His literary style is so clear and powerful that he can still be read with profit. Frequently overlooked today, he was the first to propose a workable theory of the geographical distribution of animals and, though reticent on the subject for political reasons, he clearly was leaning towards a theory of evolution.

BUGS, insects with characteristic mouthparts belonging to the order Hemiptera in which there are 40,000 different species, many of which are unfamiliar and apparently dissimilar and unrelated. There is considerable disagreement on how the bugs should be classified; some entomologists prefer to divide the group into two separate orders, while others consider they are best included under the umbrella of a single order. The second course is followed here. All Hemiptera have mouthparts which take the same form, whether the insect is an immature stage (nymph or larva) or an adult, of a beak or rostrum made up of a number of very fine bristle-like stylets which fit together to form a piercing and sucking unit. Most bugs feed by tapping plant juices but some suck blood of insects or higher animals. These feeding habits make bugs important to man. Many species damage plants of great economic importance by sucking their sap or injure growing plants by transmitting virus diseases. Similarly, some of the blood-sucking bugs transmit disease micro-organisms to man and other animals.

All bugs are alike also in having an incomplete metamorphosis; that is, the change from the immature nymph to the adult insect is a relatively minor one as far as external features are concerned. The fully developed wings, which are present in most adult Hemiptera, are represented by small buds in the older nymphs. The name Hemiptera, means literally 'half-wing' and refers to the structure of the forewings of one of the two major groups constituting the order. The true 'half-wings' are the suborder Heteroptera in which the basal part of the forewings is hardened and the tip of the wings is membranous. Well known examples are Assassin bugs, waterboatmen, Pond skaters and bed-bugs. The latter are atypical of the group as a whole because they are effectively wingless. The other suborder, the Homoptera, characteristically have forewings that are the same texture throughout, being either completely leathery or wholly membranous. Some of the best known Homoptera are the cicadas, Frog hoppers (Spittle bugs) and aphids (Plant lice or greenfly).

Mouthparts and feeding. Insects that feed on solid matter generally have a set of mouthparts which include four major types of structure. First, there are two pairs of appendages which move laterally and are termed the 'mandibles' (or jaws) and the 'maxillae'. The mandibles are structures adapted for biting or chewing and the maxillae, which usually bear jointed sensory structures called palps, frequently serve to hold the food as it is bitten by the mandibles. Completing the mouthparts are the upper and lower lip structures termed respectively the 'labrum' and 'labium'. The insect's salivary glands often open on a tongue-like structure termed the 'hypopharynx'.

The key words in the feeding of bugs are 'piercing' and 'sucking', activities made possible by modification of the basic set of mouthparts. Because the feeding habits of bugs are so uniform, the mouthparts are closely similar in most species. In the embryo mouthparts at first include biting mandibles, but as development proceeds the mandibles and maxillae sink deeper into the head and become modified into hollow stylets, the two mandibles enclosing the pair of maxillae which, when brought together form two very fine tubes, one acting as a food tube and the other as the salivary duct. When a bug is about to feed, the rostrum, which is held in a

Budgerigars in the wild are seed-eaters and like all seed-eating birds, are apt to be a menace to cereal crops. In Australia, where the photograph was taken, they live in flocks.

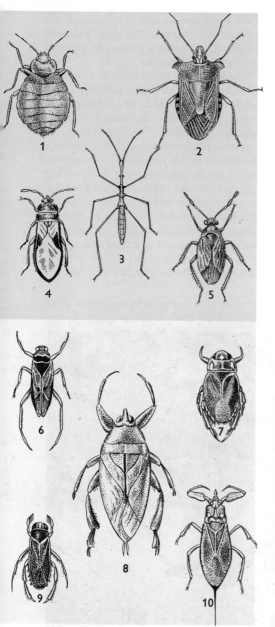

Land bugs: I. bed-bug, 2. Shield bug, *Tropicoris rufipes*, 3. Pond skater, *Hydrometra stagnorum*, 4. Chinch bug, *Blissus leucopterus*, 5. *Salda littoralis*, of the margins of lakes and rivers. Water bugs: 6. backswimmer, *Notonecta glauca*, 7. Saucer bug, *Naucoris cimicoides*, 8. Indian water bug, *Belostoma indicum*, 9. waterboatman, *Corixa geoffroyi*, 10. Water scorpion, *Nepa cinerea*.

flexed position under the body, is pointed downwards and it may probe for some time at the surface of a leaf before a particular spot is selected for penetration. Sensory setae (bristles) are present on the tip of the labium which allow the insect to find the most suitable spot for feeding. The labium does not penetrate the food surface, but serves as a grooved clamp guiding the piercing stylets into the leaf. It seems likely that the mandibular stylets are inserted into the plant first, their serrated tips cutting a path for the inner needle-like maxillary stylets. In some bugs the

labium is telescopic or retractable into the head, so that deep penetration by the stylets is possible. Two or three possible methods may be utilized to remove the sap from the plant. Most species have powerful dilator muscles in the head which, by increasing the size of the fore-gut, so reducing the pressure in it, cause the sap to flow from the plant cells into the insect's gut. It is also likely that the pressure of the fluid in the plant cells as well as capillary force take the sap into the gut. If the stylets are severed when an aphid is feeding, sap continues to exude for some time from the cut surfaces of the still embedded mouthparts, indicating that the plant juices are being forced up from within the plant.

Sound production by bugs. Cicadas are among the best known insect sound producers. The great volume of noise produced by a male cicada is the result of the vibration by powerful muscles of a pair of membranes called 'tymbals' at the base of the abdomen. Although the great French naturalist, J. H. Fabre, saw in the cicada's song 'only their peculiar means of expressing the joy of living', more recent researches suggest that the song brings individuals together and attracts sexually mature female bugs to the male singers. Several groups of bugs within the Heteroptera also produce sounds, by rubbing part of a leg, wing or rostrum against the body.

Some examples of the Bugs or Hemiptera: Homoptera. Apart from their sound-producing habit, the cicadas (Cicadidae) are interesting in that the life-cycle may be very extended. For example, the 17-year cicada, *Magicicada septendecim* of the United States has a seventeen year life-cycle in the north and thirteen year cycle in the south. The female cicada lays eggs in slits she cuts in twigs of trees, but on hatching the young

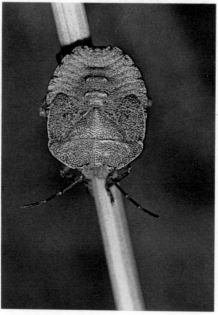

nymphs fall to the ground and spend the next 13–17 years burrowing in the soil and feeding by sucking the juices of tree roots. The only British species is *Cicadetta montana* which occurs in the New Forest in Hampshire, but some 100 species of a total world list of 1,500 species, occur in the Palearctic Region. Most cicadas occur in the warmer parts of the world.

Among the more easily recognized bugs are the Frog hoppers or Cuckoo-spit insects (Cercopidae). The most familiar of these have nymphs that suck the juices of a wide variety of different plants and envelop themselves in a frothy spume termed 'cuckoo-spit'. The adults are aptly named as their broad heads and their leaping ability make them look like miniature frogs.

The Leaf hoppers (Jassidae) are well represented by numerous small bugs which leap and fly when disturbed. They occur abundantly on hedgerow vegetation such as grass, nettles, hawthorn and wild rose. Several species are important economically. The Rice leaf hoppers, *Nephotettix,* cause very severe losses to growing rice in India and the United States.

The aphids, greenfly or Plant lice (Aphididae), familiar insects passing their lives on young succulent shoots, leaves, woody twigs,

Top: Shield bug from West Pacific islands.

Left: stinkbug nymph feeding on grass stem.

Right: Red and black East African predatory bug.

in galls or under the ground on roots, depending on the species, are of immense economic importance owing to the damage they cause to man's crops and garden produce.

Heteroptera. Although most bugs are plant feeders some feed on blood or are predatory on other insects. Of the 3,000 Assassin bugs (Reduviidae), most feed on insects but some attack man in tropical South and Central America and transmit the frequently fatal Chagas' disease. The bed-bugs (Cimicidae) form a small compact family all parasitic on mammals and birds but they are not very important in the transmission of diseases to man.

Another large family of Heteroptera are the stinkbugs or Shield bugs (Pentatomidae) which are notable for their large and usually shield-shaped bodies and the ability of many to produce obnoxious fluids. A very large family of Plant bugs, about 5,000 species, constitute the Miridae or Capsidae. Most species are small and feed on plant juices, but some are predatory on mites or other insects. When abundant, certain mirids may do considerable damage to economically important plants, including apples, black- and red-currants, tea, alfalfa, tobacco and celery. Another large family of bugs are the Chinch bugs (Lygaeidae) and many species are serious agricultural pests. Most are plant feeders inhabiting surface soil litter and low plants. The well known cottonstainer, *Dysdercus,* is a bug of the family Pyrrhocoridae.

A true aquatic bug, the predatory Water scorpion (Nepidae), is so named because of the long breathing siphon which projects from its hind end like a long sting. It can remain submerged indefinitely using its siphon as a snorkel. Another interesting aquatic group are the Pond skaters (Gerridae). These slender bodied insects are frequently seen skating gracefully over the surface of ponds, lakes and rivers using the long middle and hind pairs of legs. Other aquatic bugs are the backswimmers (Notonectidae) and the waterboatmen (Corixidae). It should be noted that backswimmers are often called waterboatmen although the two belong to quite distinct families. The notonectids swim on their backs their body being distinctly boat-shaped. The hind-legs are like oars and the bugs can row themselves rapidly through the water. Backswimmers feed on the body fluids of other aquatic insects as well as small fish, tadpoles, worms and freshwater shrimps. The superficially similar waterboatmen (Corixidae), also known sometimes as Lesser waterboatmen, are quite different in their feeding habits. They feed on diatoms or on the cell contents of green algae. The corixids may be distinguished from backswimmers as they swim the right way up, are smaller and have only a poorly developed pair of forelegs. The corixids are, furthermore, quite different in their feeding habits from notonectids. Waterboatmen consume minute particulate matter such as the single-celled plants called diatoms, and also the cell contents of green algae. ORDER: Hemiptera, CLASS: Insecta, PHYLUM: Arthropoda.   M.J.P.

BULBULS, tropical tree-dwelling songbirds with few distinctive characters to immediately identify them. There are about 112 species (authorities differ in estimates) and they vary in size from sparrow to thrush-size. They occur in southern Asia, from Syria, through northern India and central China, to southern Japan; south through the Philippines to the Moluccas and through Indonesia to Java. They are also present through Arabia and Africa to Madagascar and the Mascarene islands. They have been introduced and have established themselves in small numbers in southeastern Australia and in Florida. It is possible that the Crested berrypicker *Paramythia montium* and the Tit berrypicker *Oreocharis arfaki* are bulbuls, in which case the family extends to New Guinea also. The former species has a pointed black crest and a white nape like some bulbuls but is more colourful, having a blue body and green back and some yellow on the hind-flanks and under the tail. The latter is rather small, black and yellow on the head, yellow and brown on the underside and green on the back, and in general pattern very like the Great tit, *Parus major.*

In general bulbuls have the body plumage soft, dense and long, tending to be noticeably thick on the rump, with typically long, hair-like filoplumes on such parts as the nape or flanks. Another typical character appears to be the relative absence of feathering on the back of the short neck which, when extended, shows a rather bare patch. The wings tend to be short and rounded at the tip; and the tail is usually relatively long, the shape of the tip varying from forked to rounded. The eyes are fairly large and dark. The bill is usually slender and of a type associated with insect-eating, although for a great many of these species the most important food item is fruit, some insects being taken as well. The rictal bristles around the base of the bill are usually well-developed. Compared with birds which move and feed in similar fashion the bulbuls have legs and feet that are relatively weak and sometimes rather small.

The plumage is for the most part dull, olive-green, yellow or brown, and grey or

Sloe bug *Dolycoris baccarum*, of Europe, with its batch of eggs. These are laid on leaves of the Rose family, usually in batches of 28.

Blackcrested yellow bulbul, one of over a hundred species of starling-sized birds spread over Africa and eastwards to the Philippines.

Red-whiskered bulbul. The name 'bulbul' is from the Persian, and one species figuring in Persian poetry is called the Nightingale of the East.

black on one species, the Black bulbul *Microscelis madagascariensis*. Such plumage may, however, be varied by single patches of contrasting colour, in white, red or yellow. A number of species, particularly those in Asia, have crests that vary from a loose shaggy rounded mass of elongated crown feathers to a slender tapering conical crest. The sexes are alike in size and colour, while immature birds do not differ conspicuously from the adults.

Although nesting in scattered pairs, bulbuls are frequently gregarious at other times, travelling and feeding in small flocks, when they tend to be inquisitive and noisy. The call notes vary considerably, from the harsh or squeaky to the melodious but many species also have loud and musical songs. These usually consist of brief notes or phrases and at times some species will mimic calls of other birds. Bulbuls feed mainly on berries and other fruits which they take in quantity and where they occur in any number they are usually regarded as pests by fruit-growers. In addition to fruit they also take insects and small invertebrates, especially when feeding their young, and also buds of plants and some nectar.

Although in most species the flight is relatively weak, mainly from one bush or tree to another, some species make regular and fairly extensive seasonal movements, across forest areas or between high and low altitudes in mountain regions. Some of the Brown-eared bulbuls *Microscelis amaurotis* in Japan, regularly migrate in winter.

Bulbuls nest in separate pairs, and make fairly bulky cup-shaped nests, which in most species, are placed fairly low in trees or bushes but usually well-concealed. Larger, more conspicuous birds, such as the *Microscelis* species may choose higher and more open sites. While the male may remain in close attendance the female usually builds the nest while he accompanies her. Subsequently, however, the male takes an active part in incubating the eggs and, when these hatch into pink, naked nestlings, he also shares in feeding them. The eggs are usually white or pale pinkish in ground colour, and are finely marked with reddish or purple spots. As with most tropical birds the clutches are relatively small, two or three eggs being usual but more than one brood may be reared in the season. Nesting is fairly rapid, eggs hatching in about 12 days and the young fledging in a further 12.

The largest and most widespread genus, *Pycnonotus*, has 47 species. These are mostly brown, becoming blacker on head, wings and tail and with the drabness relieved by small patches of red or yellow on the sides of the head and on the under-tail coverts. Some species have a yellower plumage, and the Black-crested bulbul *P. dispar* of the Oriental region is an exception, being olive-yellow

The beautiful bullfinch has a bad reputation for stripping flower buds from shrubs and trees.

with a small black head and pointed crest and a shiny red throat, the iris of the eye being also red. Although some species of this genus are purely forest birds many are birds of forest edge or scrub and these have adapted themselves to the modified environment of cultivation and gardens. The Red-whiskered bulbul *P. jocosus* of southern Asia is one of these. It has red and white cheeks and a jaunty, upcurved pointed crest. It is popular as a cage-bird and has been introduced to other continents where similar changes in the environment through cultivation have created a niche for it. Another species of this group, the Red-vented bulbul *P. cafer,* also of southern Asia, has become a tame species nesting on and around human habitation, while elsewhere to the south the Yellow-vented bulbul *P. goiavier* has become a bird of gardens.

There are a number of genera of bulbuls in Africa. These include a large number of small species with slender bills and rounded tails, mostly green and yellow and in many cases showing a brown or rufous tint on the rump or tail. They are, in the main, skulking species of thick forest and undergrowth and feed much more on insects than do other bulbuls. They are sometimes referred to as greenbuls, brownbuls and leafloves. Also in Africa there are three species of bristlebills *Bleda* spp. These have a well-developed, compressed bill with a small hook at the tip and are sexually dimorphic, the females being smaller in body and bill. They are birds of forest undergrowth and one species at least, the Green-tailed

bristlebill *B. eximia,* gets its food by raiding ant columns, either for the ants or for the prey they are carrying. These bristlebills have eggs heavily blotched with brown.

Asia has also produced some bulbuls which have diverged from the typical form. The two species of Finch-billed bulbuls of the genus *Spizixos,* for example, have short thick bills with arched culmens, more suggestive of finches than bulbuls. They live at the high latitude forest fringes in the Himalayas and China. *Microscelis* species are noisy, nervous and active with shaggy crests, slightly forked tails, longish bills and small legs. They are stronger on the wing than most species. The Black bulbul *M. madagascariensis* has a variable plumage and very wide distribution, occurring from Madagascar and its adjacent islands, through India and Indo-China to China. FAMILY: Pycnonotidae, ORDER: Passeriformes, CLASS: Aves.

BULLFIGHTING, national pastime of Spain, in which men endeavour, by means of skill and courage, to kill savage bulls in a most spectacular manner.

Bullfights take place in arenas, or bullrings, according to a set of strictly observed traditional rules of procedure. Within the framework of these the matador conducts the bullfight with as much daring and skill as he is capable. The resultant display is ritualistic, more in the nature of a dramatic event than a sport. The bullfight has several phases, and there are several ranks within the hierarchy of bullfighter, each with a different function to

fulfil. Firstly, the matador enters the ring and with the initial cape work attempts to outwit the bull, avoiding its charge as narrowly and gracefully as possible. Picadors then enter mounted on armoured horses and armed with lances, which they use to fight off the attacking bull, by stabbing at the base of its neck. After another session of cape work by the matador, banderilleras take up the fight. A banderillera runs toward the charging bull and, at the last possible moment, swerves out of its path, at the same instant implanting a barbed stave in its neck. Then comes the 'moment of truth', the final slaughter of the bull by the matador. The concentrated efforts of the bullfighters cause a considerable weakening of the bull's neck muscles, so that on the final charge it carries its head low, thereby exposing the back of the neck. This facilitates the kill, the matador plunges a sword into the bull, at the junction of the neck and the shoulder blades.

The bulls used are specially selected individuals of a particularly ferocious Iberian breed, famous for the spirited way they continually charge their human adversaries. Not, it should be added, out of any aggravation caused by the red colour of the matadors cape. All cattle have no more than partial colour vision.   G.B.E.

BULLFINCH *Pyrrhula pyrrhula,* a stocky little bird, about 6 in (16 cm) long, with a short conical bill, black cap, bib, wings and tail and a white rump. In the male, the breast is pinkish-red and the back bluish, but in the female both are brownish-grey. Bullfinches extend from the British Isles, across Europe and Asia to Japan. Over most of this area, they live in conifer forests, but in western Europe they also extend south into decidu-ous woods, parks and gardens. For most of the year they eat a great variety of seeds from woody and herbaceous plants but in spring they live mainly on buds; the young are reared on a mixture of seeds and insects. Compared to other finches bullfinches eat many more seeds from fleshy fruits, like rowan and bramble.

The breeding season of the bullfinch is prolonged, up to three broods being raised each year. The nest is made of thin twigs and roots, and is placed in a thick bush in wood, hedge or garden. There are four to six eggs which are bluish white with red-brown spots. The species has several interesting courtship displays in which both sexes participate, the male puffing up the red abdominal feathers and turning his tail sideways towards the female.

In southern England, the bullfinch has much increased in recent years and become a serious pest through eating the buds of fruit trees. In fact, it now constitutes one of the greatest problems with which the fruit-growing industry has to contend. Only the

The Indian common bullfrog serves as food for other animals as well as human beings. It is also used in biology classes and laboratories in southern Asia.

small embryonic centres of the buds are eaten, those parts which would otherwise grow into the fruit, the outer scales being discarded. Bullfinches prefer the buds of fruit trees to those of native trees (the natural food in spring) and can remove them at a rate of 30 or more per minute. And since the birds often gather in groups of 12 or more, they need only a few days to devastate a large orchard, so that areas capable of producing several tons of fruit, yield only a few pounds. Certain fruit varieties are more vulnerable than others. Among pears, the varieties 'William' and 'Conference' are preferred, and among apples, dessert varieties are preferred to 'cookers'. But the least favoured varieties are spared only when the birds have a choice; otherwise they, too, are eaten. In gardens, bullfinches also eat the buds of ornamental trees, chiefly because their buds swell earlier than those of native trees, so are present when other food is scarce. It is not known what has caused the increase in bullfinches, but they have certainly learnt to live in closer association with man and in more open places than formerly. Nowadays it is the size of the ash crop which is the chief factor affecting the amount of damage done to fruit trees. Good ash crops usually occur every second year, and fruit trees are severely damaged in the alternate years when the crop fails.

Over most of its range, the bullfinch is migratory, moving in largest numbers when its food is scarce. In northern Europe the movements southward are most pronounced

The bullfrog of North America, so named from its bellowing call and its heavy build.

every third or fourth year, and in central Europe, from mountains to plains, every second year. British bullfinches, however, are remarkably sedentary. Up to 1948, over 40,000 had been marked under the National Ringing Scheme and 900 recovered. Nine-tenths of these had moved less than ten miles (16 km), and most of the rest less than 20 miles (32 km). There is no evidence for the fruit-growers claim that large numbers of bullfinches arrive each autumn from the continent to ravage the orchards of England. FAMILY: Fringillidae, ORDER: Passeriformes, CLASS: Aves.   I.N.

BULLFROGS, large frogs the males of which have a call that has been likened to the

bellowing of a bull. In different parts of the world the name refers to a particular species: the American bullfrog is *Rana catesbeiana;* the African bullfrog is *Pyxicephalus adspersus* and the Indian bullfrog is *Rana tigrina.* These are only related to one another in that they all belong to the family Ranidae or true frogs. Small frogs have a highpitched call, large frogs have a lowpitched one which is also louder.

The American bullfrog grows to 8 in (20 cm) the females being larger than the males. It is robust and powerful, a greenish drab colour with small tubercles on the skin, strictly aquatic preferring still pools with shallows and plenty of driftwood or roots along the banks. The jumping ability of American

bullfrogs is well-known and a contest is held every year in Calaveras to commemorate Mark Twain's famous tale "The Jumping Frog of Calaveras County". In fact the bullfrogs' jump, about 6 ft (2 m), is easily beaten by smaller, more athletic species of frogs from South Africa.

American bullfrogs emerge from hibernation in May and breeding lasts until July, the males calling from the edges of lakes and ponds. The tadpole reaches a length of 6 in (15 cm) and it is three years before it changes into a froglet. The adults eat anything of the right size, including mice, lizards, birds, fish, salamanders and other frogs, even those of the same species. Bullfrogs are easily caught by dangling a piece of cloth on a fish hook in front of them, and the meat of the large hindlimbs is considered a delicacy.

The African bullfrog is up to 9 in (22·5 cm), the male being larger than the female, which is unusual. It is plump and olive-coloured with many longitudinal folds in the skin. The mouth is enormous, reaching back to the shoulders and there are three tooth-like projections on the lower jaw. African bullfrogs burrow, shuffling backwards into the soil and remaining buried, with only the tip of the snout exposed. Like their American counterpart they will eat anything and are well-known for their cannibalism. They are dormant during the dry season emerging to breed at the beginning of the rains when they congregate in shallow pools. The calling of the males and the laying of eggs occurs in the daytime and the frogs are not disturbed by intruders. In fact, they are aggressive and will jump at intruders with gaping jaws and bite viciously. The males are sometimes reported to remain with the developing tadpoles and protect them. It is more likely that they are in fact feeding on them and adults have often been found with their stomachs full of tadpoles. The tadpoles are small and gregarious swimming around in large swarms. The young frogs which are about 1 in (2·5 cm) long emerge after about seven weeks and there are often enormous numbers around pools. On such occasions the young bullfrogs immediately start to eat each other.

African bullfrogs are eaten by pelicans and Nile monitors and are also considered a great delicacy by the local people in many regions.

The Indian bullfrog is a similar olive colour and reaches a length of about 6 in (15 cm). It is shy and solitary and never found far from water, preferring ditches and marshes. In most areas it breeds at the beginning of the monsoon.

They are eaten in parts of their range but in Pakistan, at least, the idea of doing so is abhorrent. There the belief is that if a woman spits in the mouth of a bullfrog and puts it back where she found it she will not become pregnant.

In South America a large species of *Leptodactylus,* not a member of the Ranidae is sometimes referred to as the South American bullfrog. FAMILY: Ranidae, ORDER: Anura, CLASS: Amphibia.   M.E.D.

BULLFROG CONTEST, the story of the jumping bullfrog is apocryphal but the popular account was told by Mark Twain. In this account a certain Jim Smiley of Angel's Camp, California, owned a bullfrog which he called Dan'l Webster. This frog was a champion jumper and had earned a lot of money by outjumping other bullfrogs. One day, so the story goes, a stranger appeared who was willing to bet against Dan'l Webster. Unfortunately he did not have a frog of his own, so Jim Smiley went to look for one, leaving Dan'l Webster with the newcomer. In due course the two frogs were lined up and prodded into action. Dan'l Webster, the champion, hardly moved and the new frog won handsomely. The stranger collected his winnings and left hurriedly. Jim Smiley is perplexed but, on examining Dan'l Webster, finds that his stomach is filled with lead shot.

In 1928 Angel's Camp celebrated the paving of its streets and one of the ceremonies included a jumping frog contest. This proved so popular that it has been repeated each year since. Because of the unpredictability of the frogs the contest is based on three consecutive jumps. The record stands at over 16 ft (5 m).

BULLHEADS, a name used for two widely separated groups of freshwater fishes having in common broad heads heavy in relation to the rest of the body. They also share the alternative name of *Miller's thumb. In Europe the bullheads are fishes of the family Cottidae (see Miller's thumb). The bullheads of the United States belong to the family Ictaluridae, more or less tadpole-shaped freshwater fishes. They are naked catfishes with four pairs of moderately long barbels. The dorsal fin is short and high, with a strong erectile spine and a long-based anal fin. The tailfin is rounded or square-ended. There are four kinds, the Black bullhead *Ameiurus melas,* Yellow bullhead *A. nebulosus* and the Marbled bullhead *A. n. marmoratus.*

The Black bullhead, up to 12 in (30 cm) or more long, variable in colour, from green to slaty-olive, lives in standing water or slow-moving rivers, from the Great Lakes to Kansas and Texas. The Yellow bullhead, up to 14 in (35 cm), coloured yellow to greyish green with dark blotches, inhabits the Great Lakes region and the Mississippi Basin. The Brown bullhead, up to 16 in (40 cm), is also found in the Great Lakes region and the eastern United States, and its related species, the Marbled bullhead, up to 18 in (45 cm), is found farther south, to Carolina and Florida.

The Brown bullhead has been introduced into European waters, where it has flourished. It has been described as providing the fisherman with a low-cost supply of protein, and like its relatives it feeds mostly on young fishes, worms, insect larvae and also fish spawn. FAMILY: Ictaluridae, ORDER: Siluriformes, CLASS: Pisces.   M.B.

BULL SNAKES *Pituophis,* common, non-poisonous snakes of North and Central America commonly about 6 ft (2 m) long. Although commonest in rocky and semi-desert country, they also frequent farming areas of states such as Iowa and Nebraska and may be encountered basking in the sun on roads. Bull snakes are attractively patterned with dark brownish diamond marks on a beige background. The Western bull snake *Pituophis catenifer* and its relative *P. sayi* are important destroyers of harmful rodents such as Pocket gophers, Ground squirrels, rats and mice which are killed by constriction or pressure. They also eat many eggs of ground-nesting game birds including quail and duck. Bull snakes mimic rattlesnakes by vibrating the tail, at the same time making a whirring noise in the throat.

This mimetic display is only part of the story. Bullsnakes have a special membrane, the epiglottis, in front of the glottis and, when air is forced past it, it vibrates like the reed in a wood-wind instrument. The note produced is staccato—a hiss amplified by the membranous flap. It has been compared with the bellowing of a bull, which is probably an exaggeration. The presence of an epiglottis is unusual in snakes. The 'bellow' is accompanied by a rapid vibration of the tip of the tail, a trick found in many snakes in moments of excitement. When the tail is near dry leaves or twigs this produces a rustling sound resembling to some degree the rattle of a rattlesnake. The effect on the human observer, if not on small animals, is enhanced by the bullsnake's habit of trying to look ferocious by blowing up its body, writhing and coiling and making sham strikes with the head.

A large number of snakes give audible warnings, as well as signalling displeasure by visual display. The commonest sound is the well-known hiss, which at times can be very penetrating, or loud as in the puff adder, said to make a noise like a horse blowing air through its lips. Yet snakes have no true voice and are deaf as well.

Instrumental music of a more remarkable kind is produced by two other North American snakes, the Sonoran coral snake *Micruroides euryxanthus* and the Western hook-nosed snake *Ficimia cana.* These draw air into the cloaca and expel it rhythmically at second-intervals, making a low popping sound. FAMILY: Colubridae, ORDER: Squamata, CLASS: Reptilia.   M.B.